SECOND EDITION

THE MARKETING
PLAN HANDBOOK

Marian Burk Wood, M.B.A.

PEARSON

Prentice
Hall

D1416402

Upper Saddle River, New Jersey 07458

Library of Congress Cataloging-in-Publication Data

Wood, Marian Burk.
  The marketing plan handbook / Marian Burk Wood.—2nd ed.
    p. cm.
  Includes bibliographical references and index.
  ISBN 0-13-148525-3
  1. Marketing—Management—Handbooks, manuals, etc.   I. Title.

HF415.13.W66 2005
658.8′02--dc22

                         2004020400

Editorial Director: Jeff Shelstad
Acquisitions Editor: Katie Stevens
Executive Marketing Manager: Michelle O'Brien
Marketing Assistant: Patrick Danzuso
Media Project Manager: Peter Snell
Managing Editor: John Roberts
Production Manager: Arnold Vila
Manufacturing Buyer: Michelle Klein
Cover Design: Bruce Kenselaar
Composition/Full-Service Project Management: Pine Tree Composition, Inc.
Printer/Binder: Hamilton Printing Company

Credits and acknowledgments borrowed from other sources and reproduced, with permission, in this text appear on page 192.

Pearson Education LTD.
Pearson Education Australia PTY, Limited
Pearson Education Singapore, Pte. Ltd
Pearson Education North Asia Ltd
Pearson Education, Canada, Ltd
Pearson Educación de Mexico, S.A. de C.V.
Pearson Education—Japan
Pearson Education Malaysia, Pte. Ltd
Pearson Education Upper Saddle River, New Jersey

10 9 8 7 6 5 4 3 2 1
ISBN 0-13-148525-3

Brief Contents

Contents

Preface

Behind every successful product is a carefully crafted, properly implemented marketing plan. Textbooks often discuss the general use of a marketing plan or contain a brief outline of one, but don't explain exactly how to develop an effective plan—yet that's what student marketers really need. *The Marketing Plan Handbook* fills this gap with concise step-by-step coverage of the structured process for formulating a creative and actionable marketing plan, including preparations for measuring marketing performance and controlling implementation. The award-winning *Marketing Plan Pro* software bundled with this book makes documenting decisions fast and easy so readers can concentrate on putting marketing principles into practice.

Real-World View of Marketing Planning

How does Nestlé use marketing planning (see Chapter 1)? What changes in customer behavior are helping JetBlue's revenues soar (Chapter 2)? How does Toyota assess global market needs (Chapter 3)? What is Home Depot doing to address the needs of different customers (Chapter 4)? Why has the nonprofit Nature Conservancy reevaluated its mission and metrics to better measure marketing performance (Chapter 10)?

These and dozens of other examples featured in *The Marketing Plan Handbook* illustrate how marketing planning is actually applied in consumer and business markets, in large and small companies, in traditional and online businesses, and in nonprofit organizations. To reinforce this real-world view, key examples also demonstrate how today's global economy and dynamic business environment can cause marketers to change their plans as new competitors emerge, budgets are cut or shifted, and new technologies overtake existing strategies. Thus, long after the marketing plan is written, savvy marketers continue charting paths to profitability and watching for threats and challenges every working day.

Special Features Support Effective Planning

The Marketing Plan Handbook supports the hands-on developme
realistic marketing plans through a series of special features:

- *Sample marketing plan.* What does a marketing plan loo
  ents a sample plan for the SonicSuperphone, an enhanc
  phone. This hypothetical sample serves as a model for
  tion of a typical marketing plan.

- *Checklists.* What questions should marketers be asking? Checklists in Chapters 2–10 summarize key areas to be examined during planning, including segmentation variables, environmental scanning, channel and logistics issues, and elements of a marketing audit.
- *Practical planning tips.* What important points and pitfalls should marketers be aware of? Each chapter includes a number of special tips to help readers make the transition from theory to application.
- *Current examples.* How are companies actually putting marketing plans to work? Every chapter showcases 10 or more recent examples of businesses and nonprofits applying the principles of marketing—including many international examples.
- *Dedicated Web site.* Visit *www.prenhall.com/wood* for hotlinks to selected marketing resources and for detailed integration guides showing how *The Marketing Plan Handbook* can be used with various Prentice Hall marketing textbooks.

Marketing Plan Pro Simplifies Planning

Palo Alto Software's highly rated *Marketing Plan Pro* software, which comes with this book, is a user-friendly program for documenting marketing plans. The software also includes sample marketing plans from a variety of organizations, including manufacturers, retailers, consulting firms, service businesses, and nonprofit groups. Preparing the financials to support a marketing plan can be tedious and time-consuming; this software streamlines the process with built-in spreadsheet and charting capabilities. Once the plan is complete, it can be printed, translated into a read-only document, exported to other programs, or exported for posting on the Web. See Appendix 2 for more details about using *Marketing Plan Pro* to prepare a marketing plan.

Supplementing Prentice Hall Marketing Texts

A value package of *The Marketing Plan Handbook* with *Marketing Plan Pro* software is available at a deeply discounted price to supplement the following Prentice Hall textbooks:

- *Marketing Management 12e* by Philip Kotler and Kevin Lane Keller
- *A Framework for Marketing Management 2e* by Philip Kotler
- *Marketing Management 2e* by Russell S. Winer
- *Principles of Marketing 10e* by Philip Kotler and Gary Armstrong
- *Marketing: An Introduction 7e* by Gary Armstrong and Philip Kotler
- *Marketing: Real People, Real Choices 4e* by Michael Solomon, Greg Marshall, and Elnora Stuart
- *Market-Based Management 3e* by Roger Best

Here is how each chapter in *The Marketing Plan Handbook* corresponds to specific chapters in three leading Prentice Hall marketing textbooks:

Chapter in *Marketing Plan Handbook 2e*	Chapter in Kotler/Keller, *Marketing Management 12e*	Chapter in Kotler, *Framework for Marketing Management 2e*	Chapter in Winer, *Marketing Management 2e*
1: Introduction to Marketing Planning	1: Importance of Marketing 2: Marketing Strategies, Plans	1: Marketing Management 2: Adapting Marketing 3: Customer Satisfaction, Value 4: Strategic Planning	1: Marketing Philosophy, Strategy 2: Strategic Marketing Framework
2: Analyzing the Current Situation	9: Dealing with Competition 19: Global Markets 20: Gathering Information, Scanning the Environment	5: Markets, Demand, the Environment 8: Dealing with Competition	6: Market Structure, Competitive Analysis
3: Understanding Markets, Customers	4: Analyzing Consumer Markets 5: Analyzing Business Markets	5: Markets, Demand, the Environment 6: Analyzing Consumer Markets 7: Analyzing Business Markets	4: Consumer Behavior 5: Organizational Buying Behavior
4: Segmentation, Targeting, Positioning	6: Identifying Market Segments	9: Market Segments, Target Markets	3: Marketing Research
5: Direction, Objectives, Marketing Support	2: Marketing Strategies, Plans 3: Creating Customer Value 11: Designing, Managing Services	4: Strategic Planning 12: Designing, Managing Services	2: Strategic Marketing Framework 15: Strategies for Service Markets
6: Product, Brand Strategy	7: Brand Equity 8: Brand Positioning 10: Product Strategy 18: New Market Offerings	10: Developing, Positioning Products 11: Product, Brand Strategy 12: Designing, Managing Services	7: Product Decisions 8: New Product Development
7: Channel, Logistics Strategy	13: Value Networks, Channels 14: Retailing, Wholesaling, Logistics	14: Value Networks, Channels 15: Retailing, Wholesaling, Logistics	10: Channels of Distribution 11: Direct Channels
8: Pricing Strategy	12: Pricing Strategies	13: Pricing Strategies, Programs	12: Pricing
9: Integrated Marketing Communication Strategy	15: Integrated Marketing Communications 16: Advertising, Promotion, PR 17: Direct, Interactive Marketing, Sales	16: Integrated Marketing Communications 17: Managing the Sales Force	9: Communications Strategy 13: Sales Promotion
10: Performance Measurement, Implementation Control	21: Forecasting Demand, Measuring Effectiveness 22: Marketing Organization	4: Strategic Planning	14: Customer Relationship Management 9: Communications Strategy

Acknowledgments

In the course of planning, writing, and revising the second edition of *The Marketing Plan Handbook*, I was extremely fortunate to have the support of many good people. I want to express my heartfelt gratitude to the many talented Prentice Hall professionals whose dedication and hard work have contributed immeasurably to this book's success: Editor-in-Chief Jeff Shelstad, Acquisitions Editor Katie Stevens, and Executive Marketing Manager Michelle O'Brien. An extra special thank you to Editorial Assistant Rebecca Lembo, whose "make it happen" attitude and attention to detail made it happen. What a joy it has been to work with everyone on this team!

A tip of the hat to Tim Berry, Sabrina Parsons, and all the folks at Palo Alto Software who are responsible for *Marketing Plan Pro*—many thanks for your ingenuity, ideas, and expertise. And I want to again thank the faculty reviewers of the first edition for their insights and helpful suggestions: Brent Cunningham, Jackson State University; Ralph M. Gaedeke, California State University, Sacramento; Dennis E. Garrett, Marquette University; Kathleen Krentler, San Diego State University; Ron Lennon, Barry University; Byron Menides, Worcester Polytechnic Institute; Henry O. Pruden, Golden Gate University; Scott D. Roberts, Northern Arizona University; Gary R. Schornack, University of Colorado, Denver; and Michael J. Swenson, Brigham Young University.

Finally, I dedicate this book with much love to two people who hold special places in my life: my beloved husband Wally Wood and my beloved sister Isabel Burk.

—Marian Burk Wood
MarianBWW@netscape.net

About the Author

Marian Burk Wood has held vice presidential–level positions in corporate and non-profit marketing with Citibank, Chase Manhattan Bank, and the National Retail Federation, as well as management positions with national retail chains. She is the author of *Marketing Planning: Principles into Practice*, a marketing plan textbook geared to the European market. In addition, Wood has collaborated with well-known academic experts to coauthor college textbooks on principles of marketing, principles of advertising, and principles of management.

Wood has extensive practical experience in marketing planning, having formulated and implemented dozens of marketing plans over the years for a wide range of goods and services. She also has developed numerous chapters, cases, marketing plans, features, exercises, and print and electronic supplements for college textbooks in marketing and related disciplines. Wood holds an MBA in marketing from Long Island University in New York and a BA from the City University of New York; her special interests in marketing include ethics, segmentation, channels, and B2B marketing.

CHAPTER 1

Introduction
to Marketing Planning

In this chapter:

Preview

Is a good product, brand, ad, Web site, or price good enough? Not when businesses, non-profit organizations, and government agencies must fight simply to capture the attention of customers, clients, and constituents. Building strong relationships is even more of a challenge in this world of global competition and ever-increasing customer choice and power. Today's customers are exposed to marketing messages everywhere they turn; they can research products, compare prices, and buy with the click of a mouse. And reputation counts: Customers (and suppliers) prefer to deal with organizations and brands that have credibility and a positive public image.

This emphasis on building and maintaining relationships is reflected in the American Marketing Association's current definition of marketing: "Marketing is an organizational function and a set of processes for creating, communicating, and delivering value to customers and for managing customer relationships in ways that benefit the organization and its stakeholders." Thus, effective marketing covers everything the company is and does—it all must be good or even great, on a consistent basis, to earn customer loyalty. However, what is good enough today may not be tomorrow: ever-accelerating change is the only constant that marketers can depend on when formulating a marketing plan.

Overview of Marketing Planning

The best way for any business, nonprofit, or government agency to move toward its goals is one marketing plan at a time, over and over. Start-ups, multinational corporations, and charitable foundations all need marketing plans to chart paths (whether success is defined by profits, donations, or people helped). Consider how one fast-growing business changed marketing plans in its quest for success:

> **Netflix.** This online DVD movie rental-by-mail company didn't exist before 1999, yet today it serves more than 2 million subscribers. Its first marketing plan called for customers to rent and pay for DVDs one at a time, plus a late fee if the DVD was not returned within a week. When this approach attracted few customers, the company changed its marketing plan. Now customers pay a flat $22 monthly fee to have three DVDs out at one time, with no return deadlines. Customers like the convenience of renting DVDs by mail, selecting from 20,000 movies, and browsing personalized recommendations from Netflix's automated system. Despite competition from Wal-Mart and Blockbuster, Netflix is moving into new markets and planning to make movies available for download in the near future.[1]

Rapidly expanding young companies like Netflix face special challenges in defining their initial and ongoing objectives, researching and analyzing the marketing environment, and developing effective strategies to build (and retain) a solid customer base. Established companies have more experience with their customers, markets, and competitors, but they are subject to the same environmental dynamics. Nestlé, for example, has been in business for more than a century but is still learning new things about customers and competitors:

> **Nestlé.** Based in Switzerland, Nestlé has a diverse product portfolio of foods, beverages, and pet foods for global markets. One of the most promising is China, which an executive calls "the fastest and most competitive market in the world" because of burgeoning demand and intense rivalry from international and local firms alike. Nestlé has profited here by creating hundreds of food items specifically for China—such as sesame-chocolate cubes—and developing an adaptable distribution system to get products to outlying communities. In Argentina, the company has prospered despite a difficult economic situation through brand-building campaigns, product introductions, and periodic price promotions.[2]

Nestlé, like Netflix, faces daily decisions about using marketing to profitably acquire, retain, and satisfy customers in a competitively superior way. Online businesses have the added complications of designing and running a Web site, handling customer service, and managing order fulfillment as they work on all the other elements of marketing strategy. Still, marketers for younger firms, like their counterparts in established companies, are most effective when they follow a structured series of steps for marketing planning.

The purpose of this handbook is to provide an overview of the process that contributes to the development of a viable marketing plan. This process is one that enables marketers in every organization, regardless of industry or product, to make informed decisions about the most appropriate marketing paths to profits and other objectives. Marketing principles and techniques are explored in the context of each step in the process, along with numerous examples illustrating their use. Despite organization-by-organization variations in the formality and timing of the process, the aim is to emerge with a plan documenting appropriate strategies and programs for the chosen markets.

Practical Planning Tip

A structured process helps you identify, assess, and select appropriate marketing strategies.

MARKETING PLANNING DEFINED

Marketing planning is the structured process of researching and analyzing the current situation, including markets and customers; developing and documenting marketing's objectives, strategies, and programs; and implementing, evaluating, and controlling activities to achieve the objectives. This systematic process enables marketers to identify and evaluate opportunities that might lead to achieving overall goals, as well as emerging threats that could interfere (see Exhibit 1.1). As noted in the preview, any aspect of the marketing environment can change at any time; thus, marketing planning must be viewed as an adaptable, ongoing process rather than a rigid, annual event.

The outcome of this structured process is the **marketing plan**, a document covering a particular period that summarizes what the marketer has learned about the marketplace, what will be accomplished through marketing, and how. All marketing plans should explain intended marketing strategies, outline the activities that employees will undertake to reach objectives, show the mechanisms for measuring progress toward objectives, and allow for adjustments if results are off course.

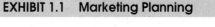

EXHIBIT 1.1   Marketing Planning

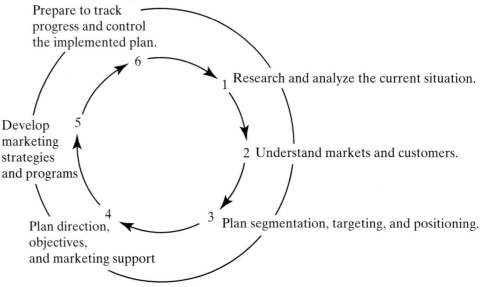

A marketing plan is one of several official planning documents created by a company. These include the business plan, which outlines the organization's overall financial and operational objectives and strategies; and the strategic plan, which discusses the organization's general long-term strategic direction. Sir George Bull, chairman of the U.K. supermarket chain J. Sainsbury, stresses that the marketing plan is distinguished from the business plan by its focus. "The business plan takes as both its starting point and its objective the business itself," he explains. In contrast, "the marketing plan starts with the customer and works its way round to the business."[3] The company's strategic plan falls in between, laying out the broad strategies that will guide the strategic management of all divisions and functions over a 3- to 5-year planning horizon. The marketing plan is created at a lower level than either the business or strategic plans, and it is intended to provide shorter-term, specific operational direction for how the organization will implement strategies and move toward achieving the targeted results.

In the past, marketing planning often was sequestered in the marketing department until the plan was reviewed by management, revised, and then distributed to sales and other departments. These days, however, marketing planning encompasses more bottom-up, organization-wide input and collaboration. At Nokia, for example, managers and employees from different units contribute ideas to be incorporated into the plan. With tweaking to allow for endless environmental shifts such as new technology and competition, this is the plan used to guide the company's marketing. Such collaboration is a necessity when, like Nokia, a company introduces dozens of new products yearly.[4] In addition to building internal consensus and cooperation, this two-way flow of information provides valuable input for strategies at all levels.

Larger organizations frequently require a marketing plan for each unit (e.g., individual stores or divisions) as well as for each product or brand. The Pontiac division of General Motors has its own marketing plan, as well as detailed plans for the Solstice, Sunfire, Vibe, and other Pontiac brands. Even a GM model like the pickup-equipped Cadillac Escalade EXT, expected to sell only 11,000 units annually (a tiny fraction of the millions of cars GM sells each year), must have a plan. "If you don't have [a plan], you're going to have a hodgepodge and people running around like a fire drill," says the general manager of GM's Hummer division.[5]

CONTENTS OF A MARKETING PLAN

Although the exact contents, length, and format may vary, most marketing plans contain the sections shown in Exhibit 1.2. (The sample plans in *Marketing Plan Pro* and the sample in Appendix 1 show how plan contents and length differ depending on the organization and its purpose.) The executive summary at the beginning of the plan is actually the final section to be written, because it serves as a brief overview of the main points. The other sections are generally drafted in the order in which they appear in the plan, with each successive section building on the previous one. Managers are unable to prepare marketing budgets and schedules, for example, until their objectives, strategies, and action programs have been set. Note that

EXHIBIT 1.2   Main Sections of a Marketing Plan

Section	*Description*
Executive summary	Briefly reviews the plan's highlights and objectives.
Current marketing situation	Summarizes environmental trends: • Internal and external situational analysis (products, markets, previous results, competitors, other environmental forces) • SWOT analysis (internal strengths and weaknesses, external opportunities and threats)
Objectives and issues	Outlines the specific marketing objectives to be achieved and identifies issues that may affect the organization's attainment of these objectives.
Target market	Explains the segmentation, targeting, and positioning decisions and analyzes the market and segments to be targeted through marketing strategy.
Marketing strategy	Shows the strategy to be used in achieving the marketing objectives.
Marketing programs	Lays out the programs supporting the marketing strategy, including specific activities, schedules, and responsibilities for: • Product • Price • Place (channel) • Promotion • Service • Internal marketing
Financial plans	Details expected revenues, expenses, and profits based on the marketing programs in the plan.
Implementation controls	Indicates how progress toward objectives will be measured and how adjustments will be made to keep programs on track.

**Practical
Planning Tip**
**Get a fresh perspective
by creating a new plan
every year, rather than
adapting last year's
plan.**

when a company changes one part of the plan, it may have to change other parts as well (such as programs and budgets), due to the interrelated nature of the sections.

Even after receiving management approval and being implemented, marketing plans should be revised in accordance with changes in competition, customers' needs and attitudes, product or company performance, and other factors. Starbucks' experience is a good example:

Starbucks. Always striving for growth and profits, Starbucks' marketing plans are about more than coffee and cafés. A few years ago, one of its marketing plans called for partnering with Time, Inc. to launch *Joe* magazine. Once they saw that customers were not overly interested, Starbucks and Time changed their plans and dropped the project. On the other hand, with increased competition and more than 7,000 stores already open—some around the clock— Starbucks has increased its advertising efforts, begun offering in-store, custom-mixed music CDs, and tested other changes to attract customers and reinforce loyalty.[6]

The success of a marketing plan depends on a complex web of internal and external relationships as well as on uncontrollable environmental factors. Look at the marketing challenges faced by Coca-Cola. Industry-wide sales of carbonated soft drinks are barely growing in North America, in part because customers are buying more bottled water and other beverages—a trend that Coca-Cola cannot single-handedly reverse. To gain market share here, the company must plan to take share away from long-time rival PepsiCo. Internationally, the company is bolstering its trademark colas with new soft drinks for local tastes. In Argentina, for example, it came up with Nativa, a sweet drink that tastes of yerba mate; in Brazil, it launched Kuat, a drink featuring extract of guarana berries. Coca-Cola's international marketing plans also call for shaping a positive public image by donating money to community schools, among other charitable works.[7]

Unexpected circumstances can alter the marketing environment profoundly, making even the most carefully crafted marketing strategies obsolete without warning. Here is how Sony's competitive situation has been changing:

Sony. Sony suddenly faces more competition in electronics than ever before, especially from companies that were not serious rivals—until now. For example, Dell, known for its computers, is marketing flat-screen television monitors; Nokia, known for its cell phones, has introduced handheld video game devices. Although Sony made its name through innovation, more nimble companies are making headlines for their stylish and popular products (such as Apple's iPod digital music players). In response to this powerful competitive pressure, Sony has changed its marketing plan by eliminating some older product lines, cutting costs, and emphasizing much newer products such as DVD recorders to boost profits.[8]

As these examples indicate, no marketing plan is ever really final. Rather, the marketing plan must be updated and adapted as the organization's situation, priorities, and performance change.

Developing a Marketing Plan

Marketing plans generally cover a full year, although some (especially those covering new product introductions) may project activities and anticipate results farther into the future. The marketing planning process starts at least several months before the marketing plan is scheduled to go into operation; this allows sufficient time for thorough research and analysis, management review and revision, and coordination of resources among departments and business units.

The Phoenix Suns basketball team, for instance, starts its planning cycle for the following season even before the current year's playoffs are over. During the early stages of working on the marketing plan, team management reviews the current season's ticket and merchandise sales performance, analyzes game-by-game attendance, weighs fan feedback and market research, and swaps best-practices ideas with other National Basketball Association teams. With months of lead time, management can examine the team's current situation, identify market segments for special attention, set objectives, and prepare forecasts of future results.[9]

The following sections introduce each of the six marketing planning steps shown in Exhibit 1.1, providing an overview for the remainder of this handbook.

RESEARCH AND ANALYZE THE CURRENT SITUATION

The first step is to study the current situation before charting the organization's marketing course. Externally, marketers study environmental trends to detect demographic, economic, technological, political-legal, ecological, or social-cultural changes that can affect marketing decisions, threats to performance, and potential profits. Marketing managers also assess the company's internal capabilities and the strategies of competitors so they can build on internal strengths while finding ways of exploiting rivals' weaknesses or emerging opportunities. In addition, they analyze how customers, competitors, suppliers, distributors, partners, and other stakeholders might influence marketing results. For example, marketers for Michaels Stores uncovered growing interest in the hobby of scrapbooking:

> **Michaels Stores.** Marketers for this Texas-based crafts retail chain noticed a sharp increase in sales of scrapbooking products and also found that suppliers were offering a wider range of albums, labels, and related items. With the Hobby Industry Association projecting that near-term sales of scrapbooking products would increase 40% or more every year, Michaels used its retailing expertise to launch a new chain of stores carrying only merchandise for this hobby. Meanwhile, Wal-Mart and other rival retailers have expanded the shelf space they devote to scrapbooking products, presenting Michaels with a potential threat.[10]

Chapter 2 contains more detail on gathering and analyzing data to examine the organization's current situation.

UNDERSTAND MARKETS AND CUSTOMERS

The second step is to analyze markets and customers, whether consumers or businesses, by researching market share trends, customer demographics, product demand, buying habits, needs and wants, and customer attitudes and satisfaction.

Marketing Plan Pro software can help you organize and document background information and decisions for your marketing plan.

Practical Planning Tip

Market and customer analyses help you decide which customers to target and how to meet their needs.

Among the many questions to be studied are: Who is doing the buying—and why? How are buying habits changing—and why? What products and categories are in demand? McDonald's has become expert at analyzing customers' preferences in different countries and then adapting menu items for local tastes: aloo tikka in Bombay, gourmet burgers in Tokyo, kosher meats in Tel Aviv.[11]

With cutting-edge technology, marketing managers can examine detailed customer buying behavior based on sales by channel and by product. The Limited retail chain, for instance, uses software to track and analyze online and in-store customer purchases hour by hour, providing critical data that helps management make timely decisions about distributing merchandise and starting or changing promotions. Carphone Warehouse Group, a London-based retailer of cell phones, checks sales every 15 minutes so it can react quickly to problems or shift resources to better-performing areas.[12]

However, marketers must not overdo customer research. To illustrate, different groups within IBM used to conduct 48 or more surveys measuring customer satisfaction with products, sales, and service; one survey involved 40,000 interviews spread over 58 countries. Some IBM customers complained about being surveyed up to five times a year. "When you're the CEO of one of our major customers, and you hear from IBM three times in a month on a survey that sounds identical to the last one you answered, you get a little annoyed," notes IBM's director of world-wide customer satisfaction management, who consolidated the surveys and responses to make research data available across the corporation.[13] (More information about analyzing markets and customers can be found in Chapter 3.)

PLAN SEGMENTATION, TARGETING, AND POSITIONING

Knowing that organizations can never be all things to all people, marketers have to apply their knowledge of the market and customers to select certain parts of the market, known as **segments**, for marketing attention. In the past, this meant dividing the overall market into separate groupings of customers, based on characteristics such as age, gender, geography, needs, behavior, or other variables. With today's technology, however, some companies can now identify and serve segments as small as a single customer, based on what they know (or can find out) about that consumer or business.

The purpose of segmentation is to group customers with similar needs, wants, behavior, or other characteristics that affect their demand for or usage of the good or service being marketed. To illustrate, Toyota segments the market for cars and trucks by buyer age, price sensitivity, geography, driving habits, design preferences, and environmental interests, among other factors. Thus, its popular, fuel-efficient Prius hybrid car was created for environmentally-conscious U.S. drivers, while its low-priced Yaris subcompact was designed for budget-conscious young European drivers.[14]

Once the market has been segmented, the next set of decisions centers on **targeting**, including whether to market to one segment, to several segments, or to the entire market, and how to cover these segments. Segmentation and targeting are vital in **business-to-business (B2B) marketing**, as well as consumer markets:

> **Intranets.com.** Based in Massachusetts, Intranets.com originally targeted businesses that use software for managing files and internal communication. With Internet usage on the rise, however, the company shifted to online services for businesses, nonprofits, and government agencies that need instant data interchange. It initially offered these services at no charge; later, 75,000 of the 600,000 most active users became paying customers after Intranets levied a monthly fee. The company is profitable on $6 million in annual sales and now serves 175,000 customers, including the National Aeronautics and Space Administration (NASA).[15]

Next, the organization formulates suitable **positioning**, which means using marketing to create a competitively distinctive place (position) for the brand or product in the mind of targeted customers. This positioning sets the product apart from competing products in a way that is meaningful to customers. For example, Apple Computer uses design to differentiate its Macintosh computers and iPod digital music players; Southwest Airlines uses low fares for differentiation. To effectively create a particular image among targeted customers, companies must convey the positioning through every aspect of marketing. This is why most Apple iPod ads focus on the product's sleek styling and Southwest's ads trumpet its no-frills service. Chapter 4 discusses segmentation, targeting, and positioning in further detail.

PLAN DIRECTION, OBJECTIVES, AND MARKETING SUPPORT

Marketing managers are responsible for setting the direction of the organization's marketing activities, based on goals and objectives. **Goals** are long-term performance targets, whereas **objectives** are short-term targets that support the achievement of goals. The marketing, financial, and societal objectives that are set (and eventually achieved) will move the organization forward toward its overall goals, whatever they may be and however they may be expressed.

To illustrate, executives at Target Stores established a mission during the 1970s to guide future growth. Although the mission has been revised periodically, one basic tenet unchanged for 30 years is the idea that Target sells "the best products at the best value." Another tenet is that the company will "give generously to the communities" where it does business. This mission provides direction for the top managers who set long-term growth goals and for marketing managers who set and document shorter-term marketing, financial, and societal objectives in the marketing plan.[16]

Like Target, most businesses use their marketing plans to support growth strategies. As shown in Exhibit 1.3, growth can be achieved in six ways; in practice, some companies pursue growth through two or more of these methods.[17] For example, Nestlé's corporate marketing strategy calls for an annual sales increase of 5%, to be achieved by selling more existing products in current markets and by introducing new products to current markets. Its business units set objectives to support corporate growth strategies and goals. Nestlé Rowntree, for instance, plans to increase its share of the U.K. chocolate market from 18% to 20%, which means taking share away from Cadbury, Mars, and other rivals.[18] Note, however, that marketing existing products (or variations) is not as risky as marketing new products or diversifying.[19] Moreover, the chosen direction and objectives need marketing support, as discussed below.

More organizations are adopting **sustainable marketing**, "the establishment, maintenance, and enhancement of customer relationships so that the objectives of the parties involved are met without compromising the ability of future generations to achieve their own objectives."[20] This requires balancing long-term goals with the short-term realities of current objectives and budgets. For instance, FedEx has set a goal of cutting air pollution by buying 30,000 low-emission diesel-electric vans over the next decade. Although the initial cost is high, eventually savings in fuel and maintenance will offset the entire cost, and FedEx will be differentiated as

EXHIBIT 1.3   Six Approaches to Growth

	Product Offers	
Penetrate existing markets with current product offers	Modify current product offers for existing markets	Innovate product offers for existing markets
Market current product offers in expanded geographic areas	Modify current product offers for dispersed markets	Innovate product offers geographically
Expand current product offers to entirely new markets	Modify current product offers for entirely new markets	Diversify by innovating product offers for entirely new markets

(Markets)

a "green" delivery company.[21] (See Chapter 5 for more about planning direction and objectives.)

DEVELOP MARKETING STRATEGIES AND PROGRAMS

At this point, the company has examined its current situation, looked at markets and customers, targeted segments and determined its positioning, and set both direction and objectives. Now management formulates strategies using the basic marketing-mix tools of product, place, price, and promotion, enhanced by customer service to build stronger customer relationships and internal marketing to bolster support within the organization.

A small but growing number of companies are customizing parts of their marketing mixes for segments of one. France's Airbus does this, adjusting its airplane configuration, pricing, and sales approach to each airline customer. As another example, Reflect.com, partly owned by Procter & Gamble, allows customers to order personal care products such as lipstick and shampoo manufactured to their individual specifications. Such customization commands a pricing premium that online customers are willing to pay—giving Reflect.com a healthy profit margin.[22]

Marketing strategies and programs must be consistent with the organization's overall direction, goals, and strategies, as Amazon.com's experience suggests:

> **Amazon.com.** Over the years, this online retailer's marketing plans have supported aggressive growth by diversifying into music, movies, kitchen gadgets, electronics, apparel, jewelry, and other merchandise. Once the company went public, CEO Jeff Bezos felt pressure to achieve profitability, so he cut costs, dropped lower-potential merchandise, expanded internationally, and began operating online stores for Target and other retailers. By 2003, the company was profitable, in part because its offer of free shipping on certain purchases had boosted sales. Amazon's marketing plans remain focused on achieving ever-higher revenues and profits.[23]

External marketing strategies are needed to build relationships with suppliers, partners, and channel partners such as wholesalers and retailers. In addition, an internal marketing strategy is needed to build support among employees and managers, ensure proper staffing to carry out marketing programs, and motivate the proper level of customer service. (See Chapter 5 for more about internal marketing and customer service; Chapter 6 for more about product and brand strategy; Chapter 7 for more about channels and logistics; Chapter 8 for more about pricing; and Chapter 9 for more about promotion [integrated marketing communication]).

PREPARE TO TRACK PROGRESS AND CONTROL THE PLAN

Before the marketing plan is implemented, the company needs to identify mechanisms and methods of measuring progress toward objectives. Most companies use sales forecasts, budgets, schedules, and other tools to set and record standards for market share, sales, profitability, productivity, and other measures against which to evaluate results. By comparing actual outcomes against daily, weekly, monthly, quarterly, and yearly projections, management can see where the firm is ahead, where it is behind, and where adjustments are needed to get back on the right path.

EXHIBIT 1.4   Marketing Control

Set marketing ⟶ set standards ⟶ measure ⟶ diagnose results ⟶ take corrective action
plan objectives   performance   if needed

The best marketing plan is useless without effective implementation, as numerous businesses have learned the hard way. The online furniture retailer Living.com, for example, wanted to revolutionize the way consumers buy furniture. Its marketing plan centered on the sale of upscale sofas and other home furnishings; too late, the company realized that few top-end manufacturers were willing to sell through Internet retailers. The company also assumed that consumers would visit local furniture stores to browse, then buy online. In reality, consumers looked at Living.com's site, then went to local stores to buy. Moreover, the company failed to plan for returned merchandise, so any returned items were simply thrown away. Living.com burned through millions of dollars before closing down.[24]

To control implementation, marketers measure interim performance of the planned programs against standards, diagnose the results, and then take corrective action if results fail to measure up. This **marketing control** process is iterative; managers should expect to retrace their steps as they implement strategies, assess the results, and take action to bring performance into line with expectations (see Exhibit 1.4). See Chapter 10 for more about measuring progress and controlling implementation.

Preparing for Marketing Planning

Marketing planning is more challenging than ever before, due to the complex and volatile business environment as well as intense competition in many industries due to ongoing consolidation. Therefore, marketers need to develop a number of professional and organizational strengths, including:

- *Knowledge of markets and customers.* Marketers need current, in-depth knowledge of what their customers want, how and why they buy, how they perceive competing products, and so on. Often technology can be employed to collect and analyze detailed data about specific customers instead of relying on a composite picture of the average customer. This allows fine-tuning of marketing actions to build one-to-one customer relationships, rather than relying on general knowledge such as knowing that the average U.S. household consists of 2.59 people.[25]
- *Core competencies.* **Core competencies** are skills, technologies, and processes—not easily imitated—that give the company competitive superiority in effectively and efficiently satisfying customers. Marketers identify these by looking at employees' talents and expertise as well as at the organization's technologies and operational processes. How can marketing build on these core competencies to satisfy customers and achieve marketing plan objectives? Just as important, how can management handle activities outside the organization's core competencies through outsourcing, forging alliances, and other methods?
- *Relationships.* Strong, mutually-beneficial links with suppliers, distributors, ad agencies, and others form the chain through which the organization creates and delivers **value**—the difference between the perceived benefits that cus-

tomers receive and the perceived price (plus other costs) they pay. The higher the perceived benefits, the higher the value to customers. For example, Cardinal Health Care coordinates its suppliers' activities to get the right mix of medical products to hospitals at just the right time. Cardinal's customers value having prepackaged trays of sterilized surgical tools delivered immediately before operations are to begin.[26] And because the marketing function must work with every other company function in satisfying customers, good internal relationships are also critical.

PRIMARY MARKETING TOOLS

Practical Planning Tip
Use your marketing plan to satisfy customers' needs in a competitively superior way.

In addition to relying on these three main strengths, marketers need to be creative in their use of the primary marketing tools: product, channel, pricing, and promotion. Some of the key elements in the marketing mix are shown in Exhibit 1.5 (and discussed further in Chapters 6, 7, 8, and 9).

Product

Although the product can be either a tangible good or an intangible service, many offerings are actually a combination of tangibles and intangibles.[27] Verizon, a major U.S. provider of cell phone services, for example, frequently offers a free or discounted cell phone (tangible) to customers who enroll in certain calling plans (intangible). In planning product strategy, therefore, think about all the components and about customers' perceptions of the offering as a whole. Piaggio, for example, has learned that customers buying its Vespa motor scooters particularly value styling and technology, not just ease of operation and fuel efficiency.[28] Branding is another key aspect, so important in certain categories that large retailers are cashing in by introducing their own brands: 7-Eleven now markets its own imported Santiago beer, and Home Depot markets the Hampton Bay brand of ceiling fans.[29]

Channel

Channel (place) strategy involves decisions about how, when, and where to make goods and services available to customers. Reflect.com, for example, markets

---

EXHIBIT 1.5   The Marketing Mix

Marketing Mix

Product Offering	Pricing	Channel	Promotion
Product variety	List price	Coverage	Advertising
Quality	Discounts	Assortments	Sales promotion
Features	Credit terms	Locations	Public relations
Brand	Payment period	Inventory	Personal selling
Packaging	Other pricing issues	Transport	Direct marketing
Labeling	New product pricing	Order fulfillment	Internet activities
Warranty	Price competition	Other channel issues	Other promotion issues
Other product issues		Levels	

beauty products directly to customers; this is an unusual channel strategy for part-owner Procter & Gamble, which typically makes Pampers disposable diapers and other products available to consumers through local stores. Aircraft manufacturers such as Boeing and Airbus also market their multimillion-dollar jets directly to the world's airlines. In contrast, many consumer products pass through one or more layers of wholesalers and retailers to reach buyers. Transportation, inventory management, and other logistics issues are an integral part of channel strategy.

Pricing

What should the organization charge for its product offering? Pricing decisions are based on a number of factors, including how customers perceive the value of the offering; how the organization positions the product; what the product's development, production, and distribution costs are; and the competitive structure of the market. Pricing can be so complex that companies such as General Electric and Home Depot use special software to set and change prices.[30] Technology is bringing new practices and new flexibility to pricing, as the travel site Orbitz (www.orbitz.com) and other Web-based businesses have demonstrated.

Careful pricing can attract new customers, boost market share, and fend off rivals. Nintendo, for example, in competing with Microsoft's Xbox and Sony's PlayStation, stimulated U.S. sales and reduced its inventory of GameCube videogame consoles by reducing prices up to 45%. Higher sales of consoles helped Nintendo sell more of its profitable game programs—but more pricing decisions are on the way for portable game units, the next industry battleground.[31] On the other hand, higher pricing to support an upscale image or better quality carries the risk that customers may perceive the price as too high relative to the product's perceived value. These are two of many considerations in pricing strategy.

Promotion

Promotion covers all the tools used to communicate with the target market, including advertising; public relations; sales promotion; personal selling; and direct marketing techniques such as catalogs, e-mail, and wireless messages. Because of media proliferation and audience fragmentation, a growing number of organizations are reducing their use of television and other mass media in favor of nontraditional promotions. Coca-Cola, for instance, cut $80 million from its television advertising budget and invested in nontraditional promotions such as opening Coke Red Lounges in major malls where teens can mingle, watch music videos, and buy Coke drinks from vending machines.[32] When using a variety of messages and media, marketers must carefully manage the overall content and impact through the use of integrated marketing communication.

SUPPORTING THE MARKETING MIX

No marketing plan is complete without strategies for supporting the marketing mix with customer service and internal marketing. Why is customer service so important? First, it reinforces positive perceptions of a brand, product, and company—and customers expect it (or even demand it). Second, good service can clearly differentiate a company from competitors. Third, poor or inconsistent customer service simply will not satisfy customers—and they are likely to tell others about their dissatisfaction, generating negative word of mouth.[33] Fourth, great service can help the organization retain current customers and bring in new ones through reputation and referral.

At the very least, marketing plans should allow for handling customer inquiries and complaints; some may also cover installation (e.g., for appliances, floor coverings, or giant turbines), technical support (e.g., for computer products), and training (e.g., for software). Online businesses may rely on Web-based FAQs and help indexes, e-mail, live text chat, live online telephony, and/or toll-free telephone contact to deliver service. Even the U.S. government is focusing on customer service, speeding up answers to inquiries submitted by mail or e-mail to the Federal Citizen Information Center (www.firstgov.gov) or by phone to the National Contact Center.[34]

The internal marketing strategy focuses all employees on serving customers and builds support for the marketing plan. For example, Green Hills Farms Store, a family-owned supermarket in Syracuse, New York, pretests promotions on its 200 employees. Once the store receives employee feedback, it adjusts programs if needed before launching them to customers. Employees also serve as goodwill ambassadors, telling their friends and family about new promotions.[35] (Chapter 5 discusses customer service and internal marketing.)

GUIDING PRINCIPLES

Supplementing the marketing strengths and tools discussed above, today's marketers should follow five guiding principles to contribute to customer value and stay competitive as they proceed through the marketing planning process: (1) expect change; (2) emphasize relationships; (3) involve everyone; (4) seek alliances; and (5) be innovative. These guiding principles, summarized in Exhibit 1.6, are explored below.

Expect Change

The global networked economy is a fact of business life, with technology enabling buyers and sellers to connect anywhere in the world. In practical terms, this means marketers can more easily link with the best suppliers, partners, resellers, and deals, because geographical distance is not the obstacle it used to be.

EXHIBIT 1.6   Guiding Principles of Marketing Planning

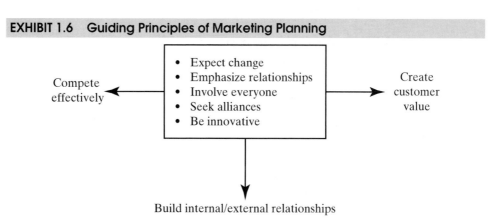

**Practical
Planning Tip**
Expect change and stay
alert for new partners,
rivals, customers, oppor-
tunities, and threats.

Still, competitors can more easily explore the territory of their rivals, so marketers must expect change and be ready to fend off rivals from anywhere at any time.

In the dynamic business environment, trends can come and go without warning. Here is how the retailer Escada plans for change:

> **Escada.** Fashion never stands still, which is why Escada, a women's apparel chain based in Germany, introduces as many as 15 full product lines every year. The company also watches for suddenly-hot looks or colors and makes these the basis of periodic "minicollections" produced between regularly-scheduled line introductions, bringing shoppers back again and again in search of the latest styles. "It is a reaction to the ever-faster fashion cycle and to retailers like H&M and Zara, who react to new trends very quickly," says an Escada official.[36]

Emphasize Relationships

Consumers, businesses, nonprofit organizations, and government agencies have access to more information and more choices in today's marketplace, giving them more power as customers. Therefore, for long-term success, marketers need to work at closer relationships with their customers (as well as suppliers, channel members, partners, and other key **stakeholders**, people and organizations that are influenced by or can influence company performance).

**Practical
Planning Tip**
Prepare for future suc-
cess by forging good
long-term relationships
with all stakeholders.

Traditionally, companies kept up a monologue by sending information to customers through advertisements and other promotion techniques. With a dialogue, however, information flows both ways—from the firm to customers, and from customers to the firm. This dialogue provides clues to what customers think, feel, need, want, and expect, helping marketers adjust current programs and plan new programs to reinforce loyalty.

Some marketers are taking dialogue a step further, connecting customers with each other and taking the pulse of the community. The auction site eBay, for example, also serves as a forum for buyers and sellers to exchange ideas and research areas of interest. Having buyers rate sellers is "a really important part of eBay's chemistry," says CEO Meg Whitman. With more than 100 million people worldwide using eBay, she adds, "A cardinal sin is not knowing what the community's concerns are"—which is why the company checks buyers' and sellers' reactions before implementing major changes.[37]

Involve Everyone

At one time, marketing and sales personnel were the only people responsible for an organization's marketing functions. Now all employees must be involved in marketing, and all contact points must be seen as opportunities to strengthen customer relationships. Everything about the company sends a signal, so companies must project the right impression and meet customers' expectations through more than marketing.

**Practical
Planning Tip**
By involving everyone,
you strengthen internal
relationships and sup-
port the marketing
plan.

To keep employees involved, they must be informed about products, promotions, and whatever else they need to satisfy customers. Many firms circulate printed newsletters, post news on internal Web sites (*intranets*), or send updates via e-mail to keep employees informed. Japanese beauty products manufacturer

Shiseido connects employees in 16,000 stores worldwide with cell phones that can download corporate information and upload comments on fast-selling products. This keeps manufacturing, sales, and home-office personnel updated about inventory, requests, sales, and more.[38]

Seek Alliances

Successful marketers work through a network of alliances with carefully-chosen suppliers, channel members, partners, customers, and community leaders (see Exhibit 1.7). The purpose is to provide the mutual support, capabilities, and innovations that the participants need to satisfy their customers, meet their objectives, and be competitive. In essence, the company's network of alliances is in competition with the networks that rival companies have assembled.[39]

Practical Planning Tip
Seek out creative ideas and insights from suppliers and other value-chain members.

- *Suppliers* not only provide raw materials, parts, and other inputs, they can offer insights regarding the external environment. Increasingly, companies are connecting with suppliers to lower costs and exchange data for mutual profitability. These alliances are critical because the quality of a product depends, in part, on the quality of suppliers' materials.
- *Channel members* such as wholesalers and retailers have daily contact with customers and can provide vital feedback about buying patterns and preferences. Channel choices are critical because customers associate the firm's brand with the quality and convenience of their shopping experience.
- *Partners* in joint ventures, outsourcing, or other arrangements contribute their core competencies and market knowledge. Linking up with a partner that has complementary capabilities and strengths gives both more marketing

---

EXHIBIT 1.7   Building a Network of Alliances

Suppliers
Raw materials suppliers
Parts and components suppliers
Suppliers of products for resale
Other suppliers

Channel members
Wholesalers
Retailers
Agents and brokers
Transportation firms
Storage firms
Other intermediaries

ALLIANCE NETWORK PARTICIPANTS

Partners
Joint venture partners
Outsource vendors
Strategic alliance partners
Research and development partners
Other partners

Customers and community
Consumers
Business customers
Product users
Purchase influencers
Community leaders
Other groups

power. In the course of developing new products, for instance, consumer products giant Procter & Gamble coordinates the efforts of 600 partners around the world.[40]

- *Customers* can be excellent partners because they are eager for products that solve their problems or, in the case of businesses, help them better serve their own customers. 3M, for example, brings in business customers to discuss their needs, and its scientists visit customer sites to see products in use. Groups within 3M that forge customer partnerships generate four times as many new product ideas compared with other groups, helping to boost revenues by $1.2 billion annually.[41]

- *Community* leaders from civic groups, charities, school groups, and other parts of the community can offer feedback about the organization's image and activities and inform management thinking about social issues, local concerns, and sustainable marketing ideas. For instance, after consulting with community leaders, Washington Mutual decided to erect affordable housing near some of its U.S. bank branches; similarly, Freeport-McMoRan Copper & Gold decided to donate money for a new medical facility near its mine in Indonesia.[42]

Be Innovative

To succeed, companies must seize every opportunity to be innovative. A return to old-fashioned personal service is a welcome "innovation" in industries where automation has reduced human contact. To illustrate, Patriot National Bank in Connecticut competes with regional and national banks by hiring employees who are known in the community and by emphasizing personal service at its seven branches. The bank's marketing plan calls for high-tech as well as high-touch operations: "We serve muffins and cookies in our offices, but we still have Internet banking," says the bank's president.[43]

Some of the most ingenious innovations are occurring online, where companies apply technology to satisfy customers and provide good service. For instance, customers at the Lands' End Web site (www.landsend.com) can create a "virtual model" by inputting their measurements and hair color so they can see how different clothing might look on them.[44] Here's how Blue Nile sells expensive jewelry on the Internet:

> **Blue Nile.** Business is brisk—especially at holiday time—for Blue Nile (www.bluenile.com), where customers can review pages of information about diamonds and design the jewelry of their dreams before they buy. Customers with broadband Internet connections can zoom in on 32,000 gems and try the stones in different settings. (Customers with slower Internet connections see less graphics-intense pages.) Because Blue Nile's jewelry sells for up to $300,000, it is not surprising that customers typically view 200 Web pages before ordering. Enthusiastic customer response has helped Blue Nile expand quickly and reach $128 million in annual sales.[45]

Technology is not the only way to innovate. Ben & Jerry's, for instance, sends tasters around the world in search of ideas for novel new ice cream flavors. After its travels, the team concocts 150 recipes and narrows the decision to about 12 new

Practical Planning Tip
Look beyond the usual to satisfy customers, build your image, and beat competitors through innovation.

flavors each year. Given that Ben & Jerry's marketing plan calls for selling fewer than three dozen flavors at any one time, 12 newcomers represent considerable innovation. The company, a Unilever division, is also known for its commitment to sustainable marketing. As one example, its Coffee for a Change flavor is made with coffee beans certified as grown in an ecological-friendly way.[46] These and other innovations attract like-minded customers, suppliers, and investors, building stronger relations for long-term success.

Summary

Marketing planning is the structured process used to research and analyze the marketing situation; develop and document marketing objectives, strategies, and programs; and implement, evaluate, and control marketing activities to achieve marketing objectives. The marketing plan documents the results of the marketing planning process and serves an important coordination function. With internal consensus, it provides direction for employees and managers; encourages collaboration; outlines resource allocation; and delineates the tasks, schedules, and responsibilities planned to accomplish objectives.

The six broad steps in marketing planning are (1) research and analyze the current situation; (2) understand markets and customers; (3) plan segmentation, targeting, and positioning; (4) plan direction, objectives, and marketing support; (5) develop marketing strategies and programs; and (6) prepare to track progress and control the plan after implementation. For marketing purposes, marketers need a number of professional and organizational strengths and the know-how to create an effective marketing mix supplemented by customer service and internal marketing. Five broad guiding principles for marketing planning are to expect change, emphasize relationships, involve everyone, seek alliances, and be innovative.

2

Analyzing
the Current Situation

In this chapter:

Preview

"Marketing and the marketplace are dynamic systems," observes Professor Don E. Schultz of Northwestern University.[1] Thus, a change in one element of the marketplace or organization can make a difference in decisions about marketing strategies, customer service, choice of channels, pricing, and other aspects of the marketing plan. This chapter explores the use of environmental scanning and analysis to understand the dynamic forces and trends affecting the current marketing situation. First is a discussion of the internal environment, including the organization's mission, resources, product offerings, previous results, business relationships, keys to success, and warning signs. The second half of the chapter examines the external environment, including demographic, economic, ecological, technological, political-legal, and social-cultural trends, as well as competitor analysis. Coverage of SWOT (strength, weakness, opportunity, threat) analysis ends the chapter, laying the foundation for market and customer analysis (see Chapter 3).

This is a good time to set up the structure of your marketing plan so you can document the outcome of your environmental scanning and analysis efforts. Use the *Marketing Plan Pro* software bundled with this book to create your plan or follow the outline shown in Exhibit 1.2 (*page 5*). For more about *Marketing Plan Pro* software, see Appendix 2. Also see this chapter's checklist (*page 22*), which summarizes key questions to ask as you analyze the environment for marketing planning purposes.

Environmental Scanning and Analysis

To map an effective marketing plan, the marketer needs to stay abreast of key factors in the **macroenvironment** that can affect organizational performance, including broad demographic, economic, ecological, technological, political-legal, and social-cultural forces. In addition, the marketer must look at specific groups in the **microenvironment** that more directly influence performance, such as customers, competitors, channel members, partners, suppliers, and employees.

Through *environmental scanning and analysis,* marketers collect and examine data about these environmental factors to better understand the company's strengths, weaknesses, opportunities, and threats as a prerequisite to developing marketing strategies and programs (see Exhibit 2.1):

Practical Planning Tip
Remember that what is a strength for one organization may be a weakness for another; the reverse holds true as well.

- *Strengths* are internal capabilities that can help the firm achieve its goals and objectives; for a car manufacturer, strengths might include a well-known brand, engineering expertise, and manufacturing efficiency.
- *Weaknesses* are internal factors that can prevent the firm from achieving its goals and objectives; high staff turnover and out-dated equipment might be two weaknesses for a computer chip manufacturer.
- *Opportunities* are external circumstances that the organization might be able to exploit for higher performance; media attention to obesity in the United States might present an opportunity for a food manufacturer or cookbook publisher.
- *Threats* are external circumstances that might hurt the organization's performance, now or in the future; for an airline, threats could include

CHAPTER 2 CHECKLIST   Areas of Focus Within the Environment

Internal Factors

✔ What is the organization's mission? How will marketing planning be affected by the purpose; main focus; and approach to creating value?

✔ What resources are available? How will marketing planning be affected by employees' skills, training, and morale; the organization's financial strength; and the available information, supplies, and technology to support marketing?

✔ What are the current offerings? How will marketing planning be affected by the product mix; product lines and prices; product age; and sales and profitability by product?

✔ What do previous results reveal about sales and profit trends, marketing effectiveness, and customer relationships?

✔ How do business relationships with suppliers, distributors, and partners affect costs, capacity, quality, and ability to satisfy customers?

✔ What special factors make the difference between good and poor performance?

✔ What critical warning signs indicate potential problems?

External Factors

✔ What demographic trends can be identified? How will marketing planning be affected by population size, composition, changes, characteristics related to product purchase or usage, business demographics, and other trends?

✔ What economic trends can be identified? How will marketing planning be affected by trends in the local, regional, national, and global economy and the target market's buying power?

✔ What ecological trends can be identified? How will marketing planning be affected by trends in materials and energy availability, pollution problems, governmental and social responses to ecological issues?

✔ What technological trends can be identified? What are the marketing planning implications of innovations that may affect customers, suppliers, channel members, marketing activities and processes, standards and regulations?

✔ What political-legal trends can be identified? What are the marketing planning implications of political shifts and legal/regulatory mandates (or proposals) applicable to the organization's marketing and operations?

✔ What social-cultural trends can be identified? What are the marketing implications of customers' nationality, religion, language, immersion in popular culture, core beliefs and values?

higher fuel costs, increased competition, and customer concerns about terrorism.

Consider how Eastman Kodak's marketers and managers examined the environment, interpreted emerging trends, and shaped the company's marketing in response:

EXHIBIT 2.1   Environmental Scanning and Marketing Strategy

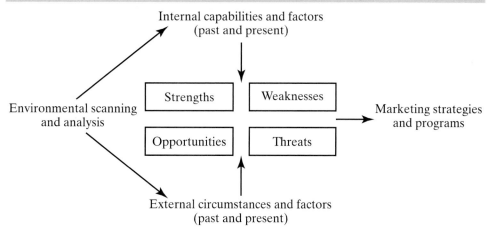

Kodak. Kodak's marketers have been studying the advance of digital photography to determine how much of the company's film and camera business it would displace—and when. They had projected a significant drop in film sales in 2006, but consumers embraced digital photography so quickly that, by the end of 2002, industry-wide film sales had plummeted and were unlikely to rebound. Increasingly popular camera-phones also became a threat to Kodak's $8 billion consumer imaging business. By leveraging its strengths—a well-regarded brand, extensive imaging expertise, and long-time relationships with channel members and partners—Kodak is now moving decisively into digital imaging. The company leads the market in photo-quality inkjet paper for printing digital images at home and is implementing plans to address opportunities in commercial and medical digital applications, as well as in the consumer market.[2]

As Kodak's experience demonstrates, environmental scanning must be an ongoing process, not a once-a-year exercise, to prevent the company from following an outdated marketing plan. If Kodak's marketers had not continually monitored the penetration of digital photography, they might have missed the unexpectedly rapid adoption of this technology as well as the increase in sales of camera-phones. Seeing the sudden upward trend in digital imaging convinced them to adopt a new marketing plan—fast. As branding expert Kevin Lane Keller observes: "A marketing plan is not a static document but must be constantly updated to reflect current developments and emerging threats and opportunities."[3] Exhibit 2.2 lists selected internal and external sources for environmental scanning.

EXHIBIT 2.2   Selected Sources for Environmental Scanning

Internal Sources	*External Sources, Microenvironmental Trends*	*External Sources, Macroenvironmental Trends*
• Company databases and files (sales; financial indicators; market share; customer acquisition, retention, churn; product lines; etc.) • Workforce (feedback, ideas from sales staff, other personnel) • Customer service records (complaints, inquiries, repairs) • Marketing research reports (market studies, satisfaction surveys)	• Customer advisory panels • Marketing research suppliers • Industry groups, publications, Web sites, databases, meetings • Competitor products, Web sites, literature • Web sites that cover business, marketing (www.hoovers.com, www.scip.org)	• Government agencies and publications (www.census.gov, www.stat-usa.gov, www.ftc.gov, www.gnet.org, www.un.org/ecosocdev) • Consumer and business media (www.cnn.com, www.msnbc.com, www.ecommercetimes.com) • Academic and professional publications, Web sites (www.stateline.org, www.norc.org) • Channel members, suppliers, partners • Community groups, other stakeholders (www.bsr.org, www.net-impact.org)

Analyzing the Internal Environment

In the course of internal environmental scanning, marketers start by looking to the organization's overall mission for direction in their marketing planning efforts. They also examine the organization's resources, offerings, previous results, business relationships, keys to success, and warning signs.

MISSION

Knowing the organization's mission helps marketers make decisions about appropriate strategies and programs. The **mission** states the company's fundamental purpose—its core ideology, in the terminology of Collins and Porras—defines its focus, indicates how it will add value for customers and other stakeholders, and outlines the envisioned future. This definition provides decision makers with direction about aligning strategy and resources to stimulate progress toward the future vision of the organization.[4]

Consider the mission of Morgan Stanley: "Connecting people, ideas, and capital, we will be our clients' first choice for achieving their financial aspirations." Such a concise yet specific mission directs Morgan Stanley's marketers to concentrate on innovations that move the company toward its vision of being the preferred service provider to help clients (individual investors, institutions, and government customers) reach their financial goals. In applying this mission, Morgan Stanley strives for market leadership and product innovation.[5] As another example, the mission of the nonprofit organization Médecins Sans Frontières (Doctors Without Borders) is "providing medical aid wherever needed, regardless of race, religion, politics, or sex, and raising awareness of the plight of the people we help."[6]

RESOURCES

Next, look at the resources the organization has or can obtain, including human, financial, informational, and supply resources. No company has unlimited resources; therefore, management must carefully balance resource allocation to ensure successful performance. Some questions to ask in examining internal resources include:

- *Human resources:* Does the workforce have the needed skills and training? Do managers have the initiative and entrepreneurial drive to support the mission? Is the company using recruitment and training to prepare itself for the future? Is morale high or low? Is turnover high or low? If applicable, what is the state of relations with unionized workers and their leaders?
- *Financial resources:* Does the company have the capital (or access to capital) to support marketing? What funding issues must be addressed over the period covered by the marketing plan?
- *Informational resources:* Does the company have the data needed to address its markets and challenges? What informational sources are available to support marketing planning, implementation, and control?
- *Supply resources:* Does the company have (or can it obtain) steady and affordable supplies of parts, components, materials, and services needed for operations and production? Are its suppliers stable and committed to the organization?

Practical Planning Tip

Check that resources are adequate to support successful completion of current marketing programs and fund future marketing strategies.

In many cases, organizations can arrange external sources or supplement existing resources through new strategic alliances and new supply chain relationships. But only by analyzing internal resources will marketers learn about gaps and strengths that can affect marketing planning, implementation, and control.

OFFERINGS

This part of the analysis looks at what the organization is currently offering in the way of goods and services. At a minimum, it is necessary to look at the product mix and the lines within that mix, asking questions such as: What products are being offered, at what price points, and for what customer segments? What is the age of each product and its sales and profit trend over the years? How are newer products faring in relation to older products? What is the market share of each product or line? How does each product support sales of the line—are some sold only as supplements or add-ons to others? How does each product contribute to the company's overall performance? Does one product account for a large portion of sales and profits? Where is each product in its life cycle, and how can marketing extend or enhance the life cycle?

Just as important, marketers must determine how the organization's offerings relate to its mission and to its resources. Do the products use the firm's resources most effectively and efficiently while following the mission? Are other offerings needed to restore the focus or fulfill the long-term purpose described in the mission? Answering these questions will give management a better sense of internal strengths and weaknesses in preparation for future marketing activities.

PREVIOUS RESULTS

The company's previous results also offer important clues to internal strengths and weaknesses that can affect results. By analyzing last year's unit and dollar sales, profits, and other financial results—and comparing these results with trends over several years—marketers can get a big picture of overall performance. Marketers also need to analyze the results of the previous years' marketing programs to see what worked and what did not.

In addition, marketers should look carefully at customer acquisition and retention costs to be sure they are appropriate for the value of the relationship. As an example, traditional catalog retailers spend about $38 to acquire a new customer. Some consumer products marketers may spend less; B2B companies and new online businesses may spend more. Netflix, for instance, spends about $35 to acquire each DVD rental customer as part of its aggressive growth strategy. "Because we're a subscription service, with an ongoing revenue stream from each customer, we expect total marketing costs will fall as a percent of revenue," notes the CEO, explaining the financial rationale.[7]

The point of analyzing previous results is to separate effective from ineffective activities and understand related costs as a prelude to planning marketing programs. Consider the situation at Procter & Gamble, where marketers examine results over time when formulating marketing plans:

> **Procter & Gamble.** With $45 billion in sales, P&G owns some of the best-known brands on the planet, including Tide and Crest. In fact, 13 of its brands each generate more than $1 billion in annual sales. P&G is always studying results, product by product and category by category, to build on its successes and identify areas for improvement. Thus, Crest debuted in 1955 as a toothpaste brand and, 50 years later, the brand remains so strong that it powers a broad range of products in the oral-care category, including manual and battery-operated toothbrushes. When a product like the Crest SpinBrush is a big hit, P&G's marketers develop plans to use its success as a foundation for future enhancements and product introductions.[8]

BUSINESS RELATIONSHIPS

A closer look at relationships with suppliers, distributors, and partners can help determine whether changes should be made in the coming year. Although cost is always a critical factor, companies also must ask whether their suppliers and distributors (1) have the capacity to increase volume if needed; (2) maintain a suitable quality level; and (3) can be true partners in adding value and satisfying customers. How has the roster of suppliers and dealers changed over time? Is the company overly dependent on one supplier or channel partner? Does the company expect its partners to provide special expertise or services? All these questions are geared toward getting a well-rounded picture of strengths and identifying weaknesses that can affect the organization's offerings and marketing plans.

A close supplier–customer relationship may be both an advantage and a disadvantage, as in the case of KH Vatec:

KH Vatec. The rise of cell phones has opened numerous opportunities for this South Korean manufacturer. Founder Nam Kwang Hee supplied Samsung with a number of parts before he invented a cheaper way to make antenna brackets and electromagnetic interference shields and priced these much lower than competitors. Now sales to Samsung represent 80% of the company's revenue. Despite this close relationship, Nam wants to diversify to avoid being overly dependent on one customer. Yet being known as a Samsung supplier makes KH Vatec attractive to other customers: "To become a supplier to Samsung, you must have the highest-quality everything at the lowest price," Nam points out.[9]

KEYS TO SUCCESS AND WARNING SIGNS

Not everything in a marketing plan is equally important. Marketers should identify, in just a few sentences, the special factors that most influence the firm's movement toward fulfilling its mission and achieving superior performance. Pinpointing these keys to success can put the focus on the right priorities in planning the year's marketing strategies and programs. For example, Wal-Mart has built its retail empire on two major keys to success: (1) controlling costs and logistics to keep prices low and (2) selecting locations that are underserved by competitors.

Likewise, every organization should scan for the major warning signs that indicate potential problems with leveraging the keys to success and performing as planned. For Wal-Mart, one such issue might be rising transportation costs: unless the chain can contain or lower such costs, it may be forced to hike prices—a problem when low prices are a key to success. Other possible warning signs for Wal-Mart: shifts in U.S. trade policy that affect imports and objections in communities where new stores are planned.[10] Paying close attention to these issues will help Wal-Mart's marketers plan to reach their objectives.

Analyzing the External Environment

Practical Planning Tip
Use this analysis to identify opportunities and threats that must be factored into your marketing decisions.

Within the external environment, marketers need to examine broad demographic, economic, ecological, technological, political-legal, and social-cultural trends. They also must pay special attention to strategies and movements of competitors. (Customer and market analysis are discussed in more detail in Chapter 3.) Whereas scans of the internal environment are designed to uncover strengths and weaknesses, scans of the external environment are designed to uncover opportunities and threats that can be effectively addressed in the marketing plan. Exhibit 2.3 shows an example using Southwest Airlines.

DEMOGRAPHIC TRENDS

Consumer and business markets are moving targets—never static, always changing. For marketers of consumer products, population trends and characteristics suggest the size of the market and strength of demand. For marketers of business products, indicators of market size and strength include trends in business forma-

EXHIBIT 2.3   The External Environment of Southwest Airlines

Element and Potential Impact	*Possible Changes in Marketing*
Demographic trends: Population shifts and changes in business concentration can affect demand; household income can affect affordability.	Consider entry into new markets; examine pricing for targeted segments; plan promotions in line with trends.
Economic trends: Growing inflation can push costs higher; economic recovery can boost demand.	To maintain profitability, trim costs or raise prices in response to inflation; gain pricing flexibility if demand is higher.
Ecological trends: Community concerns about airports being expanded and flight-related noise can affect the number of available gates and flight slots.	Research airport plans and local reaction in new markets; research local rules about early-morning flights; train flight crews for noise-abatement.
Technological trends: Higher Internet usage can shift more customers to online reservations; advanced plane design can increase fuel efficiency.	Reduce off-line customer service support, increase marketing use of Web site; consider applying fuel savings to lower ticket prices.
Political-legal trends: More stringent security rules are forcing changes in check-in procedures and baggage handling.	Consider communications to alert customers about security requirements and offer reassurances about air travel safety.
Social-cultural trends: Money-saving choices are gaining widespread acceptance; public interest in social responsibility can affect company reputation.	Communicate the financial benefits of flying Southwest and the money-saving advantages; expand Adopt-A-Pilot community educational program for fifth-grade students.
Competitive trends: Start-up airlines can increase competitive pressure; price wars can affect revenue and profits.	Continue to enhance brand image and awareness; communicate competitive superiority; maintain competitive pricing in each market.

tion and certain organizational characteristics. However, these point-in-time examinations of demographic trends must be routinely updated to reflect any changes.

Consumer Demographics

Population growth is creating and expanding markets around the world—sometimes through higher birth rates, sometimes through lower death rates, sometimes through immigration. At the same time, the population is actually shrinking in some areas as people move to other areas, such as from urban to suburban or rural markets or from one state or country to another. For this reason, marketers need to follow the population trends in the markets where they currently do business or are considering doing business, using U.S. Census data and other research.

Also explore the composition of the consumer population: age, gender, ethnic and religious makeup, education, occupation, and household size and income, as well as trends over time. When P&G, for example, examined U.S. demographics through Census reports and other data, it noticed sizable increases in certain segments, such as Hispanic consumers. Then it looked closer, says Graciela Eleta,

P&G's vice president-general manager of multicultural development: "While Hispanic household income is about $33,000 a year versus $43,000 a year for the general market, Hispanics consume more in our product categories than the general population—diapers, detergents, etc." Based on this opportunity, the company increased its Spanish-language advertising and raised awareness among Hispanic consumers by becoming active in Avanzando con tu Familia and other causes.[11]

Business Demographics

Companies that operate in business markets need to scan the environment for information about the size and growth of the industries that they sell to, as measured by number of companies, number of locations or branches, number of employees, and sales revenues. They also should pay attention to trends in new business formation, which can signal emerging opportunities to market products such as office furniture, computers, accounting services, telecommunications services, and cleaning supplies. Palo Alto Software, which makes the *Marketing Plan Pro* software packaged with this text, is particularly interested in new business formation as an indicator of demand for its marketing planning software as well as its *Business Plan Pro* business planning software.

Just as consumer marketers examine population trends in different geographic markets where they are selling or want to sell, business marketers must look at business population trends. *Inc.* and other magazines regularly publish studies of the cities and states hosting the most new start-ups, among other business population analyses that can point the way toward promising markets for B2B products such as business loans, printers, and insurance. Often urbanization and business demographics suggest opportunities for marketing to government and business customers, as in the case of Caterpillar:

Caterpillar. This Illinois-based manufacturer of earthmoving equipment— from bulldozers to backhoes and beyond—targets areas being transformed by infrastructure projects, urbanization, or business development. It is planning to attain $30 billion in annual sales by 2010, fueled in part by higher sales in Asia. Already, Caterpillar is selling the Chinese government equipment for modernizing the country's dams, railways, and roads. Private construction in India represents another marketing focus: with the expansion of business centers and new housing, Caterpillar has established a network of dealerships to sell and service its construction equipment across the country. However, the company also must plan to deal with competition from rivals such as Sweden's Volvo, South Korea's Hyundai and Daewoo, and Japan's Komatsu and Hitachi, all of which are active in Asia. And, if economic trends move downward, Caterpillar may have difficulty reaching its ambitious objectives.[12]

ECONOMIC TRENDS

In today's interconnected global economy, deepening recession in one part of the world can affect consumer and business buying patterns thousands of miles away. For Caterpillar, unfavorable economic conditions in Asia would likely slow the pace of development, thereby affecting sales of construction-related products.

**Practical
Planning Tip**
Notice how regional,
national, and interna-
tional economic trends
affect customer buying
power, supplier
strength, and competi-
tive pressures.

Thus, marketers have to keep a close eye on local, regional, national, and even global economic trends, watching for signs of change.

To better understand the buying power of consumers (or business customers), marketers should analyze buyer income, debt, and credit usage. When personal income is rising, consumers have more buying power; lower debt and more available credit also fuel consumer buying. Similarly, businesses with higher debt may not buy as much or as often as businesses with lower debt and more available credit. For planning purposes, consider how specific trends may affect the company's industry, its products, its competitors, and targeted geographic markets.

ECOLOGICAL TRENDS

The natural environment can influence businesses and nonprofits in a variety of ways. One of the most obvious is the availability of raw materials such as water, timber, oil, minerals, and other essentials for production; shortages, as one example, can cause major headaches for companies. To illustrate, after drought hurt cotton crops in China and Australia (and hiked cotton prices), Nike, Adidas, and Reebok began introducing polyester sports apparel. Cotton shortages also prompted Levi Strauss and other sportswear makers to increase the percentage of polyester used in certain items.[13]

In addition, marketers have to examine the various environmental issues that affect their organizations because of government regulation or social attitudes. What pollution or environmental problems directly and indirectly affect the business? How can the organization build on growing interest in environmentally safe goods and services? WorldWise, for example, responded to this trend by creating "green" products such as rainforest snack foods sold through Costco, Target, and other retailers. As another example, New Leaf Paper sells a line of top-quality recycled paper products.[14] Even businesses that don't position their products as ecologically sound must watch ecological trends and anticipate movements or regulations that can influence performance.

TECHNOLOGICAL TRENDS

Technology reaches into every aspect of the marketing mix, from digitally enhanced advertisements to new packaging materials and methods and beyond, making this an increasingly vital part of the macroenvironment. Key trends include the ongoing global penetration of cell phones, computers, digital media, Internet usage, and the incorporation of electronic capabilities into a wider range of products. The Internet alone has spawned countless opportunities, from online retailing and wholesaling to security solutions for viruses, stolen data, and other problems. Here is how JetBlue Airways harnesses technology for internal and external impact:

JetBlue Airways. Based in New York, this fast-growing discount airline relies on technology for efficient operation and competitive differentiation. Its pilots tote laptops for checking online flight manuals, updated instantly for changing flight conditions. Thanks to this "paperless cockpit," the pilots can complete preflight preparations and get in the air much more quickly, speeding passengers to their destination. JetBlue was also an industry leader in offering free satellite television at each seat—a feature so popular that several rivals have followed suit.[15]

Broad questions about technological trends include: What cutting-edge innovations are being introduced, and how do they affect the organization's customers, suppliers, distributors, marketing, and processes? How are these technologies affected by, or generating, industry-wide standards and government regulations? What substitutes or innovations are becoming available due to new technology, and how are these changes likely to affect suppliers, customers, and competitors? As an example, PC buyers are deserting large, box-like cathode-ray tube (CRT) computer monitors now that flat-screen liquid-crystal displays (LCDs) are more affordable. LCD monitors will soon outsell CRT monitors by four to one.[16] Understanding such trends can reveal threats (such as inventions likely to supplant older technology) and opportunities (such as quickly adopting a new technological standard).

POLITICAL-LEGAL TRENDS

As part of the external scanning process, marketers need to examine the legal and regulatory guidelines that govern diverse business and marketing practices. Numerous U.S. state and federal laws cover competitive behavior, pricing, taxation, promotion, distribution, product liability, labeling, and product purity, among other elements, in the United States. Moreover, government agencies such as the Federal Trade Commission and the Department of Justice watch for questionable business practices.

Political developments also can signal changes in legal and regulatory priorities—posing new threats or opening new opportunities. The Sarbanes-Oxley Act, which requires companies to collect and retain internal documents about their financial performance as a way of improving corporate accountability, has opened opportunities to sell software for storing e-mail, voice mail, and other messages; it has also opened opportunities for info-tech systems providers.[17] Political pressure to deregulate U.S. industries has resulted in both threats and opportunities. Deregulation freed airlines to compete through schedules, destinations, fares, amenities, and loyalty programs. However, price wars, global economic woes, and high costs took a toll, and eventually several major airlines (such as United Airlines) flew into severe financial turbulence. On the other hand, low-fare carriers such as Southwest and JetBlue have thrived, making the U.S. market more attractive for start-ups such as Virgin USA, a new discount carrier created by London's Virgin Group.[18]

Companies that operate globally need to monitor the concerns of regulators in all the countries and regions where they operate, because regulatory obstacles can derail even the most carefully planned strategies. To illustrate, Microsoft encountered serious regulatory difficulties in the European Union:

Microsoft. European Union regulators recently ruled against Microsoft in an antitrust case, saying that the integrated Media Player software in Microsoft's Windows operating system posed a threat to competitors such as RealNetworks. Microsoft's Media Player then held a 64% share of the European market for software that plays audio and video media, compared with 22% for RealNetworks' media software. Despite the ruling, appeals could keep this case alive for some time. Microsoft has plenty of cash to pay a hefty fine; however, it would have to rethink its product strategy if forced to disclose some of its software code or unbundle Media Player from Windows.[19]

SOCIAL-CULTURAL TRENDS

Increased diversity in markets—and in the workforce—is a key social-cultural trend affecting today's marketing. Using U.S. Census data and other sources, marketers can learn more about the cultural diversity of specific geographic markets—including nation of origin, primary language, and other details that can help in tailoring the offer and the message to specific groups. Diversity opened promising opportunities for EthnicGrocer, which operates U.S.-based retail sites selling foods preferred by immigrants and expatriates, such as Namaste.com (www.namaste .com) featuring Indian products. Wider exposure to other societies also creates new opportunities. Sawanee Engblom started Tuk Tuk Foods in Stockholm after she noticed that Swedish travelers returning from Thailand wanted to buy authentic Thai dishes locally. Now Tuk Tuk markets Thai meals in Swedish supermarkets and will soon export its meals to Denmark, Norway, and Finland, where people are becoming interested in Thai foods.[20]

Remain alert to the unexpected opportunities and threats created by popular culture; makers of fad products are quite familiar with the pattern of meteoric sales increases followed by sharp sales declines as another craze takes the spotlight. Yet the core beliefs and values that pervade a society or subculture, which change only slowly over time, also create opportunities and threats. Attitudes toward ethical and social responsibility issues, influenced by core beliefs and values, can affect marketing plans and corporate image, as cigarette marketers have learned. As another example, the Co-operative Insurance Society (CIS), a U.K. insurance firm, surveyed its 5 million customers about whether CIS should invest its $37 billion portfolio in certain countries or certain types of companies. "We think that the social, ethical, and environmental issues on which we engage should reflect the values of our customers," the CEO says.[21]

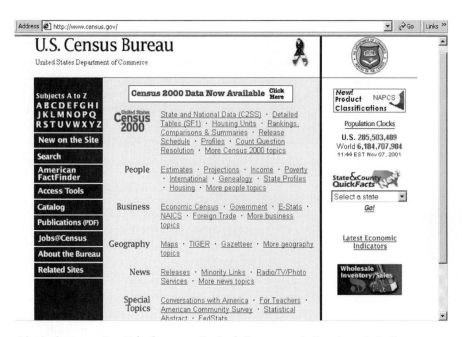

Marketers use the U.S. Census site to follow population trends in the markets where they currently operate or are considering doing business.

COMPETITOR ANALYSIS

Analyzing competitors can help marketers better understand market dynamics, anticipate what rivals will do, and create more practical marketing plans. Start by identifying current competitors and possible sources of competition in the near future, to avoid being blindsided by a new entrant. Also look at trends in market share to get a sense of which competitors are becoming more powerful. Look at the changing fortunes of Toys 'R' Us:

Toys 'R' Us. Once the dominant U.S. toy store chain, Toys 'R' Us now faces off against its fiercest rival, Wal-Mart, the market leader with an estimated 22% share of the toy market and an appetite for price competition. One recent holiday season, Wal-Mart unexpectedly cut the price of a popular toy by more than 20%—below the cost level for many stores. Toys 'R' Us felt compelled to cut its price, even though the CEO believed that the toy would have sold out at the higher price. He explained, "Our choice was short-term profit versus long-term market share; we chose to protect market share." Other changes in the market: discount chain Target is expanding and drawing shoppers with low-priced toys; specialty toy retailers (such as the Internet's SmartKids) are serving specific customer niches. Toys 'R' Us is striking back by renovating stores, investing in its Babies 'R' Us chain, and opening toy sections within Albertsons supermarkets.[22]

Practical Planning Tip

Look for new ideas by probing customers' reactions to competitors' strengths.

Exhibit 2.4 depicts Michael Porter's model of the competitive forces affecting industry profitability and attractiveness. As this model suggests, it is important to examine competitive barriers to entry and exit, which can affect the number of new entrants and the number of firms that leave the industry, as well as the power of both suppliers and buyers and the potential threat presented by substitute products. One barrier to entry may be political-legal (such as regulation), another financial (such as high costs), for example.

During this competitive analysis, marketers should learn about the unique competitive advantages of each rival (such as Wal-Mart's global buying power and ability to sell at unusually low prices). Yet customers ultimately determine the value of a firm's competitive advantage, which means that any organization can build advantage by discovering what customers need or desire and delivering it more effectively and efficiently (and perhaps more distinctively) than competitors. That's how Starbucks turned a run-of-the-mill product, coffee, into an everyday luxury and an experience for which millions of customers pay handsomely. Now any new entrants to the upscale coffee market must contend with Starbucks' established brand and leadership position.

Competitive analysis helps marketers determine which of Porter's generic competitive strategies is most appropriate for the company's unique situation.[23] With a **cost leadership strategy**, the company seeks to become the lowest-cost producer in its industry. With a **differentiation strategy**, the company creates a unique differentiation for itself or its product based on some factor prized by the target market. With a **focus strategy**, the company narrows its competitive scope to achieve a competitive advantage in its chosen segments. Which strategy a company

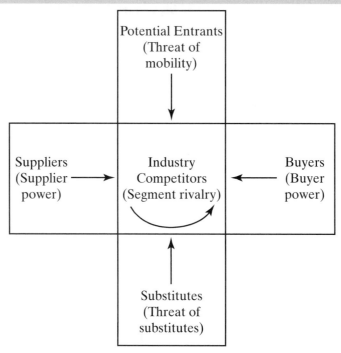

EXHIBIT 2.4   Competitive Forces Affecting Industry Profitability and Attractiveness

chooses depends, in part, on its analysis of internal strengths and weaknesses and external opportunities and threats.

SWOT ANALYSIS

All the information gathered through scanning and analysis is now distilled into a **SWOT analysis** showing the *s*trengths, *w*eaknesses, *o*pportunities, and *t*hreats of the organization. Marketers also conduct a SWOT analysis of each competitor, current and emerging, to examine the possible influence on the marketing situation, the overall industry, and the overall market.

The purpose is to understand key strengths that can be exploited through marketing and defend against vulnerabilities that competitors might detect and use against the organization. What is a strength and what is a weakness? Exhibit 2.5 shows four criteria to be used in assessing organizational resources and capabilities.

Coach uses SWOT analysis in planning the marketing of its luxury products:

Coach. One of Coach's main strengths is its well-known brand, which is associated with quality. Ten years ago, seeing Gucci and other upscale marketers give new fashion life to their venerable brands, CEO Lew Frankfort hired designer Reed Krakoff to enhance the styling of Coach's handbags and accessories. By looking for opportunities and testing products through ongoing consumer research, Coach's marketers learned that consumers were willing to pay more than $300 for the Hamptons Flap Satchel, now a company best-seller. Every proposed product is evaluated in terms of whether it detracts from the brand image (a possible weakness) or enhances the strength of the brand. Careful SWOT analysis has enabled Coach to sharply increase both sales and profit margins as it moves toward the goal of overtaking Vuitton, the world's largest luxury-goods company.[24]

EXHIBIT 2.5 Judging Organizational Strengths and Weaknesses

Past Performance Trends

Comparison against Competitors

Are organizational resources and capabilities strengths or weaknesses?

Specific Goals or Targets

Personal Opinions of Strategic Decision Makers

Summary

Environmental scanning and analysis is the process of gathering data about the environment and analyzing the findings to understand the company's strengths, weaknesses, opportunities, and threats in preparation for marketing planning. The macroenvironment consists of key environmental factors that affect organizational performance, including broad demographic, economic, ecological, technological, political-legal, and social-cultural forces. The microenvironment consists of groups that more directly influence performance, such as customers, competitors, channel members, partners, suppliers, and employees.

In scanning the internal environment, marketers examine the organization's mission, resources, offerings, previous results, business relationships, keys to success, and warning signs. In scanning the external environment, they examine demographic, economic, ecological, technological, political-legal, and social-cultural trends, as well as the competitive situation. Using the data gathered during these environmental scanning steps, marketers conduct a SWOT analysis so they can plan to take advantage of strengths and opportunities while defending against weaknesses and threats.

Understanding Markets and Customers

In this chapter:

Preview

All the world's a market—but clearly, no company can afford to sell to or satisfy everyone. Even well-heeled giants like General Electric, Carrefour, and Volvo must make informed decisions about which local, regional, national, and international markets to serve and, within each, which potential buyers they can satisfy most profitably. Likewise, smaller businesses must carefully define their markets so they can use their resources most efficiently and effectively.

This chapter discusses how to research and analyze markets and customers. The chapter starts with a discussion of how to define the broad market, research overall characteristics, and calculate market share, a prelude to selecting markets and segments to target. The next section shows how to examine the needs and behavior of consumers and business customers in light of the constant change that affects marketing activities. The chapter closes with an overview of planning for primary and secondary marketing research.

As you read this chapter and move ahead with marketing planning, continue to record your conclusions and decisions using *Marketing Plan Pro* software or in a written marketing plan. This chapter's checklist (page 38) features key questions to help you understand your markets and customers.

Analyzing Markets

A **market** is defined as all the potential buyers for a particular product. As Exhibit 3.1 indicates, market analysis is a backdrop for understanding customer needs and buying behavior—because people, not statistics or projections, constitute markets. Whether buying for themselves (or their families) as part of the **consumer market**, or buying for their companies (or nonprofit or institution) as part of the **business market**, customers are ultimately the primary focus of every marketing plan. Knowing this, marketers must perform a comprehensive market analysis so they have a context within which to understand the requirements, behavior, and attitudes of customers in the marketplace.

Understanding the market and younger buyers' attitudes toward new cars shaped Toyota's marketing plan for its Scion XB:

Toyota. American baby-boomers are big buyers of imported cars, but will the next generation follow suit? Already, teenagers and twenty-something drivers account for nearly 6% of all U.S. car sales, which is why the Japanese automaker Toyota wants to reach these U.S. customers: "We need to build the same relationship with them that we have with their parents," says a company official. Because research shows that younger drivers want cars that deliver a lot for the money, Toyota gave the Scion bold styling and standard features such as a top-notch sound system. It studied customers' viewing patterns, then aired commercials during MTV programs and other cable television programs popular with younger audiences. Finally, it stimulated word-of-mouth buzz by offering test drives outside busy restaurants and music stores. The positive response will soon make Scion profitable.[1]

CHAPTER 3 CHECKLIST   Analyzing Markets and Customers

Broad Market Definition

✔ What are the geographic and product descriptions of the market?

✔ What general consumer demographics, characteristics, needs, and preferences pertain to this product and category in this market?

✔ What general business demographics, characteristics, needs, and preferences pertain to this product and category in this market?

Changes in the Market and Market Share

✔ What specific needs do people in the market exhibit for the product and category, and how are these changing over time?

✔ What current and projected demographics in this market pertain to this product?

✔ What are the current and projected sales of or demand for the product in this market?

✔ What do projected demographic and demand trends suggest for market growth and profitability?

✔ In units or dollars, what is the market share of the company, brand, or product?

✔ What is the market share of each competitor, and how are these changing over time?

Customers in Consumer Markets

✔ What consumer needs, wants, and behaviors pertain to the product and category?

✔ Who are the customers in each market (in terms of gender, geography, etc.), and what are their buying patterns?

✔ How do users, culture, subculture, class, social connections, and personal factors influence this purchase?

✔ What main needs, wants, attitudes, behavior, and purchasing patterns are shaped by these influences?

✔ How can the marketing plan build on these influences for competitive advantage or stronger customer relationships?

Customers in Business Markets

✔ Who is involved in the buying decision, what is each participant's role, and what does each need to know during the buying process?

✔ How do the company's size and industry, share and growth, competitive situation, buying policies, finances, needs, and purchase timing affect marketing planning?

✔ Does the company buy from competing suppliers, and how does it evaluate suppliers?

✔ How can the marketing plan build on these influences for competitive advantage or stronger customer relationships?

EXHIBIT 3.1 Market and Customer Analysis

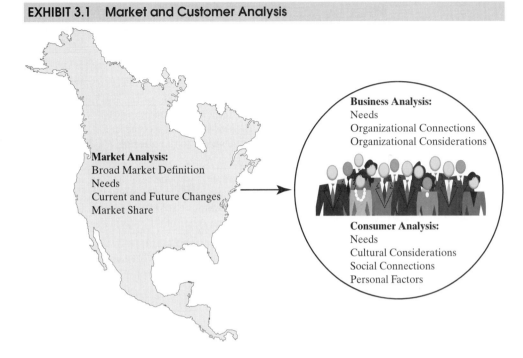

Toyota realizes that certain drivers (not all drivers) are potential customers for the Scion, and it has planned the car and the advertising with that in mind. The first step for Toyota, as for other marketers, is to broadly define the market and its needs.

BROAD DEFINITION OF MARKET AND NEEDS

It is helpful to think about five basic levels of market definition, explained in Exhibit 3.2: (1) potential market, (2) available market, (3) qualified available market, (4) served or target market, and (5) penetrated market.[2] The potential market contains the maximum number of customers that exist for a company's product; in reality, however, no single product can appeal to every possible customer. Marketers therefore want to narrow their focus by gaining a thorough understanding of the potential, available, and qualified available markets.

For planning purposes, markets may be described in terms of geography as well as by product or customer definition. "The U.S. cell phone market" is a broad description of one target market that Nokia seeks to serve. Because it markets internationally, Nokia must define each target market geographically: "The Italian cell phone market" or "the Rome cell phone market" are two examples.

The geographic description must be more precise to distinguish different markets being served. The online auction firm eBay, for instance, offers global auction listings as well as local auction listings in certain areas. Thus, eBay can define a series of markets for its services, including: "The Orange County, California, market for online auction services," "the San Francisco market for online auction services," and "the Vancouver, Canada, market for online auction services." This helps eBay's marketers focus on the needs and preferences of a particular set of buyers in each location.

Next, the company conducts research into the broad needs of the available market. Here, the emphasis is on identifying general needs prior to a more in-depth

Practical Planning Tip
When formulating your marketing plan, research and analyze the broad market for your product.

EXHIBIT 3.2 Defining the Market

Type of Market	Definition	Rental Car Example
Potential market *(broadest definition)*	All customers who may be interested in a particular offering	Any driver who needs temporary transportation
Available market *(subset of the potential market)*	Customers who are interested, possess sufficient income, and have access to the offering	Any driver who can afford the rental fees and is in the area served by rental-car services
Qualified available market *(subset of the available market)*	Customers who are qualified to buy based on age (for products that cannot be sold to underage consumers) or other criteria	Drivers in the available market who have valid licenses and meet minimum or maximum age restrictions
Target market *(subset of the qualified available market to be served)*	Customers that the company intends to target for a particular offer	Drivers in the qualified available market who need to travel from airports to final destinations in the area
Penetrated market *(subset of the target market)*	Customers who are already buying the type of product sold by the company	Drivers in the target market who have previously rented cars

investigation of each segment's particular needs. This research also helps the company identify what customers value and how its image, products, services, and other attributes can be positioned for competitive differentiation. For example:

> **Thor.** Thor is the U.S. market leader in towable recreational vehicles (RVs), with a variety of offerings for different markets and customer segments. Each brand (including Airstream and Dutchmen) and vehicle is differentiated by styling, size, features, capacity, price, and other elements. Now Thor is driving for more growth by entering the motorized RV market (designed to be driven, not towed). Studying the U.S. market, it uncovered higher consumer interest in driving vacations; learned that the median income of RV households is $56,000; and noted increased availability of longer-term loans for more expensive RVs. In response, Thor has introduced more luxurious motorized models like the Damon Escaper, outfitted with most of the comforts of home at a home-like price of $245,000.[3]

Along with a broad understanding of needs, marketers need to look at general demographics, such as the number and characteristics of the consumer or business population, to get a sense of what each market is like—in the aggregate. U.S. Census data shows the number of people and households in specific areas of the country. Then marketers look beyond sheer numbers, researching gender, age, education, marital status, income, or other characteristics that relate to their products. Thor considers income a key characteristic; Marriott's retirement complexes would look at the population and incomes of consumers aged 50 and older.

In the business market, marketers can use the North American Industry Classification System (NAICS) to classify industries and investigate industry size; the main source for such data is the U.S. Census Bureau. Additional research about industries, products, and geographic markets is available from a wide variety of sources, including international trade organizations, global banks, foreign consulates, universities, and business publications. As with consumer markets, the next step is to obtain meaningful characteristics that relate to the product, such as the annual sales, number of employees, or industries served by the businesses in the market. Texas Instruments, for example, sells computer chips to manufacturers of high-tech products around the world. Because only some businesses are potential buyers, the company must identify and research industries that incorporate chips in their products, such as PC manufacturers and cell phone manufacturers. Then it can examine each market in more detail.

MARKETS AS MOVING TARGETS

Practical Planning Tip
Consider the market of tomorrow as well as the market of today when developing marketing objectives and strategies.

Markets are always changing: Consumers move in or out, are born or die, start or stop buying a good or service; businesses change location, go into or out of business, start or stop buying a product. Thus, at this stage of the market analysis, marketers need to locate projections of demographic changes in the markets and forecast future demand for (or sales of) their type of product, as a way of sizing the overall market over time. (Common forecasting methods are discussed in Chapter 10.)

Is the population expected to grow or shrink, and by how much? How many new businesses are projected to enter or leave the market? What are the projections for total industry sales of the product over the coming years? Do these projections suggest a sizable market, a stagnant market, or a shrinking market? The answers to these questions influence decisions about targeting markets and segments and setting objectives. To illustrate, Microsoft is one of several companies attracted by the global projection that the number of corporate users of instant messaging software will triple by 2007.[4] On the other hand, Microsoft would look elsewhere if its marketers found that fewer businesspeople were using instant messaging year after year.

Much research is publicly available for major markets and for products, but marketers of ground-breaking products—such as the first satellite radio systems—often must conduct their own research to project demand and sales. This part of the marketing planning process also feeds into the SWOT analysis discussed in Chapter 2, because it can reveal new opportunities or threats that must be addressed.

MARKET SHARE AS A VITAL SIGN

Practical Planning Tip
Keep market share in mind to set realistic objectives and create appropriate standards for measuring results.

The market share held by a company and the share held by competitors usually change over time as the market grows or shrinks and competitors enter or exit. Market share information serves as a baseline for understanding historical market dynamics and a standard for setting and measuring objectives to be achieved through the marketing plan.

Market share is the percentage of sales in a given market held by a particular company, brand, or product, calculated in dollars or units (ideally, both). In simple terms, a company's share can be determined by dividing its product unit or dollar sales by the entire unit or dollar sales of that type of product in that market. Thus, if a firm sells 2 million units in the 50 states and overall market sales for all competitors selling that kind of product are 10 million units, the firm holds a 20% share of the U.S. market. Calculated in dollars, the same firm's share would be 15% if its product sales totaled $15 million and overall market sales totaled $100 million.

Market share calculation is only a point-in-time snapshot showing relative positions of the competitors during a particular period—positions that can and do constantly change. Thor has a market-leading 26% share of the towable RV market but only a 10% share of the motorized RV market (where Fleetwood, Winnebago, and Monaco are leaders). Once Thor launches its motorized RV models, its share in that market will change. These new models could very well attract customers who might otherwise have bought towable RVs, affecting Thor's share in that market as well. If Thor acquires other RV companies, that will increase its market share. In an industry with more than six dozen competitors marketing hundreds of brands, higher share can fuel economies of scale, strengthen relations with dealers, and enhance profitability.[5]

Clearly, market share is one of the vital signs of a business, to be monitored over time as a way of spotting potential problems as well as potential opportunities in the marketplace. Companies should develop share information for each product in each market, regularly update share numbers to track shifts, and examine shifts as possible triggers for control measures (discussed in detail in Chapter 10).

In addition, market share directly affects segmentation and targeting, because a company with marketing strategies to capture a larger and larger share of a shrinking market segment could end up with nearly 100% of a market too small to be profitable. On the other hand, most companies take special notice of markets in which demand is projected to skyrocket, using share over time to identify opportunities, understand competitive dynamics, and set and measure progress toward objectives. Consider the experience of Japan's Fujifilm:

> **Fujifilm.** Fujifilm targeted China during the late 1990s to capitalize on growing demand for photographic equipment and supplies. Despite its years of marketing in China, Fujifilm and another rival, Konica, hold less than 25% of the market between them. Why? Kodak, which also markets traditional film and photo printing in China, has invested in and cooperated with several local firms to become the market-share leader, with a 70%-plus share. To wrest share from Kodak, Fujifilm is working on new ways to attract buyers in this huge and potentially profitable market.[6]

Analyzing Customer Needs and Behavior

With the market analysis as backdrop, marketers use research to analyze the needs, buying behavior, and attitudes of the customers in their markets. This research forms the foundation for decisions about which segments to target, the most effective way to position the product in each market, and what marketing strategies and tactics are most appropriate for profitably satisfying customers. The chapter-ending section on marketing research briefly discusses how marketers can study and understand customers' behavior and buying decisions.

Practical Planning Tip

Analyze market needs in the context of competing offers.

Forces in the external environment can play a key role in affecting the who, what, when, where, why, and how of consumer and business buying behavior (see Exhibit 3.3). This is one of the reasons for studying the current situation, as discussed in Chapter 2. For example, when the economy is not doing well, many con-

EXHIBIT 3.3 Analyzing Customer Needs, Behavior, and Influences

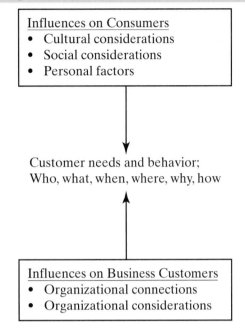

Influences on Consumers
- Cultural considerations
- Social considerations
- Personal factors

Customer needs and behavior;
Who, what, when, where, why, how

Influences on Business Customers
- Organizational connections
- Organizational considerations

sumers and business customers change their buying patterns—sometimes purchasing less or less often; sometimes seeking out lower-priced alternatives. During a recent recession, Navistar International saw its truck sales decline 40% from their peak as business customers cut spending. Once the economy improved, however, Navistar received so many orders that it quickly boosted production to meet demand.[7] Social-cultural issues such as corporate ethics and social responsibility also affect buying habits. To illustrate, more than half of all U.K. consumers have purchased a Fairtrade food product, a designation showing that the growers in developing countries receive a fair price for their coffee and other crops.[8]

The attitudes and habits of consumers and business customers are clearly affected by the marketing-mix programs implemented by different companies competing for their attention, loyalty, and buying power. From the customer's perspective, no marketing tactic stands in isolation: it is only one tactic used by the company and one of many stimuli in the market (some of which are noticed and acted upon, most of which are not). As a result, marketers must not only understand their markets and the environmental forces shaping customer actions, but also learn to see the totality of their marketing activities and the actions of competing firms through their customers' eyes.

Luckily, technology now exists to help marketers identify, research, and analyze the behavior of individual customers in particular markets, instead of relying solely on averages or aggregate data. Then, as companies establish relationships with individuals in their consumer or business markets, they can gather even more customer behavior data and track changes over time, leading to even more effective marketing plans. Wells Fargo, for instance, examines every interaction with its 10 million banking customers and correlates the data with customer-specific personal information. The bank has solidified its customer relationships by understanding both current and future needs; its customers buy, on average, 4 financial products from

Wells Fargo—considerably more than the industry average of 2.2 products per customer.[9] Yet customers are more concerned about privacy and what companies do with personal information. Thus, more online shoppers are reading privacy statements and checking for the Better Business Bureau Online seal or another indication that a site adheres to guidelines for protecting personal data.[10]

Whirlpool's marketing in the United States and India shows the importance of understanding and responding to customer needs, market by market:

Whirlpool. Although Whirlpool is based in Michigan and sells appliances all over the world, it knows that markets differ in needs and demographics. In the United States, where appliance sales are barely growing but more consumers are remodeling and redecorating, the company moved upscale with a matched washer and dryer set called the Duet, featuring futuristic styling, designer colors, and improved energy efficiency. Within just 3 years, the Duet washing machine achieved a nearly 20% share of category sales. In India, where appliance demand is rising, consumers worry about white clothes being discolored in the wash. For this market, the company created a washing machine that helps maintain the color of white clothing. Understanding this market's needs boosted Whirlpool's sales in India by 80% in 5 years.[11]

Delve below the surface when researching what customers need and want. Stated needs are generally the tip of the iceberg; customers also have unstated needs (e.g., good service) and sometimes secret needs (e.g., relating to their self-concept or other internal needs). Thus, it is vital to understand the problem each customer seeks to solve and what that customer really wants from the solution.[12] Remember that the needs, wants, attitudes, behavior, and decision-making processes of consumers differ, in general, from those of business customers. The next sections highlight important attributes that marketers need to understand when preparing plans for consumer and business markets.

CONSUMER MARKETS

As shown in Exhibit 3.3, marketers need to analyze the needs and behaviors of consumers from every angle. Who in the household or family is buying or using the product? What, exactly, are these consumers buying or using, and when, where, how, and why? What is their decision-making process for buying that product? What are consumers buying now, what did they buy before, how often are they buying, and how are their buying patterns changing? Look at both internal and external sources of data for this analysis of consumer needs, decision making, and behavior.

When making decisions about more complex purchases, such as an RV, consumers generally take more time, gather more information about alternatives, weigh the decision more carefully, and have strong feelings in the aftermath of the purchase. Inexpensive items bought on impulse, such as candy, are not usually subjected to as much analysis and scrutiny before or after the purchase. By investigating the entire process consumers follow to buy, use, and evaluate their products, marketers can determine how, when, and where to initiate suitable marketing activities.

Early in the buying process, for example, marketers may need to emphasize benefits that solve consumer problems. Later in the process, marketers may need

Practical Planning Tip

Customize your research to fit the characteristics of your products and markets.

to communicate where the product can be purchased; still later, marketers may want to stress the security of a product's warranty. The exact nature and timing of the marketing activities will depend on what the marketer learns about consumer decision making (as well as on the marketer's strategy and resources, of course).

Although the exact level of influence varies from individual to individual, consumer needs, wants, and behaviors are affected by cultural considerations, social connections, and personal factors.

Practical Planning Tip

Simply asking about needs is not enough, because many consumers are unaware of what influences their behavior.

Cultural Considerations

As buyers, consumers feel the influence of the culture of the nation or region in which they were raised as well as the culture where they currently live. This means that consumers in different countries often approach buying situations from different perspectives because of differing values, beliefs, and preferences. Without research, marketers can't know exactly what those differences are or how to address them. Consider Hering's experience selling harmonicas in different countries:

Hering. Alberto Bertolazzi, head of Brazilian harmonica maker Hering, competes with Hohner, Suzuki, and Tomba for a share of the $130 million global harmonica market. He targets two main markets: Japan, where consumers annually buy $10 million worth of harmonicas, and the United States, where consumers annually buy $7.5 billion worth of all musical instruments. Bertolazzi has found different expectations in each culture. "In the [United] States, people said Hering harmonicas were great but looked cheap, so we upgraded the plates from brass to bronze," he says. For Japan, he added markers to indicate the three octaves on each harmonica, because "the Japanese prefer them that way." Now the company is using its knowledge of customers to market guitar tuning equipment and guitars.[13]

Subcultures are distinct groups within a larger culture that exhibit and preserve distinct cultural identities through a common religion, nationality, ethnic background, or lifestyle. A variety of subcultures drive U.S. consumers' decisions and behavior. Cuban Americans frequently have different food preferences than, say, Chinese Americans. Teenagers—an age subculture—have different food preferences than seniors. To create an effective plan for reaching each subculture, marketers must research that group's behavior and buying patterns. To illustrate, Kroger, the top U.S. grocery chain, is targeting Hispanic customers in certain states with its Buena Comida private-label foods and specially-designed *supermercado* stores featuring Spanish-language signage and distinctive décor.[14]

Class distinctions, even when subtle, also influence consumer behavior. The members of each class generally buy and use products in a similar way; in addition, people who aspire to a different class may emulate the buying or usage patterns of that class. Savvy marketers learn how such distinctions operate and then apply this knowledge to decisions about products, marketing communications, distribution arrangements, price levels, and service strategies.

Social Connections

Consumers have a web of social connections that influence how they buy—connections such as family ties, friendships, work groups, and civic organizations.

Family members, for example, directly or indirectly control household spending for many goods and services. Children ask parents to buy products advertised on television; parents buy things to keep children healthy or safe; families make group decisions about vacations.

Understanding how these connections affect the buying decision is critical for marketers creating plans for products intended for specific family members, usage, or occasions. Heinz, as one example, designed its EZ Squirt ketchup packages (and developed green, purple, and blue ketchups) to appeal to children yet be acceptable to parents, knowing that children can influence food-buying patterns. Company research revealed that "3-year-olds use almost twice as much ketchup as adults," according to a Heinz executive. That was another reason to redesign the package for smaller hands. The result: 25 million bottles of colored EZ Squirt ketchup were sold in the first 30 months, and Heinz holds 60% of the U.S. ketchup market.[15]

As with class distinctions, aspirations to different social connections can be a powerful influence on buying behavior. In apparel, for example, preteens want to look as grown up as possible, so they emulate teen fashions; teenagers dress like the movie stars they admire; and managers seeking to move up follow the clothing cues of higher-level managers. Within each social group, consumers look to certain opinion leaders for advice or guidance about buying decisions. Consider how Coca-Cola's Sprite taps into social connections for marketing purposes:

Sprite. Soft-drink companies fight for the loyalty of 16- to 24-year-old consumers because this segment accounts for a significant portion of carbonated beverage sales. Based on research showing that consumers in this segment value variety and sometimes mix soft drinks with juices and other ingredients, Sprite came up with the idea for Sprite ReMix, a beverage with constantly changing tropical flavors. To launch this drink, Sprite turned to a network of entertainment and music "lifestyle influencers" such as disk jockeys, who like being in on the next big thing—and like telling others about it. This approach worked: Sprite ReMix sold 55 million cases in its first year, and frequent buyers say they enjoy the novelty of drinking a beverage with ever-changing taste.[16]

Personal Factors

Personal factors are another major category of influences on consumer buying, covering life cycle, lifestyle, and psychological makeup, among other factors. Life cycle refers to the individual's changing family situation over time—whether single, cohabitating, engaged, married, married with children, divorced, remarried, and so on. Each of these life-cycle phases entails different buying needs, attitudes, and preferences that, in turn, can be identified through research and addressed through marketing. Engaged couples, for instance, are targeted by marketers selling formal wear, wedding invitations, catering services, and other wedding products; new parents are targeted by marketers selling entirely different products (such as Huggies disposable diapers).

Lifestyle is the pattern of living that a person exhibits through activities and interests—how the individual spends his or her time. To understand the complexities of lifestyle and its influence on consumer buying, marketers use sophisticated techniques to examine variables known as **psychographic characteristics**, which together form a picture of the consumer's lifestyle. Some markets are better approached through psychographics. For example, Carnival Corporation markets to consumers who enjoy cruises, although age, income, and other demographic elements are helpful descriptors of this market. At the top end of its offerings, the Queen Mary 2 (in its Cunard line) is geared to the luxury lifestyle. Marketing according to lifestyle does not work for all products and segments: when marketing the Carnival Paradise as a "no smoking" ship did not stimulate the expected sales, the company changed the ship's port and strategy.[17]

Internal elements such as motivation, perception, and attitudes—all part of the consumer's psychological makeup—can strongly influence consumer behavior. **Motivation** stems from the consumer's drive to satisfy needs and wants. For example, the popular search engine Google is constantly adding new features—such as Google News for searching news reports and Orkut for social networking—to motivate users to return to the site again and again when searching for virtually anything. The more people who click on Google, the bigger its audience for advertising, which fuels profitability.[18]

Perception is how the individual organizes environmental inputs (such as ads, conversation, and media) and derives meaning from them. When marketers talk about "cutting through clutter," they are discussing how to make the marketing message stand out among many messages bombarding consumers throughout the day—not just to capture attention but to motivate consumers to respond. **Attitudes** are the individual's lasting evaluations of and feelings toward something, such as a product or a person.

Only through careful research can marketers become knowledgeable about the personal factors that influence their customers. When the Diamond Information Center researched women's attitudes toward jewelry on behalf of the De Beers' Diamond Trading Company, it found many women who believe that diamond rings should be gifts of love, rather than being self-purchased. To modify this attitude and encourage women in the target audience (30 to 54 years old with household incomes of $100,000 and above) to buy diamond rings for themselves, it launched a campaign emphasizing that "Your left hand says 'we,' your right hand says 'me.'" Supported by this marketing, sales of non-wedding diamond rings have risen in recent months.[19]

BUSINESS MARKETS

Like consumer markets, business markets are made up of people—individuals who buy on behalf of their company, government agency, or nonprofit organization. In the context of business buying, however, these people are generally influenced by a different set of factors. Marketers therefore need to examine organizational considerations and connections when analyzing business buying decisions and behavior.

Practical Planning Tip
Dig deeper to understand underlying needs and internal concerns of business customers.

Organizational Connections

Although exactly who does the buying differs from company to company, officially designated purchasing agents are not the only people involved with the buying decision. Buyers are usually connected with other internal players. For instance, another employee or manager may initiate the buying process by suggesting a purchase; those who actually use the product may play a role, by providing specifications, testing alternatives, or evaluating purchases; and buyers may

When forest products
are your business,

SM

planting 1.7 million trees every day is
a smart investment.

The Sustainable Forestry Initiative® program is dedicated to the future of the nation's forests, as well as the challenge of preserving rare and endangered forests around the world. Respect for nature and sound business practices are integrated to the benefit of the environment, landowners, shareholders, customers and the people they serve. And that allows us to meet the demand for wood and paper products, while helping to ensure our forests will be around forever.

SUSTAINABLE FORESTRY INITIATIVE®
Growing tomorrow's forests today.®
www.aboutsfi.org

This ad for the Sustainable Forestry Initiative explains how wood and paper manufacturers are replanting and preserving forests around the world, an ecological protection issue that can influence business buyers.

need connections to the managers who are authorized to approve a purchase. In a business that buys express delivery services, as an example, a manager in one department may make the actual decision but managers in other departments may have a say or request assistance. Knowing this, FedEx has a laboratory to test customers' packaging and suggest improvements that will ensure safe arrival of items that are shipped. This wins FedEx support among a number of internal players and helps the business satisfy its own customers.[20]

Depending on the organization and its structure, other internal players may wield some type of influence (such as insisting on compatibility with existing goods or services) or controlling access to buyers. Not every player will participate in every purchase, so marketers must understand the decision process that takes place inside key customer organizations so they can plan appropriate marketing activities to reach the right players at the right time with the right information.

Finally, learn about the organization's current relations with competing suppliers, including long-term contracts, evaluations, requirements, and other elements. Ford, Campbell's, and many other companies have long-term buying relationships with suppliers who meet preset quality and performance standards. Likewise, Apple Computer depends on its suppliers for critical components such as the chips and software that make the hit iPod music player operate. However, Apple also has a strict policy against suppliers publicly revealing anything about the business relationship, a restriction that potential suppliers must bear in mind.[21] Researching a business customer's supplier connections and requirements is a good first step toward getting on the short list of approved suppliers and making the sale.

Organizational Considerations

Organizational considerations include the company's size and industry, share and growth, competitive situation, buying policies and procedures, financial constraints, and the timing of purchases. In researching these factors, marketers need to find out, for example, whether a corporation buys centrally or allows each unit to buy on its own; whether companies participate in online marketplaces; and what funding and scheduling issues affect the purchase. Internal priorities are another organizational consideration. At General Electric, units are classified as either "growth businesses" or "cash generators." To achieve long-term growth, GE plans to invest more heavily in the growth businesses than in the cash generators—a prime consideration for suppliers that market parts, components, or services needed by the designated growth units.[22]

Business buying is also affected by **derived demand**, the principle that demand for business products in an industry is based on demand for related consumer products. For instance, demand for Internet access is growing rapidly, which opens opportunities for server manufacturers such as Cisco and, in the burgeoning Chinese market, Huawei Technologies.[23] As another example, demand for cell phones drives demand for components of cell phones. Thus, Qualcomm's ability to market specialized chips depends, in large part, on the level of demand that consumers have for new-generation cell phones. However, in high-tech industries, demand changes continually and unpredictably. Recently, major marketing initiatives by wireless service providers boosted consumer demand for new cell phones by 5 million units more than Qualcomm had anticipated. According to the California chipmaker's CEO, "We had to scramble to provide sufficient supply to meet the demand."[24]

Planning Marketing Research

**Practical
Planning Tip**

Summarize research
findings, identify addi-
tional needs, and plan
for new research in
your marketing budget.

This chapter has covered a wide range of issues that should be researched to give organizations a better understanding of markets and customers. Often the best way to start is with **secondary research**—information already collected for another purpose, such as data that the U.S. government gathers during each census. Secondary research is more readily available and less expensive than **primary research**, research conducted to address a specific situation.

Exhibit 3.4 shows selected sources of secondary research for business and consumer markets and customers, as starting points for more extensive research. Before relying on any secondary research, check the dates and sources. Some sources offer new or updated statistics and profiles on a regular basis; others provide a snapshot covering a specific period, which can be useful but may be quickly outdated. Also consider the source's credibility to be sure the information is from an unbiased and reputable source. If a source reports data but did not actually conduct the research, find out where the information came from and whether it was changed from the original. Also try to verify the information as a double-check on accuracy.

Secondary research can help marketers construct a good overview of the market, but this may be too general to answer detailed questions about particular markets and types of customers. That's where primary marketing research comes in. Marketers who are qualified to do so can conduct primary research on their own, work with internal research specialists, or hire outside specialists to collect and interpret data through surveys and other methods. One technique gaining attention is **ethnographic research**, observing how customers behave in actual product purchase or usage situations:

EXHIBIT 3.4   Selected Sources of Secondary Research

Market	*Source*
Consumer	• U.S. Census Bureau (www.census.gov/population/www/index.html) • Conference Board Consumer Research Center (www.crc-conquest.org) • Social Science Information Gateway (http://sosig.ac.uk) • CyberAtlas Web usage (http://cyberatlas.internet.com) • Global Statistics (www.geohive.com)
Business	• NAICS industry classification data (www.census.gov/epcd/www./naics.html) • CEO Express business links (www.ceoexpress.com) • *Inc.* magazine (www.inc.com) • *Industry Week* magazine (www.industryweek.com) • *E-Commerce Times* online (www.ecommercetimes.com)

> **Ethnographic Research.** Frontier Airlines, Whirlpool, and Microsoft are among the companies using this technique. Microsoft, for instance, has specialists on staff to observe children and parents at home as they use the MSN online service. Based on ethnographic research, Microsoft decided to rename its "parental control" features (which log the sites that children have visited) as "safety and security" features to encourage more frequent use. As another example, Frontier Airlines' researchers followed families through Denver International Airport and noticed their delight with the animals painted on Frontier's jets. This led the airline to feature the animals in its advertising, adding an emotional connection to the communication.[25]

In planning primary research for marketing planning, detail what exactly the company wants to find out and how that knowledge will be used in developing and implementing a more practical or effective marketing plan. If marketing research is not available or must be carried out, indicate this in the marketing plan and include the research as part of the plan's budgets and schedules. Also plan ongoing marketing research to help measure results during implementation. Research studies of customer satisfaction, market share changes, and customer attitudes and buying patterns can be valuable for spotting and analyzing clues to the company's effect on the market and on customers as well as how competitors are doing.

Finally, be aware that marketers are often forced to make decisions based on incomplete data; given the fast pace of the global marketplace, marketers rarely have enough time or money to conduct exhaustive research. Each company therefore must assess the risk of waiting for more research compared with the risk in seizing an opportunity before it slips away or before competitors gain an edge.

Summary

In analyzing markets, companies start by broadly defining the general market and its customer needs. Markets are always changing, as consumers or business customers enter or leave, start or stop buying a product. For this reason, marketers should project market changes and demand prior to selecting a specific segment to target. Many companies track their market share over time, compared with that of competitors, to understand market dynamics and establish a standard for measuring marketing results.

Research is important for analyzing consumers and business customers. In consumer markets, cultural considerations, social connections, and personal factors are important in shaping needs, wants, and behavior patterns. Marketers also must research how consumers think and act in each stage of the buying decision process. Business buyers are influenced by both organizational considerations and organizational connections. Companies can use secondary research and primary research to gain a better understanding of their markets and customers. However, marketers may be forced to plan marketing activities based on incomplete data in order to keep up with fast-moving market opportunities or parry competitive initiatives.

CHAPTER 4

Planning Segmentation, Targeting, and Positioning

In this chapter:

Preview

For a long time, marketers could successfully follow one marketing plan to satisfy the entire market—think of the milk market, for instance. These days, however, markets are increasingly fragmented and diverse, with customers exhibiting a much wider variety of needs, attitudes, and behaviors. Companies also are under intense competitive pressure and therefore must differentiate themselves more clearly in the markets where they compete. The result is a move away from *mass marketing*—using one marketing mix to reach the entire market—and toward *segment marketing,* marketing to certain groups (segments) within the market. Consider milk: a huge variety of milk products are now available, including low-fat milk for weight-conscious consumers, soy milks for health-conscious consumers, and flavored milks for children.

This chapter explains how to use segmentation, targeting, and positioning during marketing planning. The first section reviews the major steps and explores how to select the consumer or business market, how to apply segmentation variables, and how to assess and select segments for targeting. The next section discusses targeting and coverage strategies; the final section looks at how to use positioning for competitive advantage.

After reading this chapter, continue creating your marketing plan by summarizing your decisions and noting any issues using *Marketing Plan Pro* software or in a written marketing plan document. See this chapter's checklist (page 54) for ideas about segmenting consumer and business markets.

Segmenting Consumer and Business Markets

Market segmentation is the process of grouping customers within a market according to similar needs, habits, or attitudes that can be addressed through marketing. The point is to identify distinct segments, defined in Chapter 1 as sizable groupings of consumers or business customers with similarities (such as similar needs, buying preferences, or attitudes) that respond to marketing efforts. In the milk market, for instance, one segment consists of people who want to limit their fat intake and therefore want low-fat varieties; another consists of people who prefer flavored varieties; and a third consists of people who buy milk products for health reasons. Within each segment, customers have similar needs or are seeking the same benefits, and react differently to marketing-mix stimuli than do people in other segments. If all the people in all the segments (either consumers or business customers) reacted the same way to the same marketing mix, there would be no need for segmentation.

Even within a large segment, marketers often can identify **niches**—smaller segments with distinct needs or benefit requirements, such as people who buy low-fat milk in individual serving sizes at meal time. Over time, tiny niches can expand into sizable segments, an evolution that Beiersdorf's Nivea is encouraging for the niche of men who buy skin-care products:

CHAPTER 4 CHECKLIST   Applying Segmentation Variables

Segmenting Consumer Markets

✔ Can demographics be used to group consumers according to needs or responses that differ by gender, household size, family status, income, occupation, education, religion, race, nationality, social class?

✔ Can geographic variables be used to group consumers according to needs or responses that differ by nation, region, state, city, postal code, climate, distance?

✔ Can psychographic variables be used to group consumers according to needs or responses that differ by lifestyle, activities, interests?

✔ Can behavioral and attitudinal variables be used to group consumers according to needs or responses that differ by benefits expected, usage occasion, user status, loyalty status, technological orientation, attitudes, price sensitivity?

Segmenting Business Markets

✔ Can demographics be used to group business customers according to needs or responses that differ by industry, business size, business age, ownership structure?

✔ Can geographic variables be used to group business customers according to needs or responses that differ by nation, region, state, city, climate, postal code, distance?

✔ Can behavioral and attitudinal variables be used to group business customers according to needs or responses that differ by benefits expected, usage occasion, user status, loyalty status, technological orientation or usage, purchasing patterns, attitudes, supplier standards and evaluation?

Beiersdorf. Nivea, a division of Germany-based Beiersdorf, has a well-established women's skin-care brand. Now Nivea for Men is putting marketing muscle behind a line of men's skin-care products, including lotions, shaving gels, and cleansers. This relatively small niche has more than tripled in size during the last two years due to higher interest in healthier looks and lifestyles. Focusing on this opportunity, Nivea for Men is promoting its products as a way to keep skin fit. The company is facing off against a number of competing products, including Bullie and Brave Soldier, that want to capture share in this growing niche.[1]

Using technology and in-depth knowledge of segments and needs, some organizations tailor their marketing mix for one customer at a time. Here's what the post office in Canada is doing with product personalization:

Canada Post. Consumers and businesses can now order customized postage stamps from Canada Post. The process is simple: submit an order form with a noncopyrighted photo and payment, and receive the personalized postage stamps in just three weeks. The price is double that of ordinary stamps, yet the opportunity to feature a favorite child or a company logo on a stamp is drawing thousands of orders every week. In this way, Canada Post is boosting revenues by fitting its product—a key part of the marketing mix—to the needs of individual customers.[2]

Segmentation allows marketers to focus their resources on the most promising opportunities. This improves marketing efficiency and effectiveness as the organization gets to know each segment's customers and what they want and need. Such customer intimacy also enables marketers to notice changes in the segment and respond quickly. Finally, it gives marketers the choice of entering segments where only a limited number of competitors are active or where their most powerful rivals are not competing.

As shown in Exhibit 4.1, segmentation lays the foundation for decisions about targeting and coverage strategy. The **target market** is the segment of the overall market that a company chooses to pursue. With these decisions, marketers are ready for positioning, giving the brand or product a distinctive and meaningful place (position) in the minds of targeted customers, as discussed later in this chapter.

EXHIBIT 4.1   Segmentation, Targeting, and Positioning

Segmentation
- Select the market
- Apply segmentation variables
- Assess and select segments for targeting

Targeting
- Select number and priority of segments for entry
- Select segment coverage strategy

Positioning
- Select meaningful attributes for differentiation
- Apply positioning through marketing strategy and tactics

Practical Planning Tip
Use market and customer analysis to broadly define the market, then drop inappropriate markets or segments.

SELECT THE MARKET

The first step in segmentation is to select the general market(s) in which the company will target customers, based on the market definition, situational analysis, and SWOT analysis (see Chapter 3). Eliminate markets or segments that have no need for the product or are inappropriate for other reasons, such as geographic distance, lack of purchasing power, ethical issues, or troubling environmental threats. Cosmetics giant Avon Products selects its markets carefully:

Avon. Russia was not part of Avon's global marketing plan until 1995, when the country was democratic, purchasing power was rising, and capitalism was encouraged. To tap this promising opportunity, the company recruited independent sales representatives and gave them cosmetics samples to show customers. By 1999, Avon's Russian business was ringing up $22 million in annual sales; by 2002, annual sales had skyrocketed to $142 million. With a new Moscow-area factory and nearly 200,000 reps in place, Avon's president says the company is ready to "meet the rapidly escalating demand from the nation's vast population of sophisticated beauty consumers" in moving toward its 2007 objective of $500 million in annual sales in Russia, supporting stronger global profits.[3]

Now marketers start to search for segments within the markets they have defined. People and businesses differ in many ways, but not every difference is meaningful from a marketing perspective. The purpose of segmentation is to form groups of customers that are internally similar yet sufficiently different that each group will not react in exactly the same way to the same marketing activities. If all segments were similar or responded in the same way to marketing, there would be no need for segmentation—the company could simply use one marketing plan for the entire market. Therefore, marketers create segments by applying one or more variables to the chosen consumer or business market.

APPLY SEGMENTATION VARIABLES TO CONSUMER MARKETS

Marketers can isolate groupings within consumer markets using demographic, geographic, psychographic, and behavioral and attitudinal variables (see Exhibit 4.2). Consumer markets can be segmented with just about every one of these variables; the choice depends on the company's detailed marketing research profiling customers and analyzing their buying behavior. Sophisticated marketers often apply geographic, demographic, and psychographic or behavioral variables in combination to create extremely well-defined segments or niches for marketing attention.

Common sense also plays a role: some variables simply don't lend themselves to certain markets. For example, the consumer market for paper towels might be segmented in terms of education, but will the resulting groupings reveal differing

EXHIBIT 4.2	Segmentation Variables for Consumer Markets
Type of Variable	*Examples*
Demographic	Age, gender, family status, household size, income, occupation, education, race, nationality, religion, social class
Geographic	Location (by country, region, state, city, neighborhood, postal code), distance, climate
Psychographic	Lifestyle, activities, interests
Behavioral and attitudinal	Benefits perceived/expected, occasion/rate of usage, user status, loyalty status, attitude toward product and usage, technological orientation, price sensitivity

Practical Planning Tip
Use marketing research to profile customers and identify variables for meaningful segmentation.

needs or responses to marketing efforts? On the other hand, income and household size are likely to be better variables for segmenting this market, since either (or both) may result in groupings that have different needs or respond differently to marketing activities. The following sections take a closer look at the main consumer segmentation variables.

Demographic Variables

Demographic variables are popular for segmentation because they are common and easily identified consumer characteristics. In addition, they often point to meaningful differences in consumer needs, wants, and product consumption, as well as media usage. For instance, Beiersdorf and other skin-care marketers segment customers on the basis of gender, because men and women have different needs, attitudes, and behavior patterns. Segmenting on the basis of income can help marketers of upscale goods and services, such as Tiffany's, identify consumer segments with the means to buy. It also can help marketers of lower-priced products focus on customers who need to stretch their dollars; an example is Dollar General, which segments by income and geography.[4] In fact, discount store sales volume has grown so rapidly that Procter & Gamble and other manufacturers are creating products and brands specifically for lower-income segments.[5] Combining demographic variables can focus marketing even further; Charles Schwab looks at household income, investment assets, and several other variables when segmenting the market for brokerage services.[6]

Yet marketers must avoid stereotyping customers when using demographic variables such as race, nationality, and income. Adding behavioral and psychographic variables linked to customers' underlying wants and needs will reveal customer motivations and benefits that can be addressed, segment by segment, through marketing. To illustrate, General Motors Acceptance Corp. is one of several companies with special marketing programs for the home-buying needs of new immigrants. Recognizing that many immigrants live with extended families, GMAC's Settle America program takes into consideration the income of cousins, aunts, and uncles when a family applies for certain mortgages. "There are qualified people who are outside the [homeownership] walls, but they are quality customers," comments GMAC's executive vice president.[7]

The ready-to-eat cereal industry is another example:

Cereal Marketing. In many families (demographic variable), children's changing tastes and motivations (behavioral and psychographic variables) are the major influence on cereal purchases. Knowing that preteens particularly like free gifts in or on cereal packages, manufacturers have arranged for freebies and special package graphics to attract kids' attention. In the United Kingdom, for instance, Sugar Puffs (made by Quaker) has given away stickers featuring famous soccer players; Cheerios and Shreddies (made by Cereal Partners) have given away paperbacks by top children's authors; and Kellogg has given away BeyBlade tops. Experts caution that in-depth customer knowledge is vital to avoid poor choice of premium or poor timing: A cereal will sell slowly or lose market share if preteens have never heard of the in-pack gift or have moved on to the next fad.[8]

To research consumer demographics, try Web sites such as Marketsegment .com (www.marketsegment.com), which provides data on different U.S. subcultures. Also see Economy.com's Free Lunch page (www.economy.com/freelunch), with links to reports and statistics covering consumer markets, economic trends, industry analyses, and other demographic issues. Another source is Hispanic Business (www.hispanicbusiness.com), which offers statistics and articles about Hispanic businesses. Many sources listed in Chapters 2 and 3 also provide demographic information.

Geographic Variables

As shown in the earlier Avon example, companies routinely use geography to segment consumer markets. The decision to use geographic variables may be based on a company's ability to sell and service products in certain areas or climates, its interest in entering promising new markets, or its reluctance to sell in certain areas due to environmental threats or unfavorable climate. For instance, Somerfield, a large U.K. grocery chain, segments on the basis of neighborhood to identify locations for its smaller Kwik Save food stores. Tesco, the dominant U.K. grocery chain and a Somerfield competitor, also segments by geography to identify neighborhoods for new Tesco Express convenience food stores.[9]

Still, companies that segment by geography should note meaningful differences within each area or similarities that cross geographic boundaries. Waitrose, a Southern England grocery chain, competes with Tesco, Somerfield, and other rivals by featuring organic foods and emphasizing quality and service. Because customers all over the United Kingdom are interested in organic foods, Waitrose can broaden its segmentation beyond the boundaries of current store locations, serving a wider geographic area through online shopping.[10]

Psychographic Variables

Segmenting on the basis of psychographic variables such as lifestyle, activities, and interests can help companies gain a deeper understanding of what and why consumers buy. Sometimes psychographic segmentation is the only way to identify a consumer group for special marketing attention, because activities and interests tend to cross demographic and geographic lines. People who share an interest in sports, for instance, may live anywhere in the United States—or in another country—and be of almost any age or gender.

Marketers who apply both psychographic and demographic variables may be able to create one or more segments that will respond to different marketing initiatives. The key is to identify the specific psychographic variables (and any other variables) that correspond to meaningful differences. Home Depot has done this:

Home Depot. The home improvement retailer Home Depot is tapping a significant profit opportunity by segmenting according to gender and interest in do-it-yourself projects. Based on research showing that many women like to pick up tools and work on home renovation, the company tidied up its stores, started a gift registry program, and initiated "Do-It-Herself" workshops to teach skills such as flooring installation. "Historically, we have overmarketed to men and undermarketed to women," explains a store executive. "The reality is of an increasing partnership. Women are definitely equal partners in home renovations." This segment also is a driving force behind purchases for kitchen makeovers and other projects.[11]

Thus, segmentation not only identifies the segment (in this case, women do-it-yourselfers) but also provides clues to how it can be reached through marketing (through workshops and better-organized stores).

Behavioral and Attitudinal Variables

As with psychographic variables, behavioral and attitudinal variables are often the best way to identify a consumer group for marketing purposes, because benefits expected, usage occasion and status, loyalty status, technological orientation, and attitudes toward products or usage generally cross demographic and geographic lines. Segmenting by benefits helps marketers think about what, exactly, a group of consumers expects from a particular good or service.

For example, air travelers look for different benefits—business travelers may put more value on convenient schedules, while vacation travelers may put more value on affordability—so marketers will use a different marketing message for each segment. Airline marketers could segment by behavior and demographics or other variables, putting the emphasis on what people need rather than who they are. As another example, many weight-conscious consumers seek out foods with reduced carbohydrate levels. Knowing this, Smart Ones and other firms market low-carbohydrate meals to this consumer segment.[12]

Segmenting by usage occasion helps marketers group consumers based on the occasion(s) when they buy or use a product. User status—whether a consumer has ever used the product, is a first-time user, or is a regular user—is particularly important when a company wants to increase sales by selling to nonusers, first-time users, or light users. Do consumers in the market tend to be brand-loyal or do they constantly switch—and why? Companies often mount one marketing program to reinforce loyalty and another to court switchers from other brands. Attitudes and

Spread harmful germs.

Kill harmful germs.

Only LYSOL Sanitizing Wipes contain
the power of LYSOL to clean and disinfect.
So don't just wipe up, wipe out 99.9% of germs.

Lysol is appealing to consumers who want the dual benefits of cleaning and disinfecting household surfaces.

behavior toward technology—whether consumers use cell phones, for example—are key variables for firms like Guangzhou Mobile:

Guangzhou Mobile. This division of China Mobile knows that many cell phone users are eager to have the latest gadget-equipped phones. Under pressure from China Unicom and other competitors, Guangzhou Mobile has segmented the market on the basis of service usage and affinity for new phones. It found that the revenue generated by a heavy user is equivalent to the revenue generated by 20 average users. Therefore, the company offered to sell new Sony-Ericsson cell phones at a fraction of the regular price to heavy-usage customers who prepaid a set amount of future call charges. Lighter-usage customers who prepaid a minimum amount could buy the phone at a discount of 30% or more. Not only did segmentation allow Guangzhou Mobile to identify and retain its most profitable customers, it also brought in new, younger customers and polished the company's image as the area's dominant service provider.[13]

APPLY SEGMENTATION VARIABLES TO BUSINESS MARKETS

As Exhibit 4.3 shows, business marketers can segment their markets using three major categories of variables: (1) demographic, (2) geographic, and (3) behavioral and attitudinal. In many cases, marketers use a combination of variables, including industry (a demographic variable), size of business (another demographic variable), location (a geographic variable), and purchasing patterns (a behavioral variable). Again, the purpose is to create segments that are internally similar but don't have the same needs or don't respond exactly the same as other segments when exposed to the company's marketing activities.

Demographic Variables

The main demographic variables in business markets are industry, business size, business age, and ownership structure. Industry segmentation is a good starting point, but doesn't necessarily result in groupings that are sufficiently different to warrant different marketing approaches. Therefore, marketers typically segment further on the basis of size (as measured by annual revenues or unit sales, number of employees, or number of branches) or even rate of growth, reasoning that business

EXHIBIT 4.3 Segmentation Variables for Business Markets	
Type of Variable	*Examples*
Demographic	Industry, business size, business age, ownership structure
Geographic	Location (by country, region, state, city, neighborhood, postal code), distance, climate
Behavioral and attitudinal	Purchasing patterns and process, user status, benefits expected, supplier requirements and evaluation, attitude toward product and usage, technological orientation, loyalty status, order size/frequency, buyer/influencer/user attitudes

of different sizes or growth rates have different needs. As an example, Esselte segments the market for office supplies according to business size. It recently created its first advertising campaign directed at small business owners and entrepreneurs to highlight the company's main brand names—which include DYMO and Pendaflex—and the wide range of products it offers for office organization and administration.[14]

Marketers that segment according to business age are looking for differing needs or purchasing patterns that relate to how long the business has been in existence. Businesses in the formation stage often have a higher need for office or factory space, computers and equipment, accounting and legal services, and other products. In contrast, older businesses may need repair services, upgraded computers and equipment, and other goods and services. Segmenting by ownership structure also can reveal meaningful differences. For instance, the insurance and accounting needs of sole proprietorships are not the same as those of corporations. Only by segmenting the market can marketers identify these differences for appropriate marketing attention.

Geographic Variables

Business marketers, like their consumer counterparts, can use geographic variables such as nation, region, state, city, and climate to segment their markets. This allows grouping of business customers according to concentration of outlets, location of headquarters, and geography-related needs or responses. Consider the experience of WebEx Communications:

> **WebEx.** This provider of online meetings segments the business market by geographic distance. Multinational firms like Texas Instruments, with offices spread over vast distances, need a cost-effective way of enabling far-flung personnel to meet and exchange information. That's where WebEx comes in: Customers can easily log on to a secure site for private teleconferences or other types of meetings, complete with shared documents or multimedia information. Countrywide Financial, a mortgage banking business, saves $4 million annually by holding meetings online through WebEx. Because online meetings are less expensive than flying staff members to one location, WebEx has attracted a solid customer base and holds a commanding 64% share of the online conferencing market.[15]

Behavioral and Attitudinal Variables

Segmenting by behavior or attitude (such as purchasing patterns, user status, attitude toward technology, loyalty status, price sensitivity, order size/frequency, attitudes, or benefits expected) can help a company better understand and satisfy specific business segments. Purchasing patterns can vary widely; for example, companies have differing buying policies and practices and buy at different times or intervals. Understanding buying cycles and policies can help marketers design and deliver the right offer at the right time. Similarly, companies that are frequent users may require a different offer or message than first-time buyers.

Segmenting on the basis of expected or required benefits can be effective for B2B marketers. To illustrate, when 3M's sales representatives asked television manufacturers about the benefits that consumers want in the next generation of flat-screen models, they learned about two desirable benefits: a wider viewing area and a darker background color. The profit potential of this segment is so attractive that 3M immediately started refining optic films for improved television displays.[16]

ASSESS AND SELECT SEGMENTS FOR TARGETING

Practical Planning Tip
Determine criteria for assessing the attractiveness of segments under consideration.

Once the company has applied segmentation variables, it must evaluate each segment based on attractiveness and fit with the firm's resources and core competencies, goals and objectives, and offerings (identified during the analysis of the current situation). Segments that require a different set of specialized skills or resources that are beyond the company's reach will be less attractive, for instance. The point is to screen out unattractive or unsuitable segments and gauge the remaining segments' attractiveness.

To illustrate, France's Alpha M.O.S., which makes electronic odor and taste sensors, eliminates segments of business customers that require customized "noses" or "tongues," because of the additional research and development cost. Instead, Alpha segments by industry and benefit to put its marketing emphasis on large segments (such as wineries, food manufacturers, and breweries) within which customers seek to save money by using one type of electronic nose to test products for quality.[17]

Exhibit 4.4 shows factors used to evaluate segments and identify the most promising for marketing attention. As this exhibit indicates, one key measure of attractiveness is the market segment itself, including current and future opportunity for sales and profits. Large, more profitable, or faster-growing segments are generally more attractive than smaller, less profitable, or slower-growing segments.

EXHIBIT 4.4 Assessing Segment Attractiveness

Fit with company resources and competencies

Market factors	**Economic & technological factors**
Size; growth rate; life cycle stage; predictability; price elasticity; bargaining power of buyers; cyclicality of demand	Barriers to entry and exit; bargaining power of suppliers; technology utilization; investment required; margins
Competitive factors	**Business environment factors**
Intensity; quality; threat of substitution; degree of differentiation	Economic fluctuations; political and legal; regulation, social; physical environment

Identify most promising segments and order of entry

In assessing opportunity, marketers also look at how each segment would affect the company's ability to reach its overall goals, such as growth or profitability.

The auction site eBay is a good example of a company selecting segments in both the consumer and the business markets:

eBay. Consumers who buy and sell collectibles were the first segment eBay targeted when it opened. Then the site sought out additional consumer segments and soon began courting corporations with excess inventory or out-of-season merchandise to sell. Later, it began targeting smaller businesses that want to expand their customer base through eBay's global presence. One testimonial ad quoted a farmer who bought agricultural equipment for less than half price "from home after my regular work was done." Although Yahoo and Amazon.com both operate online auctions, eBay remains the leader with more than 90% of the Web's auction participation.[18]

A second factor is the potential for competitive superiority. Can the company effectively compete or lead in the segment? How intense is the competitive pressure in each segment? How well differentiated are competing products and companies already targeting each segment? A third factor is the extent of environmental threats. Based on the environmental scanning and analysis, what macroenvironmental threats, such as more restrictive regulatory guidelines, exist now or could emerge to hamper the company's performance in the segment? Economic and technological factors are the fourth category; these include investment required for entry, expected profit margins, and barriers to entry/exit in the segment.

Targeting and Coverage Strategies

Through segmentation, the company has identified various segments within the larger consumer or business market and screened out segments it will not enter. Now it selects and ranks the remaining segments in order of priority for entry. Some marketers do this by weighing the evaluation criteria to come up with a composite score for each segment. This shows which segments are more attractive and allows comparisons based on higher profit potential, faster projected growth, lower competitive pressure, or other criteria. Different marketers plan for different ranking systems and weighing criteria, based on the mission and objectives, resources, core competencies, and other considerations. As shown in the simplified ranking in Exhibit 4.5, some segments may score higher for competitive superiority but lower for fit with organizational resources, for instance. The overall score generally determines which segments are entered first; here, segment B has the highest overall score and will be the top priority for marketing attention.

Other marketers prefer to rank segments according to similar customer needs or product usage. Harrah's Entertainment, which operates casinos in Las Vegas and elsewhere, segments the consumer market by frequency of usage and loyalty. It puts its main marketing focus on the segment of people who visit casinos most frequently; these customers receive free or discounted transportation to Harrah's casinos, plus communications and gifts to reinforce loyalty. In contrast, competitors generally segment according to the amount of money spent in the casino and rank

Practical Planning Tip
Summarize your ranking and targeting decisions in the marketing plan.

EXHIBIT 4.5   Sample Segment Ranking

Segment	Score for segment growth, potential	Score for competitive superiority	Score for fit with resources, core competencies	Score for economic, technological factors	Score for environmental threats	Overall score
A	3	5	2	4	3	17
B	5	4	4	3	4	20
C	4	2	3	2	5	16

Scoring key: 5=highly attractive, 4=moderately attractive, 3=average, 2=moderately unattractive, 1=highly unattractive

the biggest spenders as the top priority.[19] Another factor to consider, especially in high-tech markets, is the rate of change.

After ranking, the company can determine which segments to enter and what coverage strategy to use. Many companies identify the most attractive segment and concentrate their marketing only on that one, which is **concentrated marketing**. The advantage is that the company can focus all its marketing activities on just one customer grouping. However, if the segment stops growing, attracts more competition, or changes in other ways, it might become unattractive almost overnight.

At the other extreme, a company may decide to target all segments with the same marketing strategy, which is **undifferentiated marketing**. This mass-marketing approach ignores any segment differences, assuming that a single marketing strategy covering the entire market will yield results in all segments. Although undifferentiated marketing requires less investment in product development, advertising, and other tactics, it is rarely used today because it doesn't adequately address the needs of fragmented, diverse markets.

Instead, companies that target multiple segments generally use **differentiated marketing** to create a separate marketing strategy for each segment. Colgate, which once used mass marketing to target everyone who needed toothpaste—one product for all, one benefit for all, one campaign for all—has become expert at differentiated marketing. It targets an immensely diverse group of segments with individual marketing mixes: people who want whiter teeth, people who want less tooth tartar, people who have sensitive teeth, and so on. Traditional phone companies are also embracing differentiated marketing. AT&T, for instance, not only offers regular "land-line" phone service but also Internet access (dial-up and broadband), voice-over-Internet protocol (VoIP) phone service, and other services for specific segments. This pits the company against companies that use concentrated marketing to target one segment, the way Vonage markets VoIP services to the segment of customers with Internet access who want to cut their long-distance phone bills.[20]

Differentiated marketing requires considerable marketing research to understand each segment's needs and entails higher costs for different products, different advertising campaigns, and so on. These costs must be taken into account when preparing the marketing plan and related budgets. If the company's resources won't stretch to cover all the targeted segments, a rollout strategy may be needed for entering one segment at a time, in order of priority.

Positioning for Competitive Advantage

After selecting segments for entry and determining the coverage strategy, the next step is to decide on a positioning strategy to differentiate the brand or product on the basis of attributes that customers find meaningful. Marketing research can uncover customers' views of the brand and its competitors, revealing key attributes that influence customer buying decisions. Then the marketer must determine which attribute (or combination of attributes) supports the most meaningful differentiation and conveys a competitive advantage that will lead to achieving sales, market share, or other objectives.

Practical Planning Tip

Be sure your positioning taps into what customers value and differentiates your product from competing products.

MEANINGFUL DIFFERENTIATION

Companies can differentiate their brands and products by physical attributes such as product features; service attributes such as convenient installation; channel attributes such as wide availability; pricing attributes such as bargain pricing; and other attributes. The choice depends on what customers value and how competitors are perceived. If customers value wide availability of a product, that point of differentiation is a potentially meaningful basis for positioning. However, it won't be a powerful point of differentiation if a competitor has already used that attribute to differentiate its product or brand. Also, a positioning will not work if it conflicts with the company's mission, goals, or resources.

Here are some examples of positioning based on meaningful differentiation:

- FedEx: fast, reliable, on-time delivery
- Southwest Airlines: affordable, no-frills air travel
- Rolex: status-symbol fashion accessory
- eBay: *the* virtual marketplace to buy or sell anything

In each case, the positioning conveys the value that the brand provides and sets the brand apart from competitors in a sustainable way. FedEx's positioning on the attribute of on-time delivery—backed up by day-in, day-out performance—has given the company a distinct image and competitive edge. What about two competitors that share a meaningful attribute such as low pricing, the way Southwest and JetBlue do?

> **Southwest and JetBlue.** Southwest's positioning on the attribute of affordable air travel—backed up by low fares and few frills—has given it a distinct image and helped it build market share in a turbulent industry. Rival JetBlue also stresses low fares but its new jets, leather seats, and personal video screens add a dimension of comfort that sets that airline apart. Even if Southwest decides to add onboard entertainment, it won't allow assigned seating—something JetBlue allows—because that would slow turnaround time and raise costs. Southwest is known for its friendly humor; JetBlue is known for its style and efficiency. Just as important, Southwest and JetBlue are differentiated from major carriers such as American and USAir, which do not emphasize no-frills affordability.[21]

POSITIONING AND MARKETING LEVERAGE

Positioning alone won't build competitive advantage, although it can act as the driving force for marketing strategies and programs, setting the tone for the rest of the marketing plan. Thus, to leverage the company's investment in marketing, all marketing programs should support and reinforce the differentiation expressed in the positioning. Consider how Agfa, a photographic and digital imaging firm, supports its positioning as a B2B problem-solving provider of imaging solutions:

Agfa. When the U.S. division of Agfa wanted to position itself as a specialist in "heavy-thinking as opposed to heavy metal," the company created a Web-based tool called a "1 to 1 Profiler" to help businesses evaluate their imaging technology needs. Business managers answer a series of questions and then receive a response geared specifically to their answers. "It's not a sales proposal," explains Agfa's director of marketing communications. "What [businesses] get back is an objective and highly refined document. It generates a large amount of goodwill and brands us as a leader in our industry." Globally, the company is strengthening its B2B problem-solving positioning by acquiring cutting-edge technology that can save industrial customers time and money.[22]

Organizations of all kinds should reevaluate the basis of their differentiation as the environment changes or customer perceptions change. This applies to countries and states marketing themselves to attract investment; tourist areas and attractions seeking to bring in travelers; and communities seeking to build pride and retain residents. The high school in Manchester, Connecticut, decided to reposition itself after the school's image suffered due to reports of crowding, student fights, and other problems. The head of the local parent–teacher association said the new marketing plan would communicate the school's positive qualities without camouflaging its problems. The school adopted a new motto, "Manchester High School—Our Future, Taught Today," to convey "the far-reaching impact the high school has on this community," a parent–teacher official explained. Other marketing actions included opening the school for senior citizen events and arranging for students to speak with civic groups.[23]

Summary

Market segmentation is the process of grouping customers within a market according to similar needs, habits, or attitudes that can be addressed through marketing. The purpose is to form groupings that are internally similar yet sufficiently different so that each grouping will not react in exactly the same way to the same marketing activities. Segmentation is the basis for targeting decisions about which market segments to enter and the segment coverage strategy to use. Once segments have been chosen, the company creates a positioning strategy for effective differentiation.

The market segmentation process consists of three main steps: (1) select the market, (2) apply segmentation variables, and (3) assess and select segments for targeting. Consumer markets can be segmented using demographic, geographic, psychographic, and behavioral/attitudinal variables. Business markets can be segmented using demographic, geographic, and behavioral/attitudinal variables. After segmentation, each segment is evaluated, unsuitable segments are screened out, and remaining segments are ranked in order of entry, using concentrated marketing, undifferentiated marketing, or differentiated marketing for targeting coverage. Finally, the company must create a positioning strategy to differentiate the brand or product on the basis of attributes that are meaningful to customers, supported by the company's marketing mix.

5

Planning Direction, Objectives, and Marketing Support

In this chapter:

Preview

The ultimate purpose of the marketing plan is to help the organization achieve a number of *objectives*—short-term performance targets—that will, in turn, bring it closer to achieving its *goals,* long-term performance targets tied to the purpose described by the mission. The planning process started with a thorough examination of environmental factors, strengths and weaknesses, markets, and customers, followed by targeting and positioning decisions about reaching selected consumer or business segments.

As discussed first in this chapter, marketers are now ready to determine the overall direction for the marketing plan. Whether or not growth is chosen, the direction has to be consistent with the organization's priorities and strengths. Next, the chapter explains how to set effective marketing, financial, and societal objectives for the coming year or whatever period the plan covers. The final section in the chapter discusses how customer service and internal marketing provide marketing support for decisions about product, place, price, and promotion.

After reading this chapter, take a few minutes to document your chosen direction, objectives, and marketing support decisions using *Marketing Plan Pro* software or in a written plan. Consult the checklist below for questions to ask when developing objectives for your marketing plan.

Determining Marketing Plan Direction

The home improvement retail chain Lowe's and the insurance firm Progressive both want to expand within the United States; the fast-food giant McDonald's and the car manufacturer Toyota want to expand internationally. These companies, like many businesses and nonprofit organizations, have created marketing plans specifically for growth. Growth is not always an appropriate direction, however; to deal with constant and inevitable change, some companies may strive to maintain current sales or revenue levels during certain years and others may move in the direction of retrenchment (see Exhibit 5.1). Toys 'R' Us, for example, recently

---

CHAPTER 5 CHECKLIST   Do Your Objectives Measure Up?

✔ Is the objective specific?

✔ Is the objective time defined?

✔ Is the objective measurable?

✔ Is the objective realistic?

✔ Is the objective challenging?

✔ Is the objective consistent with the organization's mission?

✔ Is the objective consistent with the organization's overall goals?

✔ Is the objective consistent with the organization's internal resources and core competencies?

✔ Is the objective appropriate given external environmental opportunities and threats?

EXHIBIT 5.1   Options for Marketing Plan Direction

Higher-level objectives and strategies

Growth
- Market penetration
- Market development
- Product development
- Diversification

Maintenance
- Sustain current revenues or market share
- Wring short-term profits from existing products, markets
- Prepare for future growth

Retrenchment
- Exit markets
- Drop products
- Downsize all marketing
- Limit distribution
- Close down in orderly fashion

Marketing plan objectives, strategies and programs

Practical Planning Tip
Be guided by the organization's mission, goals, and situational analysis when planning your direction.

retrenched by closing its 146 free-standing Kids 'R' Us stores. The majority of the Kids 'R' Us leases were bought by Office Depot because the office supply retailer's marketing plan called for growth in those markets.[1]

What are the choices for growth strategies and nongrowth strategies? The next two sections explain what each choice entails and the implications for marketing planning.

GROWTH STRATEGIES

If an organization wants to pursue growth, marketers can develop plans for one of these four broad strategies[2]:

Market penetration is a growth strategy in which the company sells more of its existing products to customers in existing markets or segments. This is the strategy followed by the multinational financial services firm HSBC. Its HSBC Bank Malaysia unit, as one example, is pursuing growth by marketing more products to existing customers and adding new customers in existing segments. According to one official, "The greatest challenge for the bank will be to gain market share in a slow growth market environment and increasing competition. This will be achieved through clear segmentation of our customer base and reaching out to them in meeting their needs through relationship management."[3]

Clearly, market penetration is especially viable for companies that can build on established customer relationships and brands. As an example, the toy company Hasbro has grown through global market penetration of Monopoly, Trivial Pursuit, Playskool, and other successful brands. In turn, its drive for growth has led to setting and accomplishing objectives for higher sales revenues and operating profit margins.[4]

Market development involves identifying and reaching new segments or markets for existing products. The Daryl Roth Theatre in New York City has grown by attracting audiences drawn from a new segment: local college students. The theater offers discounted tickets to students at New York University and other nearby colleges who have signed up to receive text-message promotions via cell phone. "We are constantly looking for ways to tap into new markets," notes the theater's general manager.[5]

Product development is a growth strategy in which the company sells new products to customers in existing markets or segments. Consider Mattel's marketing plan for capitalizing on the popular Barbie brand in Japan by selling adult clothing, handbags, jewelry, and other items to style-conscious women. "Our three-year plan was [to make] $22 million and [after one year] we are beating that," notes Mattel's senior vice president of consumer products. "If we continue on this road, we will have a $50 million business in Japan alone and that's not even in the kid's market"—another key segment that figures in the company's growth strategy.[6]

Diversification is a growth strategy of offering new products in new markets to take advantage of new opportunities, through internal product development capabilities or by starting or buying a business for diversification purposes. B2B marketer Cisco Systems, for example, has expanded beyond its main business of making networking products to offer wireless security cameras and Web-enabled cell phones for consumers, among other new products for new markets. Because near-term projections for networking gear show minimal growth, diversification helps Cisco expand and increase profits.[7] Diversification can help an organization avoid overreliance on a small number of products and markets; on the other hand, too much diversification can dilute available resources and open the organization to competitive attacks on multiple fronts.

Corporations with significant resources may plan to pursue multiple paths to growth around the world, as Yum Brands is doing:

Yum Brands. KFC, Pizza Hut, and Taco Bell are just three of the fast-food brands in Yum's global empire. Outside the United States, Yum is pushing for higher penetration within China, where it has 1,000 KFC restaurants and 120 Pizza Huts. Within the United States, the company is growing through product development, selling low-fat, low-calorie pizzas at Pizza Hut and oven-roasted chicken at KFC. Interestingly, U.S. customers like going to Yum restaurants that feature more than one brand, such as KFC and Pizza Hut under one roof. "The volume is higher than our straight business; the margins are good," says CEO David Novak.[8]

NONGROWTH STRATEGIES

Growth is not always desirable or even possible. In tough economic times, for instance, organizations often marshal their resources and strive to simply maintain current sales or market share. Another maintenance strategy is to seek the highest possible profits from current products and current customers without trying for growth. At times, companies can be forced into a period of retrenchment because of rising costs, slower sales, lower profits, or a combination of all three. Consider the situation of Rallis India. After suffering losses for more than a year because of lower purchasing power in its main market, the company divested itself of seeds and other products to concentrate on marketing its top-selling pesticides for farmers.[9]

Decisions to withdraw from certain markets, delete particular products, cut back on marketing, limit distribution, shutter a division, or close down the entire company call for different marketing objectives and programs than those used for growth. With sufficient time, management attention, and judicious investment, the most drastic change of direction—bankruptcy—sometimes leads to successful turnarounds. The U.K. telecommunications firm Cable & Wireless put one division into bankruptcy not long ago, even as it planned for retrenchment in its main market and pursued growth in other markets:

Cable & Wireless. The telecommunications business has high barriers to entry and higher barriers to exit, not to mention intense competition in nearly every market. After going into considerable debt to build share in the U.S. market, Cable & Wireless America went into bankruptcy so the parent company could focus its resources on other markets. Now Cable & Wireless is retrenching in the United Kingdom by reducing its product offerings, speeding up new-customer connections, and streamlining sales and marketing. At the same time, it has added personnel and increased spending on expansion in India and other markets with high growth potential.[10]

Setting Marketing Plan Objectives

After choosing a direction for the marketing plan, marketers must set objectives as short-term destinations along the path toward longer-term organizational goals. Step by step, the achievement of each objective will bring the organization closer to fulfilling its purpose. The exact objectives set will depend on the marketer's knowledge of the current situation, environmental issues and keys to success, customers in targeted segments, the organization's mission and goals, and the chosen positioning.

Practical Planning Tip
Review the SWOT analysis to identify potential problems and sources of strength for achieving objectives.

As summarized in this chapter's checklist, objectives will be effective for guiding marketing progress only if they are:

- *Specific, time-defined, and measurable.* Objectives must be specific and include both deadlines and quantitative measures so marketers can plan the timing of activities and evaluate interim results. Marketers also should be able to measure progress by looking at sales figures, customer counts, satisfaction surveys, or other indicators. USAA, an insurance company headquartered in San Antonio, Texas, makes customer retention its highest priority and monitors results by counting how many customers defect during each period. Not surprisingly, USAA has one of the best records for customer retention of any insurance firm anywhere.[11]
- *Realistic but challenging.* Marketing plan objectives should be rooted in reality yet be sufficiently challenging to inspire high performance. Consider eBay's experience: In 2000, when CEO Meg Whitman announced the goal of reaching $3 billion in revenues by 2005, that was considered an extremely aggressive goal. Thanks to savvy marketing and achievement of year-by-year objectives, eBay achieved its 5-year goal a full year early.[12]
- *Consistent with the mission and overall goals.* Objectives set for the marketing plan should support the organization in fulfilling its mission and advancing toward its long-range goals. Establishing a factory tour to support the marketing objective of building goodwill is one example. Ford recently set an objective of attracting 250,000 visitors annually to the new visitor's center in its Dearborn, Michigan, plant. For $14 per person, visitors can see pickup trucks rolling along the assembly line and watch multimedia explanations of the company's operations and history. The center's designer comments that Ford

"will never have a better chance or a more attentive audience to explain its corporate values and its mission."[13]

- *Consistent with internal environmental analysis.* Challenging objectives are empty words unless the organization has the appropriate resources, core competencies, and strengths to further their achievement.
- *Appropriate in light of opportunities and threats.* Objectives must make sense in the face of marketplace realities, opportunities, and threats. Newman's Own, which donates all profits to charity, has conducted research to size the U.S. market for premium salad dressing, one of its most popular products. Nationwide, the product category represents a $1.4 billion opportunity—and Newman's Own's current share is just 5%. Despite competition from many other brands, seeking higher market share is a reasonable and appropriate objective, given the size of the opportunity. Moreover, using marketing to increase share and revenues will help Newman's Own boost its charitable donations beyond $18 million annually.[14]

Marketers usually set three types of objectives in their marketing plans (see Exhibit 5.2). **Marketing objectives** are targets for managing specific marketing relationships and activities; **financial objectives** are targets for managing certain financial results; and **societal objectives** are targets for achieving particular results in social responsibility. The next sections explain how to use each type of objective.

MARKETING OBJECTIVES

Marketing objectives should include targets for managing customer relationships because these are so critical to company success. E-marketing expert Judy Strauss advises: "Objectives to raise profit, increase market share, or change stakeholder attitudes and behaviors are meaningless unless companies make effective plans to manage their most valuable asset: customer relationships."[15] Depending on the industry,

---

EXHIBIT 5.2   Marketing Plan Objectives

Type of Objective	*Purpose*	*Samples*
Marketing	To use marketing to manage key relationships and activities	• Customer relationships • Channel relationships • Market share • Product development • Order fulfillment • Brand awareness
Financial	To use marketing to attain certain financial results	• Sales revenue by product • Sales revenue by channel • Break-even by product • Return on investment • Profitability
Societal	To use marketing to achieve results in social responsibility	• Greener/cleaner operations • Charitable activities • Energy conservation • Community involvement

direction, mission, and available resources, marketers may set targets for acquiring new customers, retaining customers, increasing customer loyalty, and increasing customer satisfaction. Acquisition and retention are especially vital in mature markets such as express delivery, which is why FedEx uses marketing for such objectives.[16]

Some firms set additional objectives for managing relationships with other stakeholders, such as channel partners. Nonprofits usually set objectives for managing relations with members and contributors, as well as for attracting donations, grants, and corporate sponsorship. In Canada, the nonprofit organization Doctors Without Borders recently set the marketing objective of attracting 1,000 new contributors within a year.[17] Other objectives in this category might cover marketing activities related to market share, new product development, and other vital areas.

Some sample marketing objectives might include:

Practical Planning Tip
Check that objectives in one category do not prevent you from achieving objectives in another category.

- *Customer acquisition:* Expand the customer base by adding 200 new customers each month for the next year.
- *Customer retention:* Reduce the annual customer defection rate to 10% by the end of the year.
- *Customer satisfaction:* Score 96% or higher on the next 4 customer satisfaction surveys.
- *Channel relationships:* Expand distribution by placing products in 4 additional supermarket chains within 6 months.
- *Unit sales:* Sell 500 units in each targeted segment during every month next year.
- *Market share:* Capture 2% of the U.S. market by March 31.
- *Product development:* Develop and introduce 5 new products by December 31.
- *Order fulfillment:* Cut the time for fulfillment of orders from 48 to 24 hours by May 15.

To illustrate, Bentley's marketers have objectives for higher sales but also face the challenge of retaining buyers during the long wait for a car:

> **Bentley.** Owned by Volkswagen since 1998, Bentley recently set a one-year objective of selling 9,000 super-luxury cars, sharply higher than the few thousand sold worldwide just two years earlier. The restyled car is hipper than ever, due in part to publicity about celebrity customers such as the Osbourne family. To attract new customers, marketers have planned dozens of exclusive preview parties for those able to afford the car's $150,000-plus price tag. They also have put the car on display at high-end boat shows and charitable affairs. Because production is carefully controlled to maintain quality, however, demand far outstrips supply. As a result, Bentley is using marketing to maintain good relations with customers who will not get their cars for 12–18 months.[18]

FINANCIAL OBJECTIVES

Although the exact financial objectives will vary from organization to organization, businesses generally quantify sales volume and product targets; profitability targets such as margin or pretax profit; return on investment (ROI) targets for marketing; and break-even targets (discussed in Chapter 8). Nonprofits might set targets for fundraising, among other financial objectives. For example, Canada's Doctors Without Borders knew it would have to invest in marketing to attract new donors, so it also set the financial objective of breaking even on these costs within 4 months.[19]

To be effective, financial and marketing objectives must be consistent. Thus, Doctors Without Borders recognized that it would have to spend money to acquire new contributors, so it set a realistic marketing objective and a corresponding financial objective for this marketing plan. On the other hand, key financial objectives may have to give way if a company is to achieve a particularly coveted marketing objective. Experiencing lower revenues from consumer and business long-distance services, AT&T recently decided to match rivals' discounts so it could achieve and build share in a market that is both mature and highly competitive. "We don't intend to lose on price," stated the CEO, who acknowledged that the company's profit margins would also be squeezed.[20]

**Practical
Planning Tip**
Be sure your objectives
are achievable, given
your resources, compe-
tencies, and marketing
tools.

Some sample financial objectives might be:

- *Sales revenue:* Achieve $150,000 yearly sales revenue by December 31.
- *Product sales revenue:* Sell $3,000 worth of Product A every month.
- *Channel sales revenue:* Increase monthly Internet sales to $50,000 by end of year.
- *Profitability:* Increase the gross profit margin to 25% by end of year.
- *Return on investment:* Achieve 17% ROI on funds invested in direct marketing activities.
- *Break-even:* Reach the break-even point on Product B by June 30.

Consider Camp Jabulani's break-even objective:

Camp Jabulani. A high-end safari lodge and game reserve in South Africa, Camp Jabulani is home to cheetahs, lions, and other animals native to the area. Here, a double room rents for $1,500 per night; however, the reserve's expenses include $20,000 per month to feed 20 Zimbabwean elephants, not including the cost of medical care and personnel costs for the elephants' grooms. To break even, Camp Jabulani set a one-year objective of achieving at least a 40% occupancy rate. This is significantly higher than the 10% occupancy rate of the lodge's first 6 months, but rising interest in ecotourism and higher awareness of the reserve's beauty could be deciding factors in achieving the objective.[21]

SOCIETAL OBJECTIVES

These days, customers, suppliers, employees, civic leaders, and other stakeholders are looking more closely at what companies do for society; as a result, more organizations are including societal objectives in their marketing plans. As shown in Exhibit 5.2, some societal objectives may call for cleaner operations or "greener" (more ecologically friendly) products, charitable donations, volunteerism or other involvement with community projects, energy conservation, and other socially responsible actions.

Fulfilling societal objectives polishes company or brand image and shows that the organization is doing something constructive about important issues. Setting objectives is not enough—stakeholders often follow the company's progress. For this reason, a growing number of firms are posting social responsibility reports on their Web sites or producing printed versions for customers and employees. Find out more about corporate social responsibility on the Business for Social Responsibility site (www.bsr.org) and the Corporate Social Responsibility Newswire site (www.csrwire.com).

Cause-related marketing falls under the umbrella of social responsibility because it links the marketing of a brand, good, or service to a particular charitable cause. Although the charity benefits, this is not outright philanthropy because of the explicit marketing connection. For example, the Red Lobster restaurant chain operates an annual cause-related program called Cobs and Lobsters, in which a portion of sales revenue is donated to Special Olympics. Olive Garden restaurants also plan an annual cause-related marketing program, Pasta for Pennies; since 1990, this program has raised $15 million for leukemia and lymphoma research and treatment. According to Olive Garden's media relations director, "An emotional something happens when your restaurant develops a relationship with its community in this way. It lets people know and feel your dedication and concern—that there's more than profit on your mind."[22]

Some sample societal objectives might include:

Practical Planning Tip
Choose a cause that makes sense for your organization, your customers, and your employees.

- *Conservation.* Reduce each store's use of electricity by at least 5% annually.
- *Reduce waste.* Increase the proportion of recyclable product parts to 50% by the end of next year.
- *Issue awareness.* Inform customers about substance abuse prevention by printing flyers for distribution with the February direct-mail campaign.
- *Community involvement.* Encourage employees to volunteer for local projects on company time, receiving pay for up to 40 hours of volunteerism per year.

Putting resources toward social responsibility can be controversial, as in the case of Petróleos de Venezuela:

Petróleos de Venezuela. This state-run oil company, known as Pdvsa, is putting much more emphasis on social responsibility. "Pdvsa used to function as a transnational company only interested in maximizing oil sales," says the president, Alí Rodríguez. "Now, Pdvsa is working with other state institutions to reduce Venezuela's exceedingly high rate of poverty." It is paying for agricultural development programs, low-income housing, and basics such as digging new wells. Critics say that Pdvsa's $1.7 billion annual social responsibility spending diverts resources that should be used to increase oil output. But many residents are benefiting and therefore starting to see the company in a new light. "I'm so happy that we're finally going to have water in the house," comments one. "This is the first time the company has ever done anything for us."[23]

Planning Marketing Support

Before marketers plunge into the details of planning the marketing mix, they need to set objectives for two aspects of marketing support: customer service and internal marketing (see Exhibit 5.3). Customer service is important in any business because it offers opportunities to reinforce competitive differentiation and start or strengthen customer relationships. **Internal marketing**—marketing to managers and employees inside the organization—is equally important for building internal relationships as a foundation for implementing the marketing plan and satisfying customers. Decisions to be made in setting objectives for these two areas of marketing support are discussed in the following sections.

CUSTOMER SERVICE

From the customer's perspective, service is part of the product or brand experience, and thus has a major influence on customers' perceptions and responses. When setting customer service objectives, then, marketers must understand what customers need and expect, what they consider satisfactory, and how service reflects on the brand or product. Although good customer service cannot make up for a bad product or spotty distribution, it can enhance the brand's image and may even allow management to raise prices despite intense competitive pressure or other challenges.

Practical Planning Tip
Because they are interconnected, coordinate service objectives with internal marketing objectives.

In general, customers have different customer service needs and expectations at different points in the buying process:

- *Customer service before the sale.* Before they buy, customers often need assistance obtaining information about the product and its usage, features, benefits, and warranty; matching the right product to the right situation or need; researching add-ons like availability and pricing of replacement parts; and understanding how installation, training, or other postsale services operate.
- *Customer service at the moment or point of sale.* When they are about to buy, customers may need help choosing a specific model; scheduling delivery, pickup, or use; choosing among payment options or preparing purchase orders; arranging trade-ins or taking advantage of promotional offers; completing paperwork for warranty registration; or handling other sale-related issues.
- *Customer service after the sale.* After the purchase has been completed, customers sometimes need assistance installing a product; reordering refills or spare parts; scheduling maintenance or repair services; training users; or dealing with other postsale needs. Bank of America calls new customers a few weeks after they open accounts to answer questions and follow up on problems or needs. "It's low-tech, but it can have a tremendous impact on the quality of new customer relationships," says a marketing official.[24]

EXHIBIT 5.3 Customer Service and Internal Marketing Objectives

Internal Marketing Objectives	Support marketing objectives and the marketing mix	Customer Service Objectives
• Keep employees focused on customers		• Meet targeted segment's needs, expectations
• Keep employees involved in marketing		• Attract, retain, satisfy customers
• Keep employees informed about marketing		• Reinforce the product or brand positioning
• Improve employee performance and satisfaction		• Allocate service resources appropriately

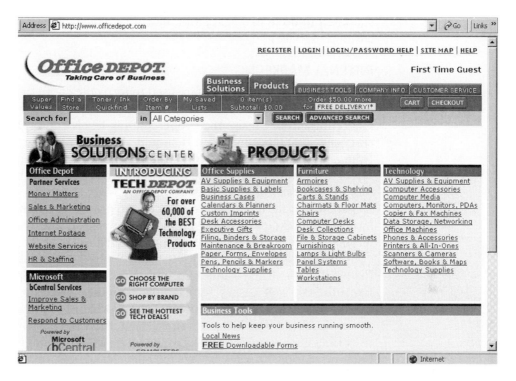

Office Depot recently set and achieved the goal of becoming the largest online retailer of office suppliers.

The marketing plan also should set objectives for allocating service resources to deliver the appropriate level of customer service for each segment. Some marketers choose to offer a lower level of customer service support to less profitable segments while providing more profitable segments with more service, as Merrill Lynch does:

> **Merrill Lynch.** Merrill Lynch has segmented its 9 million brokerage accounts, determined each segment's profitability, and assigned each to an appropriate customer service level. The smallest and least profitable accounts (those with balances under $100,000) receive customer service through call centers; the largest and most profitable accounts get personal attention from money-management specialists. This customer service strategy, along with aggressive internal cost-cutting, boosted Merrill Lynch's profit margin from 17% to 28% within 2 years and freed up personnel and capital to invest in marketing to wealthier customers who need (and can pay for) multiple investment services.[25]

Knowing that customer service is rarely perfect every time, marketers should include objectives for **service recovery**, how the organization will recover from a service lapse and satisfy its customers. Research shows that if customers are satisfied with the way their complaints are resolved, 70% will continue the relationship. In fact, those who are pleased will be more likely to tell others about their experience, bringing the company new customers through positive word of mouth.[26] In setting service recovery objectives, companies should think about the process (such as what customers must do to register a complaint and what employees are supposed to do in response) and the results (such as measuring satisfaction with customer service).

INTERNAL MARKETING

Internal marketing objectives are used to focus the entire organization on the customer and generate support for the marketing plan. At the very least, internal marketing should ensure the proper staffing levels and organization structure to carry out the marketing plan. It should also help marketers secure cooperation from other departments involved in implementation, such as operations and research and development, and keep employees informed about marketing activities so they can communicate effectively with customers and with each other. Depending on the company's resources and priorities, internal marketing communication can take place through internal newsletters and Web pages; training and marketing or sales meetings; and other techniques.

Upward communication is also vital, because it gives senior managers a feel for what the market wants and how marketing is meeting customers' needs. Executives of Walt Disney, for example, periodically suit up as Mickey or another Disney character and walk through Disneyworld or Disneyland to see what is happening firsthand. The company stresses internal cooperation and commitment to delivering quality service at every contact point. "Our goal is to treat one another the way we treat our guests," says the manager of performance and training.[27]

Another objective of internal marketing is to increase employee performance and satisfaction in a job well done, especially important in service businesses:

> **Commerce Bancorp.** Based in Cherry Hill, New Jersey, Commerce Bancorp sends a "Wow team" on the road, appearing without warning at any of the 150 branches to reward staff members for special service achievement. In turn, branch personnel are encouraged to identify opportunities and situations in which they can go beyond the expected to "wow" their customers. Superior customer service has become Commerce Bancorp's most powerful competitive weapon, fueling rapid growth in new customers and new deposits even though the bank pays relatively low rates on savings and certificates of deposit.[28]

Shaping the Marketing Mix

As shown in Exhibit 5.4, the organization's mission, direction, goals, and objectives (at the top of the pyramid) are the guiding force behind decisions about the marketing mix, marketing support, and specific marketing programs. Managers look to the priorities reflected in the top of the pyramid as they determine action steps and allocate resources. All the tactics and programs developed during the remainder of the marketing planning process must not only be consistent with the mission, direction, goals, and objectives in the marketing plan, they must actually support them.

Thus, by properly implementing the programs in the marketing plan and measuring the results periodically against preset standards, the organization should be able to move in the chosen direction and progress toward accomplishing its financial, marketing, and societal objectives. Understanding this essential link between

Practical Planning Tip

The strategy pyramid shows how marketing programs are driven by strategic decisions.

EXHIBIT 5.4   Strategy Pyramid

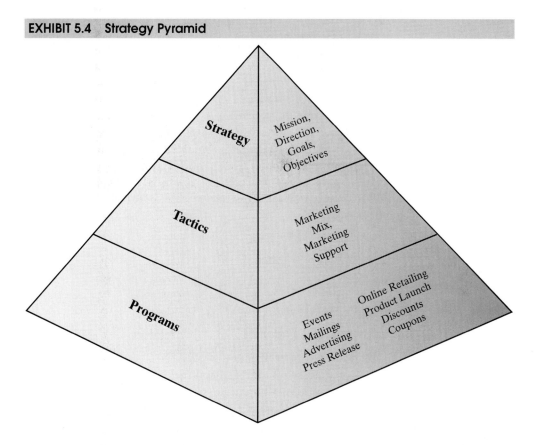

strategy, goals, objectives, tactics, and programs can help marketers make appropriate, effective, and productive marketing-mix decisions.

Summary

A marketing plan may point the way toward growth (including market penetration, market development, product development, and diversification), maintenance of current sales levels, or retrenchment. Once the direction has been set, marketers establish objectives for the marketing plan that are specific, time defined, and measurable; realistic but challenging; consistent with the mission and organizational goals; consistent with resources and core competencies; and appropriate for the external environment. Marketing objectives are short-term targets for managing marketing relationships and activities; financial objectives are short-term targets for managing financial results; societal objectives are short-term targets for managing social responsibility results.

For marketing support, marketers need to set objectives for customer service and for internal marketing. Customer service can be provided before, during, and after the sale, with service geared to customer segments and marketing plan objectives and with appropriate objectives for service recovery. Internal marketing involves marketing to people inside the organization, necessary for building external relationships and implementing the marketing plan. The strategy pyramid illustrates the principle that marketing tactics and programs must support the mission, direction, goals, and objectives.

Developing Product and Brand Strategy

In this chapter:

Preview

Of the 33,000 new food, beverage, personal care, household, and pet products launched in any given year, some will succeed and many will not.[1] Meticulous research, in-depth customer knowledge, careful planning, and good implementation make all the difference. In formulating product strategy, marketers must determine how existing and proposed products fit with the chosen direction and objectives and how each can contribute to building relationships with targeted customers. Branding plays a vital role in positioning and relationship-building as well. Strong brands—such as Nokia, John Deere, and Starbucks—can create sufficient customer value to enhance the effectiveness of the entire marketing mix.

This chapter opens with an exploration of the main decisions in planning product strategy, the first of the four Ps in the marketing mix. These decisions cover tangible and intangible products; features, benefits, and supplementary services; quality and design; packaging and labeling; and product development and management. The second part of the chapter explores the basics of branding, including how branding works with positioning and how brand equity affects customer loyalty and lifetime value. Once you have finished this chapter, document your decisions and observations using *Marketing Plan Pro* software or in a written plan. The checklist on page 84 suggests questions for analyzing offerings and developing product strategy.

Planning Product Strategy

What value can each product (existing and proposed) provide by satisfying the needs of specific customer segments? How can each product help the organization attain one or more marketing, financial, and societal objectives? These are two key questions underlying the development of product strategy. From the customer's perspective, a product's value derives from the benefits delivered by its features and supplementary services, quality and design, packaging and labeling, and branding (see Exhibit 6.1). The marketer must therefore make decisions about each of these elements to formulate a strategy for offering goods, services, and other products that suit the organization's unique situation and satisfy or exceed targeted customers' needs and expectations.

Practical Planning Tip
For existing products, review your strategy and research market changes to plan for adjustments.

GOODS, SERVICES, AND OTHER PRODUCTS

During planning, organizations must determine what, exactly, constitutes the product to be offered. Products can be:

- *Tangible goods* such as electric motors and jewelry, which customers can buy, lease, rent, or use.
- *Services* such as cell phone service or Internet search engines, which are primarily intangible but may involve physical items (cell phone or computer).
- *Places* such as geographic regions courting tourists, states vying for business investment, or cities seeking to host activities such as the Olympic games.
- *Ideas* such as eating healthy or supporting human rights, with the objective of shaping the targeted segment's attitudes and behavior.
- *Organizations* such as a corporation or a government agency, with the objective of affecting the targeted segment's attitudes and behavior.

CHAPTER 6 CHECKLIST   Analyzing and Planning Product Strategy

Current Offerings
- ✔ What products are being offered, at what price points, and for what customer segments?
- ✔ What are the unit sales, revenues, and profit trends of each product over the years?
- ✔ What is the age of each product? How are newer products faring in relation to older products?
- ✔ What is the market share of each product or line?
- ✔ How does each product support sales of the line, i.e., are some sold only as supplements or add-ons to others?
- ✔ How does each product contribute to the company's overall performance and goals?
- ✔ Which product accounts for the largest proportion of sales and profits?
- ✔ How do product sales vary according to geography?
- ✔ How do product sales vary according to channel?
- ✔ What are the strengths and weaknesses of the current offerings?

Product Plans
- ✔ How does each product support the organization's objectives and strategic direction?
- ✔ What opportunities for adding value through product modifications or introductions exist in each segment?
- ✔ What strengths and core competencies apply to product strategy?
- ✔ What weaknesses and threats pose risks to product strategy? How can these be minimized or overcome?
- ✔ How do each product's features and benefits, quality, packaging, services, and branding provide value for customers? What enhancements would add value and help the company achieve its goals?
- ✔ How do each product's features and benefits, quality, packaging, services, and branding compare with competitive offerings?
- ✔ Where is each product in the life cycle, and what is required to align its stage and sales with the strategic direction and marketing plan objectives?
- ✔ How can product introductions be managed to minimize cannibalization?
- ✔ What changes to product lines and product mixes will help the company pursue its goals?

- *People* such as the NBA star Yao Ming or the music group No Doubt, with the objective of affecting the targeted segment's attitudes and behavior.

In designing a service, marketers should think about who or what is being processed and whether the service activity is tangible or intangible (see Exhibit 6.2). Remember that the processing experience is as important as the end results, because customers are present during many service operations. Therefore, when

EXHIBIT 6.1   Elements of Product and Brand Strategy

Customer needs and response

Organizational resources and value

Decisions about:
- Features, Benefits, Related Services
- Quality and Design
- Packaging and Labeling
- Product Development and Management
- Branding

planning services, marketers must focus on delivering benefits through the appropriate combination of activities, people, facilities, and information.

FEATURES, BENEFITS, AND SERVICES

Features are specific attributes that enable the product to perform its function. In physical goods such as backpacks, features include padded shoulder straps and strong zippers; in intangible services such as online banking, features include integrated display of all account information and one-click funds transfer. Companies incorporate features to deliver **benefits**, the need–satisfaction outcomes that customers want from a product. For example, customers who buy cordless drills are seeking the benefit of creating holes for nails and screws, although some may seek additional benefits such as convenience or status. Thus, consumers and business customers buy products not for the features alone but for the value in providing benefits that fulfill needs or solve problems (which marketers can uncover through market and customer analysis).

Exhibit 6.3 shows some sample needs, features, and benefits for two tangible products and one service. Each product targets a different consumer or business segment that is described according to behavior (do-it-yourselfers) or demographics (first-time home buyers, small business owners). In each case, note how the benefit interprets the feature in relation to each segment's specific need. Taking the analysis down to this level, feature by feature, helps marketers understand the

EXHIBIT 6.2   Designing a Service

Tangible activities	*People Processing*	*Item Processing*
	• Health care	• Package delivery
	• Hotel accommodations	• Janitorial service
	• Mass transit	• Parking garage
Intangible activities	*Mental Processing*	*Information Processing*
	• Entertainment programs	• Banking
	• Management consulting	• Legal services
	• Local phone service	• Accounting services

Including the UPS logo in each marketing communication reinforces the brand name and identity.

value that each product offers to satisfy customer needs—at a given time. Needs and environmental influences can change at any point, so marketers must factor this into their analyses and plans.

A product will be at a competitive disadvantage if its features deliver benefits not valued by the targeted segment. Even if these customers value the benefits, the features must also be of value to the organization, consistent with the marketing plan's objectives. If a feature supports an objective such as capturing higher market share, it is valuable to the organization. For instance, TCC Teleplex has put pay phones equipped for Internet access on some corners in New York City. The Internet access feature is valuable to people who want the benefit of being able to

EXHIBIT 6.3 Sample Needs, Features, and Benefits				
Product	*Targeted Segment*	*Need*	*Feature*	*Benefit*
Cordless drill (tangible)	Do-it-yourselfers (behavioral description)	Drill holes without electricity	Extra battery pack included	Drill can be used for long periods of time
Mortgage loan (intangible)	First-time home buyers (demographic description)	Obtain money to buy a home	Low down payment	Less money needed up front to buy a home
Laser printer (tangible)	Small business owners (demographic description)	Print documents economically	Draft-quality printing mode uses less toner	Saves money by making toner cartridge last longer

check e-mail or visit a Web site while on the street. However, if a feature does not contribute to achieving an objective (because it is too expensive to be profitable, for instance), it is not valuable to the organization—even if it is highly valuable to customers. Verizon, which operates pay phone networks all over the country, tested Web-enabled pay phones in busy areas and decided against this product. Users valued Web access but Verizon saw limited demand and limited profit potential for this costly feature.[2]

Practical Planning Tip
Seek ways to add value while achieving societal and marketing objectives, not just financial objectives.

More companies are building customer loyalty and profits through a product strategy calling for **mass customization**, creating products, on a large scale, with features tailored to the needs of individual customers. General Electric does this with industrial plastics formulated to meet the specific needs of corporate customers. Some customers need unusually strong plastics, some need especially flexible plastics, some require multiple benefits that are delivered by a variety of features. Now more than 70,000 customers order custom-developed plastics from the GE Plastics Web site. Because customers use the site to configure their plastics formulas and submit orders, GE can respond to needs more quickly.[3] Mass customization is available for consumers as well:

Lands' End. This catalog and Internet retailer, owned by Sears, has been offering custom-ordered jeans and chinos since 2001. Customers provide their body measurements and proportion of torso to legs, then select the features they like, such as plain or pleated front, color, length, and so forth. Two weeks later, they have pants that fit much better than pants bought off the rack. Despite the significantly higher price, customized pants became so popular that within a year, they accounted for 40% of all Lands' End jeans and chinos sold online. The company has profited by offering mass-customized versions of dress shirts and other garments.[4]

Although many Lands' End customers are willing to pay for benefits they receive from the features of customized clothing, not all customers value the entire bundle of features and benefits inherent in a particular product. Marketing research is therefore a critical element in planning features. For instance, Ducati uses online research, listing the features of motorcycles in development on a page of its Web site and asking for customer comments before deciding which to actually include when production begins.[5] Studying sales trends of current offerings and researching customer reactions to those products also yields clues as to how well features satisfy customers' needs.

In planning product strategy, marketers should consider how the supplementary services related to a product can deliver valued benefits to satisfy customer needs, now and in the future. Some supplementary services may supply information for better use of the product, as in training; some may offer consultation for problem solving or customization of the product; some may involve safety or security, as in storage of products or data. IBM exemplifies this range:

IBM. Big Blue markets stand-alone computer hardware and software but puts its main marketing emphasis on product–service bundles that more precisely address business customers' problems and needs in 12 industry groups, including telecommunications, utilities, vehicles, and banking. Consider FinnAir airlines, which once bought mainframe computers from IBM. Still an IBM customer, FinnAir now buys some hardware, some services (such as outsourced data center operations), and some product/service combinations (such as specialized marketing software with services tailored to FinnAir's requirements). The changes in purchasing reflect changes in FinnAir's needs and IBM's marketing of product–service bundles to meet those changing needs.[6]

QUALITY AND DESIGN

Often defined in terms of performance capabilities, the most important definition of **quality** is how well the product satisfies customers. By this definition, a high-quality product is one that does a competitively superior job of fulfilling customer needs. Savvy marketers know that the basic functionality of acceptable quality is the price of entry in the contemporary global marketplace. Word-of-mouth (or online word-of-mouse) can quickly sink a product with inferior quality—and just as quickly generate interest in a product with excellent quality. Good quality is no guarantee of success, but it can help companies attract new customers, retain current customers, capture market share, charge higher prices, earn higher profits, or meet other objectives.

Practical Planning Tip
Determine how customers perceive your product's quality compared with that of competing products.

The marketing plan should take into account customers' tendency to switch to a competing product if they believe its quality is superior (meeting their needs more consistently or more quickly). Quality is a major concern among cell phone users, for example, which is part of the reason for the higher **customer churn** (turnover in customers) at some phone service carriers. When Cingular bought AT&T Wireless to form the largest U.S. cell phone service carrier, Cingular's chief operating officer stated, "We will be the market leader from here on out, with unsurpassed coverage. We'll have less dropped calls and more reliability. On top of that, we will have sufficient spectrum to migrate to 3G," the next generation of wireless technology. At the time, *Fortune* magazine reported that Cingular's annual churn was 2.7% and AT&T's was 2.6%, compared with rival Verizon's annual churn of 1.7%. Pricing and other factors account for some churn, but Cingular's focus on quality, as defined by its customers, should bring the churn rate down and encourage loyalty.[7]

Another focus of product strategy is design, inextricably linked to quality. A good design means more than style—it means that the product can perform as it should, can be repaired easily, is aesthetically pleasing, and meets other needs. Services are affected by design as well: New York's Long Island College Hospital recently changed its emergency room design to add efficiency as well as comfort, cutting in half the waiting time for medical attention.[8] Design is at the forefront of many product categories, from computers and entertainment electronics to home appliances and workshop tools. When good quality is the minimum that customers will accept, the "emotional quality" of design is the marketing battleground that more companies are choosing for differentiation. "A car can't exist in the future if it doesn't show passion," says Volkswagen's head designer.[9] Ford and Volvo are steering in that direction as well:

Ford and Volvo. Ford's latest designs follow "the golden rules of touch," how a car's features feel to the driver. "Everyone has discovered the importance of craftsmanship and quality in the interior," says Ford's chief designer. "Now it's an all-out war" around such features as dashboards and turn-signal levers. As one example, Ford's newest Mustangs allow customers to choose among 125 different color combinations for dashboard gauge displays. Meanwhile, Volvo (owned by Ford) recently exhibited a driver-friendly concept car designed by a five-woman team. Among the special features: gull-wing doors and retractable door sills (benefit: easy entry/exit); dirt-resistant paint (benefit: keeps exterior clean); and removable, washable seat covers (benefit: keeps interior clean). Little by little, Volvo will incorporate some of these features into car designs to continue boosting quality according to plan.[10]

PACKAGING AND LABELING

From the customer's perspective, packaging adds value by keeping tangible products safe and in convenient containers until they are used; labeling adds value by communicating product contents, uses, and warnings. Thus, Kellogg's Corn Flakes stay fresh and uncrushed in the plastic-lined cardboard packaging, and Advil pain reliever tablets are kept out of tiny hands by child-resistant containers; both packages bear labels with information about product ingredients and consumption. When planning for labels, check on compliance with regional, national, or local laws and requirements mandating warnings (such as about the health hazards of cigarettes or alcohol), allowable use of certain phrases (such as "low fat"), and even the size or type of words (for warnings or other details).

A growing number of companies are planning packaging and labeling to burnish brand image by highlighting healthy or ecologically friendly benefits before

Practical Planning Tip
Consider the needs of channel members as well as customers when planning packaging and labeling.

required or beyond minimum legal/regulatory requirements. Look at Frito-Lay's labeling initiative:

Frito-Lay. More than 2 years before the Food and Drug Administration required manufacturers to label foods with the total amount of trans fats in each product, Frito-Lay took the initiative and reformulated its snacks to eliminate trans-fat oils. Retaining the same taste in Doritos and other snacks was a challenge, but once the company made the switchover, it added a green and yellow ribbon to call attention to the "Great Taste, Smart Snack" benefits. Frito-Lay's positioning on health and taste benefits gave it a head start on building awareness and preference in advance of the FDA's 2006 deadline for trans-fat labeling.[11]

As the Frito-Lay example shows, packaging and labeling play an important marketing role by highlighting points of differentiation, explaining the product's features and benefits, reinforcing what the brand stands for, and attracting attention among customers and channel partners. In certain product categories, marketers plan innovative packaging as an effective point of differentiation. To illustrate, shelf-stable aseptic containers are gaining popularity for beverages, soups, and other foods, because they preserve taste and require no refrigeration until opened. Baby foods in aseptic packaging instead of glass jars? An executive at Gerber Products says: "We looked at a lot of [packaging] technologies, but aseptic was the most appropriate in terms of cost effectiveness and making parents' lives easier by providing lighter containers that won't break as well as providing a good-tasting, shelf-stable product."[12]

Marketers should plan packaging and labeling to "sell" from the shelf, because more than 70% of shoppers make their buying decisions while in the store. One reason that Listerine's PocketPak breath strips became a hit is that the package looked "cool and functional," notes an executive with Listerine's parent company. Research confirmed that customers found the package attractive and consistent with the brand. Even before Listerine kicked off its advertising campaign, shoppers noticed PocketPaks and bought them on impulse, giving the new product considerable sales momentum.[13]

PRODUCT DEVELOPMENT AND MANAGEMENT

The fourth major element of product strategy is managing movement through the **product life cycle** of introduction, growth, maturity, and decline (see Exhibit 6.4). Even experts have difficulty predicting the exact length and shape of a product's life cycle, which limits the practical application of this theory. However, marketers can look at sales trends for clues to a particular product's life-cycle stage: new products with low but growing sales are in the introduction stage; young products with rapidly increasing sales are in the growth stage; existing products with relatively level sales are in maturity; and older products with decreasing sales are in decline. These stages can be influenced by factors such as competition and societal attitudes—which are constantly changing—so marketers need to carefully monitor the environment as they plan to manage their products throughout the life cycle.

EXHIBIT 6.4   Product Strategy from Development through the Life Cycle

Idea Generation and Screening	*Initial Concept Testing*	*Business Analysis*	*Design Prototype*	*Market Testing*	*Commercialization*
• Based on customer needs and wants, identify new product ideas	• Research customer value of product concepts	• Estimate development, production, and marketing-mix costs	• Design and produce working prototypes	• Test customer reaction through limited market trials or simulated testing	• Plan targeting and timing of launch
• Screen out unprofitable or unsuitable ideas	• Refine concept based on research	• Compare costs with potential share, sales, profitability to identify good candidates	• Test prototype functionality, customer appeal	• Test different marketing-mix combinations for support	• Plan production and marketing-mix support for launch

Introduction	*Growth*	*Maturity*	*Decline*
• Launch the new product	• Enhance product (new features, improved quality, added services, new packaging)	• Add brand or line extensions	• Reposition, reformulate, or cut struggling products
• Support launch with marketing-mix programs to build customer awareness, make product available, and encourage trial	• Support rising sales with expanded channel coverage, pricing for market penetration, and communications to start and reinforce customer relationships	• Defend market share through competitive pricing, channel expansion, communicating differentiation, and promotion to reinforce customer loyalty	• Manage profitability through careful pricing, pruning channel outlets, and minimal or highly targeted communications

**Practical
Planning Tip**
**Aim to have different
products in different
stages of the life cycle
at any one time.**

Deciding to cut older products in decline is not an easy decision, and it has a ripple effect far beyond the targeted segments, as GM found with Oldsmobile:

Oldsmobile. The Oldsmobile product line was 107 years old when GM deleted it because of lack of profitability. Big hits like the Cutlass helped sell more than 1 million Olds vehicles annually during the 1980s, but by the time GM announced in 2000 that the line would be discontinued, only 289,000 vehicles were being sold yearly. GM will continue servicing Olds vehicles and will make key parts available for more than a decade—well after the last new Olds car rolled off the assembly line in 2004. GM also signed phase-out agreements with its dealerships and paid them for losing the line (some dealers closed and others planned to sell other lines). By one estimate, GM has retained roughly half of its Olds customer base by selling them Chevrolet, Buick, or the last of the Olds vehicles. GM CEO Rick Wagoner says that cutting the line was the right decision: "We've devoted a lot of resources in bringing out new Olds products over the last several years. I have a clear conscience that we gave it a chance."[14]

New Product Development

Just as GM's future marketing plans will include activities to encourage Oldsmobile owners to buy other GM brands when they shop for new or used cars, the company's plans will also include development of new vehicles. Like their counterparts in other companies, GM's marketing planners look closely at potential opportunities for providing value in each segment, build on internal strengths and core competencies to create competitively superior products, and think about how to deal with any weaknesses and external threats. Planning for new product development covers these basic steps:

- *Idea generation.* Collect ideas from customers, managers and employees, suppliers, distributors, and other sources.
- *Screening of new ideas.* Eliminate inappropriate or impractical ideas early in the process to avoid wasting time and resources later.
- *Initial concept testing.* Test to discover whether customers in the targeted segment understand and like the most promising new product ideas; refine or drop concepts that test poorly.
- *Business analysis.* Assess the business prospects of the remaining ideas and eliminate any that could be too expensive or will not contribute to the marketing plan's objectives. W.L. Gore, which makes Gore-Tex and other products, analyzes the business case by researching the size of the market segment, the product's value to customers, the potential profitability, and the ability to maintain a competitive advantage.[15]
- *Prototype design.* Design and produce a prototype to determine the practicality and cost. If different technology or skills are needed, making a prototype will bring such issues into focus before full production.
- *Market testing.* Test the new product and various introductory marketing activities to gauge demand and competitive strength. Often companies test different introductory tactics to find the most effective combination.

- *Commercialization.* Introduce the new product in some areas or across the entire market, with the support of channel, pricing, and promotion strategies.
- *Monitoring of customer reaction.* Monitor customer reaction; if a new product does not fare as well as expected, the company faces decisions about changing the marketing mix (including the product), repositioning the product, or pulling it from the market.

In many cases, companies make decisions about new products and life-cycle movement to avoid or minimize **cannibalization**—allowing a new product to eat into sales of one or more existing products. Some cannibalization is inevitable in high-tech markets, where life cycles are relatively short because competitors race to launch the next breakthrough product. Companies often believe that if they don't cannibalize their own products, rivals will seize the opportunity to grab both sales and customer relationships. Rather than completely cannibalize a product, however, the firm may prefer to reposition it for other uses or segments. For example, expensive computer chips that were state-of-the-art last year may be priced lower than today's top performing chips and repositioned for use in computers designed for segments where speed or power is less of a priority and customers are more price sensitive. Intel routinely does this when it introduces speedy new chips and lowers prices on existing chips to make them more attractive to different segments.[16]

Product Lines and the Product Mix

Product strategy also covers the management of each **product line** (products that are related in some way) and the overall **product mix** (the assortment of all product lines offered). The existing mix was analyzed as part of the current situation; after examining each product and line individually, marketers plan product decisions that will affect the length and width of lines and mixes (see Exhibit 6.5). One way to grow is by putting an established brand on a new product added to the existing product line, creating a **line extension**. Another is to plan a **brand (or category) extension**, putting an established brand on a new product in a different category for a new customer segment.

Longer product lines and wider product mixes typically require more resources to develop and sustain, but they help companies grow and pursue ambitious objectives. In contrast, shortening or narrowing lines and mixes can help the firm concentrate its resources on the most promising products and segments for survival, maintenance, or growth. When GM deleted the Oldsmobile product line, it narrowed its product mix and freed up resources for investing in more popular lines and in new product development, with the overall aim of growth. Clearly,

EXHIBIT 6.5 Product Line and Mix Decisions	
Decision	*Result*
New product	Lengthens product line
Line extension	Lengthens product line
New line	Widens product mix
Brand extension	Widens product mix
Product deletion	Shortens product line
Line deletion	Narrows product mix

decisions about the product mix and individual product lines must fit with the organization's situation, direction, and objectives.

Here is how and why Sony is rethinking its product mix and certain lines:

> **Sony.** Sony wants to accelerate growth and fatten profit margins, but it is not meeting its objectives because of ever-higher competitive pressure. Now the company is reducing the assortment of product lines in its mix and lengthening particular lines to support long-term growth. The PlayStation video game console has been so profitable that it retains a prominent place as the cornerstone of a popular line of accessories, games, and other related items. But newer product lines such as digital cameras, sophisticated computer chips, and DVD recorders are receiving more investment as the company allocates resources to higher-potential opportunities in a quest to increase profit margins to 10% or higher. The company is also planning for new products that will reinforce its innovation image.[17]

Planning Branding

Branding gives a product a distinct identity and differentiates it from competitive products using words, designs, and symbols. After customers learn to associate a brand with a particular set of product elements (such as features, benefits, and quality), they simplify the decision-making process by routinely buying that brand rather than stopping to evaluate every alternative on every shopping occasion. A product may carry:

- *Company name and individual brand* (Courtyard by Marriott, Marriott Marquis).
- *Individual name* (for a product, a category, or targeting a segment; Gap and Old Navy are separate brands, under the same ownership, geared toward different segments).
- *Private-label brand* (used by one retailer or wholesaler, such as Wal-Mart's Equate and George brands).
- *Multiple brands* (by *cobranding,* in which two or more organizations put their brands on one product; or by *ingredient branding,* in which an ingredient's brand is featured along with the product's brand, as when Dell PCs showcase Intel computer chips).

Practical Planning Tip
Pay attention to brand symbols because they can become as recognizable as brand names.

Brands should be recognizable and memorable, capable of being legally protected, and suitable for international markets if and when the company expands globally. Online brands are not immune to these basic branding guidelines. Amazon.com, eBay, and Yahoo! have become strong and distinctive brands through constant, consistent marketing-mix support, whereas online brands without clear differentiation or marketing reinforcement have struggled or been acquired by other companies.

Branding decisions made during the planning process are closely tied to product positioning and other marketing activities for building customer relationships through brand equity, as the next two sections explain.

BRANDING AND POSITIONING

Every consumer or business product faces some competition in the marketplace, from direct competitors (Huggies disposable diapers compete with Pampers disposables), substitutes (Huggies disposables compete with cloth diapers), or both. In this context, the brand not only identifies a particular product, it reminds customers of what sets that product apart from all others—why that product is both distinctive and competitively superior. The brand name should trigger associations with those points of differentiation, the way the hair-growth treatment Rogaine triggers associations with the word "regain."[18]

The Google brand, for example, is reminiscent of the mathematical term *googol* (1 followed by 100 zeroes). The positioning relates to the benefit of speedy searching for a high number of relevant result listings. The brand thus stands for what customers perceive and believe about this product compared with competitors (which the company can influence but cannot control) as well as the features, benefits, design, and other points of differentiation that the company can control. Consistency counts: if a marketing-mix strategy or implementation conflicts with the positioning, customers can become confused about what the brand stands for.

What if customers are not aware of a brand and what it stands for? Here's how Germany's BASF used branding to compete more effectively in the B2B world:

BASF. Fifteen years ago, the chemical manufacturer BASF was aggressively pursuing global growth but "being unknown put us at a serious disadvantage against larger and better-known competitors like DuPont and Dow," according to a former marketing manager. BASF's marketers and advertising agency analyzed the competitive situation as well as the needs and perceptions of customers in the targeted segments. After testing the positioning power of three attributes (innovation, diversity, and commitment), they created an advertising campaign to link the BASF brand with innovation. Given the company's track record in producing chemicals that are incorporated into innovative new products—and its quality customer service—the campaign successfully communicated a point of differentiation that customers value. This gave BASF the competitive strength to build worldwide revenues to nearly $34 billion by 2004.[19]

THE POWER OF BRAND EQUITY

The stronger the brand, the more it encourages customer loyalty and boosts **customer lifetime value**, the total amount a customer spends on a brand or with that company during the entire relationship. As one example, the Louis Vuitton brand has developed such a loyal long-term following among the status-conscious that sales have continued to rise year after year, even under unfavorable economic conditions. Vuitton also illustrates the power of **brand equity**, the extra value customers perceive that enhances their long-term loyalty to the brand. Customers are extremely aware of the Vuitton brand, understand the image and performance that it stands for, respond positively to it, and want an ongoing relationship with it—all hallmarks of high brand equity (see Exhibit 6.6). As a result of high brand equity, Vuitton's profit margins are much higher than the industry average for high-end fashion accessories.[20]

And although LVMH is the parent company, it is the Vuitton name that brings the value of brand equity to customers and to the organization, not the corporate name. This is also the case with a number of consumer product giants such as Procter & Gamble (well known for individual brands such as Pampers and Tide)

Practical Planning Tip

High brand equity can help defend share when a product is mature or faces fierce competition.

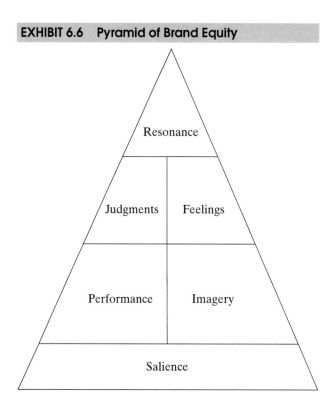

EXHIBIT 6.6   Pyramid of Brand Equity

and B2B marketers, including the U.K.-based manufacturer Tomkins, which offers industrial, automotive, and other business products under individual brands such as Fedco and Trico. In contrast, Sony and Honda build the equity of their corporate brands by showcasing them on diverse product lines and in marketing communications across targeted markets (think Sony Discman and Honda Accord).[21]

Brand equity should be addressed in the marketing plan because it can insulate a company against competitive threats and, just as important, become a driver for growth. Thanks to brand equity, Vuitton's revenues have grown fivefold since 1989, and its profit margins have risen at an even faster rate.[22] As another example, consumer packaged goods manufacturer Unilever says that 75% of its revenues come from 20 global brands. When it lavished extra marketing attention on 6 personal-care brands, they achieved double-digit revenue growth—despite ongoing competition and sluggish economic conditions—plus higher profits.[23]

In addition, brand and line extensions can help a new product achieve customer acceptance, if marketing research shows that the brand has a positive image consistent with the segment's needs, expectations, and perceptions. Giorgio Armani is a good example: its luxury brand appears on a wide variety of products, from clothing and fragrances to a new chain of upscale hotels and resorts to be designed by Armani and managed by professionals.[24] The PetsMart retail chain is extending its brand to pet hotels, targeting owners who want kennel services for dogs and cats, complete with television (for an extra fee).[25] Yet extending a brand too far from its roots can dilute the image, especially if the new line or product does not completely deliver on the brand's promises of quality, status, need satisfaction, or another point of differentiation.

Summary

Product strategy covers decisions about features, benefits, and supplementary services; quality and design; packaging and labeling; product development and management; and branding strategy. Products can be tangible goods, services, places, ideas, organizations, or people. Features are the attributes that enable the good or service to perform its intended function and deliver benefits, the need-satisfaction outcomes customers want from a product. Product-related supplementary services deliver valued benefits to satisfy customer needs as part of the product strategy.

Product quality means how well the product satisfies customers, and it is closely linked to design. Packaging and labeling deliver value to customers (storing products, keeping them safe, explaining ingredients and usage) and to organizations (polishing brand image, communicating product features and benefits, attracting interest). Product strategy includes planning for the 4 stages of the product life cycle (introduction, growth, maturity, and decline) and for new product development. It also covers the management of each product line and the overall product mix. Branding gives a product a distinct identity and differentiates it from competitive products. Moreover, it supports the chosen positioning for a product in a targeted segment and helps build customer relationships for long-term loyalty and brand equity.

Developing Channel and Logistics Strategy

Preview

The second major component of the marketing mix is channel (place) strategy, covering decisions about how, when, and where to make goods and services available to customers. Because of the complexities of channel strategy, such decisions must be carefully coordinated with other marketing decisions. Channel strategy also must be based on a thorough understanding of the targeted segment (including how customers expect or prefer to gain access to the product), the environment (the effect of competition, legal and regulatory considerations, geography, technology, costs, and other realities), the product's characteristics (such as price or perishability), and its life cycle (appropriate channels for introduction, growth, maturity, and decline).

This chapter opens by exploring the connections and flows in the value chain and how various participants add value to the offering that customers buy. The next section explains the major influences on channel strategy and the decisions to be made about channel functions, levels, and members. The closing section looks at logistics strategy, including decisions about transportation, storage, inventory management, and other functions. After reading this chapter, document your marketing decisions using *Marketing Plan Pro* software or in a written plan. See the checklist on page 100 for issues to consider when working on the channel and logistics section of your marketing plan.

Planning for the Value Chain

Every good or service is made and marketed as part of a **value chain**, also known as a *supply chain,* a series of interrelated, value-added functions plus the structure of organizations performing them to get the right product to the right markets and customers at the right time, place, and price. The marketer (shown as "producer" in Exhibit 7.1) manages supplier relationships and logistics on the inbound side to obtain the inputs (such as parts, shipment dates, and cost figures) needed for creating goods and services. On the outbound or demand side, the marketer manages logistics and **channels** (also called *distribution channels*), the functions that must be completed to meet demand by making a product available to the customers in each market.

Practical Planning Tip
Think ahead: altering channel arrangements can be difficult and time-consuming.

During the planning process, marketers analyze how value is added at each connection in this chain of functions, from inputs on the inbound side to finished products moving outbound to meet customer demand. Here is the value chain in action at the PC manufacturer Acer:

> **Acer.** Based in Taiwan, Acer makes the CD and DVD drives, keyboards, and many of the other components it incorporates into the PCs it markets in many countries. This vertical integration allows Acer to tightly control the quality and timing of inbound flows to its plants, builds profits, and enhances competitive advantage. On the outbound side, Acer uses channels geared to the needs and behavior of different markets and segments. In the U.K. market, Acer sells directly to big corporate customers and through retailers that

serve individual consumers, like PC World. It also sells through catalog or online retailers and small, independent computer dealers that provide personalized service to consumers and businesses. As Acer's managing director notes, "We realize that one size doesn't fit all." Although one independent dealer may not sell as many PCs as a huge chain, total volume in this channel is substantial—and is growing fast enough to attract Acer's rival Hewlett-Packard, which has started its own Independent Retail Initiative.[1]

CHAPTER 7 CHECKLIST   Channel and Logistical Issues

Channel Issues

✔ What is the flow of product, data, and money through the value chain, and where are the opportunities for participants to add value?

✔ How do the organization's goals and objectives, resources and competencies, direction, need for control, and marketing mix affect channel choices?

✔ How do current channel arrangements contribute to current objectives?

✔ Which channels and members perform the best, and at what cost to the organization?

✔ How do product characteristics and life cycle affect channel choices and costs?

✔ How do positioning and priority of target segment entry affect channel decisions?

✔ How do customers expect or prefer to gain access to the product, and what is the impact on channel decisions?

✔ How do market, environmental, competitive, and availability factors affect channel decisions?

✔ How many levels and members are needed or desirable to make products available to targeted segments?

Logistical Issues

✔ What logistical functions must be performed and by which channel members?

✔ Who will transport and store supplies, parts, and finished products—how, where, and when?

✔ Who will manage inventory levels—and how?

✔ Who will collect, analyze, and exchange data about orders, billing, and payment—and how and when?

✔ How do production- and sales-related objectives affect logistical plans?

✔ How are logistics affected by customer requirements and preferences, channel and company capabilities, and product plans?

✔ Will the organization handle its own logistics or hire others to handle some or all of the functions?

EXHIBIT 7.1   Major Links in the Value Chain

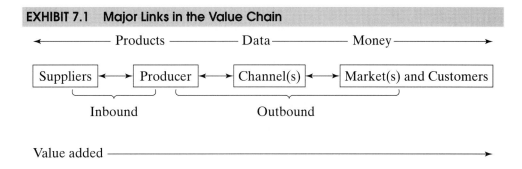

Acer has chosen to make some physical inputs on the inbound side so it can manage the cost (money), delivery (products), and specifications (information) of these components—the three flows shown in Exhibit 7.1. In the context of the value chain, the flow of products refers to physical items such as raw materials and product packaging (on the inbound side) and finished products (on the outbound side) plus other items that move from outbound to inbound (such as products returned for repair). The flow of data refers to information such as the number of items ordered (moving inbound or outbound); customer requirements and feedback (passed along from channel members or directly from customer to producer); and other information that adds value through effectiveness and efficiency. The flow of money refers to payments for supplies (on the inbound side); reseller or customer payments for finished goods (on the outbound side); and other money movements between participants.

Clearly, marketers need to plan for movement of all three flows in both directions. At times, they also plan for flows between noncontiguous links in the value chain, such as the flow of a rebate check from a producer directly to a customer who has purchased a product from a retailer. These flows are all part of channel and logistics strategy.

Note that the inbound side of the value chain is always B2B; in this example, Acer is the business customer being served by suppliers or industrial distributors that provide raw materials, components, and other inputs. After manufacturing its PCs, Acer makes them available on the outbound side through retailers and other partners that sell to consumers, businesses, and corporate customers—the channel and logistics part of its marketing plan.

ADDING VALUE THROUGH THE CHAIN

Each participant adds value to satisfy the needs of the next link (the immediate customer) as well as the ultimate customer at the end of the value chain. On the outbound side, the big retailers that market Acer's PCs have the computers in stock and ready for purchase so consumers can take them home the same day; the independents can customize an Acer PC with the exact hardware and software each customer desires; and Acer itself can market PCs geared to the specific needs of corporate customers that buy directly. The price paid by each successive participant reflects the value added by the previous link; customers at the end of the chain ultimately pay for the combined value added by all participants, a key aspect of pricing strategy (see Chapter 8).

Increasingly, producers and wholesalers, retailers, industrial distributors, or other channel members are teaming up for competitive advantage by adding value in unique ways. For instance, LG and its channel partner, Verizon, have forged a close relationship to add value for cell phone users:

> **LG Electronics and Verizon.** The Korean cell phone maker LG Electronics works closely with the U.S. phone service provider Verizon to provide handsets that meet the needs of the carrier as well as its subscribers. Because Verizon (like its competitors) has direct customer contact through stores, service representatives, and other methods, the carrier hears firsthand what the market wants—and uses the information to shape its services and the offerings of cell phone manufacturers. Verizon's marketing experts collaborate with LG's engineers to develop phones with features tailored for and marketed only to Verizon customers. Everyone benefits: LG gets its products into the hands of U.S. customers, building sales and share in an important market; Verizon gives customers what they want and ensures that the phones support newer, higher-profit services such as photos by e-mail.[2]

SERVICES AND THE VALUE CHAIN

Marketers planning for restaurants, financial services, or other intangible products need to map all the flows within their value chain. The inbound flows relate to ordering, paying for, and receiving shipments of supplies that support service delivery (such as office supplies or food). The outbound flows help customers arrange to receive the service (such as making airline reservations). Because services are generally produced and used simultaneously, marketers must plan flows to match supply and demand. McDonald's needs timely shipments of beef, buns, and potatoes to meet daily and weekly sales objectives for Big Macs and fries; Bank of America must stock each ATM with sufficient $20 bills and receipt paper for the anticipated daily usage.

Value for services, like tangible products, is added inbound through the chain as the producer incorporates a variety of inputs. Outbound, channel members add value by promoting the service, communicating with the customers, making appointments or selling tickets, managing payments and paperwork, and handling other functions to give customers access to the service at an appropriate price, place, and time.

Channel strategy should satisfy customers' needs in such a way that the organization's objectives can be met as well. The travel Web site Travelocity, for example, serves as a channel for services such as rental cars, airlines, and hotels. The site was recently redesigned with a distinctive look and simpler navigation so travelers can find what they want quickly and easily. "We did a lot of consumer research, and [consumers] told us all the Web sites look alike," the chief marketing officer explains. "They're all visually cluttered." Travelocity's site now features simpler graphics plus color to direct attention to key services, such as the Total Trip service, which offers one-price packages to popular destinations, complete with tickets, rooms, and cars. By adding value through convenience, speed, and simplicity, Travelocity attracts customers and builds sales and profits.[3]

Planning Channel Strategy

Although many aspects of channel strategy are invisible to customers, this part of the marketing mix is a vital ingredient in any product's success. Channel strategy made a best-seller out of *The Da Vinci Code,* published by Doubleday:

Doubleday and Barnes & Noble. Doubleday originally planned to print 60,000 copies of Dan Brown's thriller. Then a fiction buyer for the Barnes & Noble chain read an advance copy. The buyer ordered 15,000 copies, raised the order to 30,000, and raised it again to 80,000 copies. Doubleday quickly increased its print run, even though its president admits that "I was terrified—230,000 copies for an author nobody had ever heard of?" To promote *The Da Vinci Code,* Doubleday created store posters and shelf tags, held online contests, and e-mailed notes to opinion leaders. Barnes & Noble prominently displayed the novel, posted sales ideas on its intranet, and had employees talk the book up to shoppers. Propelled by channel attention and media coverage, the novel topped the *New York Times* best-seller list in its first week, stayed on the list for nearly a year, and has become the fastest-selling novel ever for the adult market.[4]

In the course of developing channel strategy, each organization has to decide which channel functions must be covered; who will handle each function; how many channel levels to use; and how many and what type of channel members to choose. (In addition, marketers face decisions about logistics, as discussed later in the chapter.)

CHANNEL FUNCTIONS

What channel functions are needed for the product, market, or targeted customer segment, and who will handle each? The channel as a whole must perform a variety of value-added outbound functions such as matching the volume, amount, or offer to customer needs; providing intermediaries and customers with product and market information; contacting and negotiating with customers to maintain relationships and complete sales; and transporting and storing products prior to purchase.

During planning, producers must identify the channel functions needed for each product, determine which functions intermediaries should handle, and estimate the compensation each channel member should receive for the value it adds. Some producers prefer to assume many or all of the functions themselves because they want more control over customer contacts, pricing, or other elements; others delegate selected functions to reduce costs and focus resources on other tasks. Even within the same industry, a channel strategy that works for one company may not be suitable for its competitors. Consider the different PC marketing strategies of competitors Dell and Gateway:

Dell and Gateway. Dell, the market leader in PCs, handles its own channel functions, from taking orders and processing payments to shipping computers and providing technical support. By marketing directly to customers, the company can continually upgrade features without making store inventory obsolete, custom-build PCs to order, and adapt prices instantly for competitive reasons. Dell also hears immediately when a problem arises or customers want a new feature. Rival Gateway markets directly to buyers and opened a retail chain in 1996 to encourage customers to try before they buy. However, the chain did not turn a profit, so the company shut it down in 2004 and changed strategies, supplementing its direct channel by marketing through selected computer retailers as well.[5]

CHANNEL LEVELS

The experiences of Gateway and Dell illustrate a crucial decision in channel strategy: How many channel levels are needed or desirable? The higher the number of channel levels, the more intermediaries are involved in making the product available (see Exhibit 7.2). Each channel level adds value in some way by having the product in a convenient place for purchase, for instance, or providing information and demonstrations. In exchange, each level expects to profit from the sale to the next level or to the final customer, costs that must be factored into the ultimate selling price.

A *zero-level channel* refers to a direct channel linking seller and buyer. Dell uses this approach, marketing directly to consumers and business customers and bypassing wholesalers and retailers. However, Dell entered the market during the growth stage of the product life cycle, when PCs were selling strongly, so customers knew enough about such products to risk ordering without a demonstration. In contrast, new products often need considerable support from channel members, which may mean using a one-level, two-level, or even three-level channel for certain markets or segments.

In a *one-level channel*, the seller works with a single type of intermediary, such as Doubleday working with book stores like Barnes & Noble to reach consumer markets. Gateway is using a one-level channel, marketing through retailers in local

Practical Planning Tip

Plan for research to stay in touch with customers' needs when using two- or three-level channels.

EXHIBIT 7.2   Channel Levels

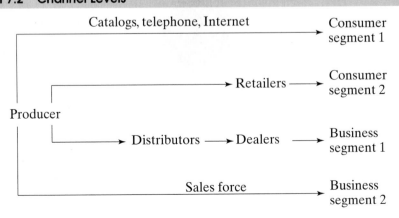

markets plus marketing directly to PC buyers. Many producers choose a one-level channel so they can build strong channel relations and facilitate product, data, and financial flows through the value chain. Consider what Dunhill is doing in China:

> **Dunhill.** Known for its upscale clothing, accessories, and other luxury products, Dunhill relies on a one-level retail channel in China. The company carefully screens stores and provides extensive product training and support so store sales personnel understand the brand's differentiation and the segments that Dunhill is targeting, such as business executives. Dunhill knows that the way stores present its merchandise and serve its customers will reflect on the brand and influence public perceptions of it. "We want to enhance control over our own brand, to protect our brand image," says Dunhill's general manager in China.[6]

Some products, such as automotive parts and accessories, are customarily distributed through two- or three-level channels. Therefore, producers with something new must find ways of breaking into those channels to reach targeted segments, not always easy with an unproven product or brand. In certain industries or countries, a company's marketing plan also must allow for reverse channels to return products for exchange, repair, or recycling. As an example, for a $49 fee, Dell will take customers' unneeded computers, strip hazardous parts, recycle salvageable materials, and wipe personal data off the hard drives.[7] Marketers must investigate applicable laws or regulations, such as the European Union's strict rules mandating recycling of certain products and materials, when planning channels in various markets.

Companies may add or eliminate levels at any time, depending on the product, its position in the life cycle, buying patterns, and other factors. Tupperware recently changed its channel strategy in the United Kingdom and the United States:

> **Tupperware.** Tupperware, which makes food storage containers, has decided to close its direct home-party channel in the United Kingdom. Seeing that U.K. consumers were not buying as much through home parties, the company instead added a channel level to sell through retailers and other businesses. In the United States, Tupperware added a new channel to sell through Target discount stores as well as through home parties, then pulled its products out of the stores after only 8 months. Sales through Target were so strong that the company did not want to threaten the direct channel of home parties, which the CEO called "our most productive source of sales," accounting for the vast majority of Tupperware's U.S. revenues.[8]

CHANNEL MEMBERS

How many and what type of channel members will be needed at each channel level? Customers' needs and habits are important clues to appropriate channel choices and to identifying creative new channel opportunities for competitive advantage. Financial considerations are another key factor. Channel members have certain profit expectations and customers have their own perceptions of a product's value; both affect the marketer's pricing strategy and profit potential.

In addition, the choice of channel members depends on the product's life cycle, the positioning, and the targeted segment. At introduction, an innovative new product may be offered in a very limited number of outlets *(exclusive distribution)* to reinforce its novelty and enable store staff to learn all about features and benefits. In maturity, the company may try to keep sales going by getting the product into as many outlets as possible *(intensive distribution)*. Frito-Lay, for example, uses intensive distribution to get its potato chips into thousands of convenience stores across China, a market that is growing by 10% each year.[9] In decline, companies may sell through fewer channel members *(selective distribution)* to keep shipping costs down (see Exhibit 7.3).

EXHIBIT 7.3   Intensive, Selective, and Exclusive Distribution

	Marketer Benefits	*Customer Benefits*	*Planning Considerations*
Intensive Distribution (in many outlets for maximum market coverage)	Increase unit sales; market impulse items; cover more of each market; reduce channel costs per unit sold.	Convenient, wide access to frequently used or impulse products; price may be lower due to competition.	• Will service be adequate? • Will product be displayed and sold properly? • Will conflict arise between outlets?
Selective Distribution (in a number of selected outlets)	Cover specific areas in each market; reduce dependence on only a few outlets; supervise some channel activities; control some channel costs.	See product and receive sales help in more outlets within each market; obtain some services as needed.	• What is the optimal balance of costs, control, and benefits? • Will outlets be convenient for customers? • Do sales staff understand the product and customers' needs?
Exclusive Distribution (in few outlets for exclusivity within each market)	Choose specific outlets to introduce an innovative product; support product or brand positioning; build closer channel relationships; better supervise service, etc.	Receive personalized attention; access to delivery, alterations, customization, and other services.	• Will channel costs be too high? • Will product be available in all targeted areas? • Will price be too high, given channel profit requirements? • Will outlets be committed as marketing partners?

Relations with channel members should be reexamined periodically to be sure the organization is achieving its objectives and determine whether channel members and customers are being satisfied. Here's how IBM does this:

IBM. The technology giant IBM sets sales and fulfillment targets for its own sales force and for channel members, monitors weekly progress, and has a structured process to get channel members the leads, products, education, and support they need to achieve objectives. Its marketers regularly calculate return on investment to assess the financial payback of the channel strategy and to consider changes. They also hire researchers to survey thousands of channel members twice a year in each market. The purpose is to solicit feedback about IBM's support and training, reseller margins, and responsiveness as a business partner—in short, to find out whether channel members are satisfied with value-chain flows and if not, what can be done to increase satisfaction and loyalty.[10]

INFLUENCES ON CHANNEL STRATEGY

All the channel decisions discussed above are influenced by a number of internal and external factors, summarized in Exhibit 7.4. The major internal factors for marketers to consider during this part of the planning process include:

- *Direction, goals, and objectives.* The channel strategy must be consistent with the organization's chosen direction, its higher-level goals, and its marketing plan objectives. For instance, when Xerox set an ambitious one-year objective of increasing sales of color printers in North America by 85%, it boosted financial incentives to encourage resellers to sell more printers.[11] Companies with green marketing objectives need to plan reverse channels for reclaiming recyclable products or parts.
- *Resources and core competencies.* If the company has the resources and competencies to handle certain channel functions, it may do so while keeping costs in line by hiring others for different functions. Companhia Brasileira de Distribuiçã, the largest retail firm in Brazil, has the resources to manage quality and inventory by storing fish and seafood in one specialized distribution center and flowers and plants in another.[12]

EXHIBIT 7.4 Influences on Channel Strategy

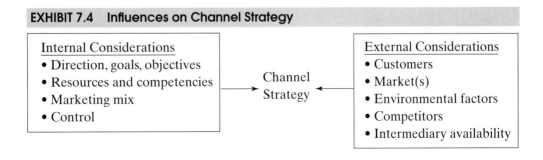

- *Marketing mix.* Channel decisions must work with, not against, the organization's product, pricing, and promotion strategies. Unusual or unexpected combinations (like marketing fine art through Costco's Web site) can be successful, but require careful planning and top-notch implementation.[13]
- *Control.* Does the company want or need tight control over channel functions for quality or image reasons? Can the company afford this kind of control or must it give up some control in exchange for other benefits, such as lower costs or wider coverage in certain areas?

The major external factors influencing decisions about channel strategy are:

- *Customers.* Channel choices should be consistent with what customers want, prefer, expect, or will accept. To illustrate, more people who used to shop for new or used cars in the classified ads and at local dealerships are now willing to buy from megadealers like AutoNation or online from sites such as eBay Motors. This is why AutoNation rings up $20 billion in annual sales and eBay Motors rings up $7.5 billion in annual car sales.[14]
- *Market(s).* New channel options are emerging for reaching far-flung markets. For example, eBay Motors is gaining popularity as a channel for selling cars in Europe, used by individuals and by dealerships that want to reach a larger geographic area. Sometimes companies prefer more control or want wider distribution in targeted markets. As another example, Boise Cascade, a U.S. lumber and paper company with an office products distribution unit, bought the OfficeMax superstore chain to enhance coverage nationwide and reach small businesses and consumers.[15]
- *Environmental factors.* Channel choices should reflect the marketer's analysis of technological, legal-regulatory, social-cultural, and other factors in the environment. For instance, many New York City retailers sell athletic shoes, but Nike makes a point of getting new styles into Training Camp stores, which draw hip-hop stars and other opinion leaders who set fashion trends.[16]
- *Competitors.* How can the company use channel strategy to gain a competitive edge? Philips Lighting did this by negotiating exclusivity with Home Depot. Now Philips is the only brand of lightbulbs sold by the huge home improvement chain—a competitive advantage for Philips.[17] Sometimes going outside the usual channels can be more effective than using the same channel members as most competitors, if customer behavior and costs allow.
- *Availability of intermediaries.* What intermediaries are available in each market, what are their strengths and weaknesses, and what is their reach? Marketers with frequently-purchased consumer products often seek distribution through large retail chains, for instance, but each chain has its own locations, strategy, and so on. Organic food companies had relatively limited choices just a few years ago; now the expansion of chains such as Whole Foods Market allows wider distribution. As another example, a pet food company seeking intensive U.S. distribution would want to know that Petco has more stores in California and in northeastern states than PetsMart—and find out how many new stores each chain will open during the coming months.[18]

Planning for Logistics

The mechanics of managing the flows through the value chain from point of origin to point of sale or consumption are addressed by **logistics.** Marketers aim for a logistics strategy that is responsive to customer needs yet meets internal financial targets. This is a delicate balancing act: Companies do not want to overspend to get supplies and products, information, and payments where and when they should be. On the other hand, they risk losing customers if they take too long to fill orders; have too few units or the wrong assortment on hand to fill orders; have a confusing or complex ordering process; cannot easily track orders and shipments; or make it difficult for customers to return products.[19]

Practical Planning Tip

Estimate the total cost of logistics for different service levels before making a final decision.

Still, responding to customers' needs entails some costs (for delivery, inventory, order confirmation, etc.). Thus, when planning for logistics, it is important to weigh the total cost of logistics against the level of customer responsiveness that is appropriate to meet the organization's marketing plan objectives.

For example, the world's largest retailer (a major player in the outbound section of many manufacturers' value chains) keeps logistics costs as low as possible so it can keep prices low for competitive advantage:

> **Wal-Mart.** Wal-Mart has the best logistics in the business. Even as it stocks the shelves of 5,000 stores in North America, Europe, and Asia to serve 138 million shoppers every week, it cuts prices and boosts margins. Buying directly from manufacturers rather than from wholesalers where possible saves time and money. Also, by forecasting demand months in advance, sharing forecasts with key suppliers, and calculating inventory levels for each store, the retailer ensures enough time to plan timely, cost-effective transportation and delivery. Whether goods are shipped to one of Wal-Mart's 150 distribution centers or directly to individual stores, the logistics are so smooth that more than two-thirds of the products are in shopping carts and through the checkout before Wal-Mart pays its suppliers.[20]

Wal-Mart minimizes the total cost of logistics and operates self-service stores, a balance that supports its market share and profit objectives. Like Wal-Mart, every marketer must consider four main logistical functions when preparing a marketing plan (see Exhibit 7.5):

- *Storage.* Where will supplies, parts, and finished products be stored, for how long, and under what conditions? Sometimes suppliers agree to warehouse goods, sometimes the marketer warehouses goods until needed to fill customer orders. More storage facilities means higher costs—faster response time. Wal-Mart locates its huge distribution centers no more than one day's drive from each cluster of stores so it can replenish shelf stock quickly. In addition, each outlet has refrigerated storage and other special storage arrangements for perishable, tiny, outsize, or fragile products.
- *Inventory.* How many parts, components, and supplies must be available inbound for production? How many finished goods are needed on the outbound side to meet customer demand and organizational objectives? How do

Chico's marketing plan must cover the logistics of making its apparel available through catalogs, online retailing, and store retailing.

projected inventory levels affect storage and transportation decisions? Lower inventory means lower costs but may cause delays in filling customers' orders if products are out of stock. In the high-tech world, however, companies often minimize inventory of parts and finished goods to avoid obsolescence. When cell phone sales in China slowed not long ago, local handset manufacturer TCL Mobile Communication had 33 days' worth of inventory on hand, up from 18 days' worth one year earlier. Nokia, the global market leader, typically holds about 27 days' worth of inventory.[21]

EXHIBIT 7.5 Logistics Decisions

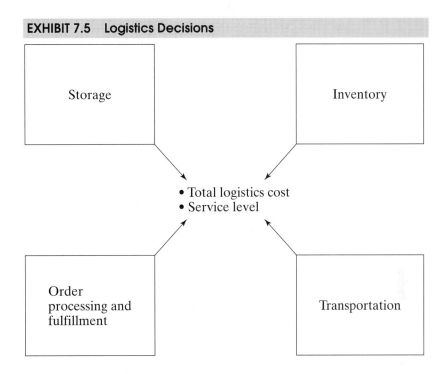

- *Order processing and fulfillment.* Who will be responsible for taking orders, confirming product availability, packing products for shipment, tracking orders in transit, preparing invoices or receipts, and handling errors or returns? How will these tasks be accomplished, relevant information be tracked, and in what time frame? Such tasks are as vital to companies offering services as to companies offering tangible products. The Royal Mile Pub in Maryland is one of many restaurants where staffers use wireless handheld computers to record orders and transmit them to the kitchen, reducing errors and expediting service. The system also calculates the bill for each table and allows management to track demand and responsiveness.[22]
- *Transportation.* How will supplies, parts, and finished products be transported inbound and outbound? Who will pay? Where and when will goods or materials be picked up and delivered? For door-to-door pickup and delivery, marketers often use truck transport. When schedules are flexible and products are heavy or bulky, they may choose less-costly rail or water transport; when deadlines are short and products are perishable or precious, marketers may use fast (but expensive) air transport. Corky's BBQ, a Memphis restaurant, uses FedEx overnight delivery for food ordered as holiday gifts. Corky's electronically creates labels, arranges for pickup, and tracks packages in transit. "We cook it, freeze it, label it, but then we don't worry about it anymore," says the chief financial officer.[23]

The marketing plan need not contain every detail of the logistics strategy, but it should contain a general outline, explain the balance of total costs versus responsiveness, and indicate how logistics functions will support other marketing decisions. It should also justify the logistics budget. Few companies spend as much for logistics as General Mills, which annually spends $400 million just for shipping goods in volume from factories to distribution centers to stores. The company's approach to logistics management shows how attention to everyday functions such as transportation can boost the bottom line. General Mills' shipping costs account for a whopping 60 percent of the expense of getting its products to supermarkets. Seeking higher profitability, its marketers found they could save $24 million by sharing truck space for supermarket deliveries with other consumer products manufacturers.[24] Even on a smaller scale, logistics decisions can make a real difference in any marketing plan.

Summary

Products reach markets at the right time, place, and price through the value chain, a series of interrelated, value-added functions and the structure of organizations performing them. Each organization adds value to satisfy the needs of the next link (the immediate customer) as well as customers at the end of the chain. The marketer manages suppliers and logistics on the inbound side to obtain inputs, then manages channels and logistics to meet demand on the outbound side. Marketers must plan for the movement of products, information, and money in both directions along the value chain. Service marketers also need to understand all the flows in the chain, determine how value is added and by which participant, and manage flows to balance supply and demand.

Channel strategy covers decisions about which channel functions must be performed and by which participant; how many channel levels to use; how many and what type of channel members to choose. In a zero-level channel, the marketer deals directly with customers; in a one-level channel, the marketer works through one type of intermediary. Influences on channel strategy include direction, goal, and objectives; resources and core competencies; other marketing-mix decisions; control issues; customers' needs and preferences; market factors; environmental factors; competitors; and intermediary availability. Logistics involves managing the mechanics of products, data, and information flows through the value chain from point of origin to point of sale or consumption, based on objectives that balance total costs with customer responsiveness levels. The four main logistics functions are storage, inventory, order processing and fulfillment, and transportation.

CHAPTER 8

Developing Pricing Strategy

In this chapter:

Preview

Pricing strategy, the third major component of the marketing mix, is vital because it directly produces revenue, whereas other marketing functions represent expenses (outlays of money, time, or effort). Most pricing decisions can be implemented relatively quickly, whereas product, promotion, and distribution changes usually take longer and cost more to complete. For many products and markets, marketers rely on **fixed pricing**, in which customers pay the price set (fixed) by the marketer—the figure on the price tag; in other cases, marketers use **dynamic pricing**, varying prices from customer to customer or situation to situation. Numerous B2B marketplaces selling commodities, industrial supplies, and parts feature dynamic pricing. Many Web sites targeting consumers also use dynamic pricing: the travel site Hotwire electronically analyzes and changes prices for certain airline destinations every day.[1]

This chapter opens by exploring customers' perceptions of value, how demand operates, and the role of pricing. The following section examines pricing objectives and the various internal and external influences on pricing decisions. Finally, the chapter concludes with a look at how and why marketers should plan to adapt prices. Once you have completed this chapter and made your pricing decisions, take a few minutes to document them using *Marketing Plan Pro* software or in a written plan. The checklist on page 115 covers three key areas to be considered when formulating pricing strategy.

Understanding Value and Pricing

As noted in Chapter 1, customers see the *value* of a product as the difference between the total perceived benefits they receive and the total perceived price they pay. Exhibit 8.1 shows the components of total benefits and total price that customers take into account when evaluating value. The more weight customers give to benefits in relation to perceived price, the higher the value they perceive in that product. Thus, marketers must research and analyze customers' perceptions of the total price—including shipping, maintenance, and any additional or later costs—as well as perceptions of the product's benefits when planning pricing strategy.

In practice, the value of a product is not considered in isolation; customers look at value in the context of the benefits and prices of competing or substitute products. Even if customers perceive all products as being priced the same (whether or not their perceptions match reality), no two customers are likely to place exactly the same value on the total perceived benefits. To add value, the marketer must either enhance the perceived benefits (e.g., by improving quality or introducing new features) or reduce the perceived price (e.g., by lowering the purchase price or offering more affordable financing).

Practical Planning Tip
Research the key benefits that customers value to satisfy needs or solve problems.

Consider Procter & Gamble's experiences with Swiffer and WetJet:

Procter & Gamble. P&G launched a new product category with the Swiffer, a lightweight mop handle to be used with disposable floor cleaning cloths. Four months after introduction, the new product had grabbed 25% of the broom and mop market. As competitors entered the market, P&G enhanced the total benefits through new features and accessories for cleaning larger areas and more surfaces. Two years later, P&G launched the bucketless WetJet, a mop that sprays cleaning solution from a self-contained reservoir. When Clorox introduced a competing product at half the price, P&G reduced WetJet's price twice in 3 months to enhance its perceived value. P&G's newest floor mops have more features and are priced to encourage purchases of the company's cleaning formula and replacement cleaning pads.[2]

CHAPTER 8 CHECKLIST   Planning Pricing Strategy

Internal Factors
- ✔ What does the organization want its pricing strategy to achieve?
- ✔ How can pricing be used to support positioning and targeting decisions?
- ✔ How can pricing be used to manage the product life cycle and product line objectives?
- ✔ How can pricing support the marketing and financial objectives?
- ✔ How do channel decisions affect pricing?
- ✔ How do promotion decisions affect pricing?
- ✔ Is the emphasis going to be on price or nonprice competition?
- ✔ What are the product's costs, and how do they affect the price floor?
- ✔ What is the break-even point at different volume levels? How do different prices affect revenues, volume, and break-even?

External Factors
- ✔ How do industry customs affect pricing?
- ✔ How do customers perceive the balance between a product's price and its benefits?
- ✔ Are customers in the targeted segment price-sensitive? Are customers in other segments less price-sensitive?
- ✔ What are the prices and costs of competing products, and how do they affect the price ceiling?
- ✔ What nonprice alternatives exist for reacting to competitive price changes?

Price Adaptation
- ✔ Are discounts an appropriate tactic for achieving pricing objectives?
- ✔ Are allowances an appropriate tactic for achieving pricing objectives?
- ✔ Is bundling an appropriate tactic for achieving pricing objectives?
- ✔ Is product enhancement an appropriate tactic for achieving pricing objectives?
- ✔ Is loss-leader pricing an appropriate tactic for achieving pricing objectives?
- ✔ Is it necessary or advisable to raise prices, and if so, how?
- ✔ How do organizational resources, capabilities, goals, and strategic direction affect pricing and price adjustments?

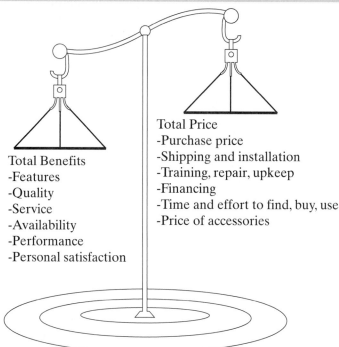

EXHIBIT 8.1   Perceptions of Total Benefits and Total Price

Total Price
-Purchase price
-Shipping and installation
-Training, repair, upkeep
-Financing
-Time and effort to find, buy, use
-Price of accessories

Total Benefits
-Features
-Quality
-Service
-Availability
-Performance
-Personal satisfaction

When competition appeared, P&G defended its market share by changing customers' perceptions of the value of the Swiffer and the WetJet. Adding to the total benefits worked for the Swiffer; reducing the price worked for the WetJet. All told, P&G has generated more than $315 million in sales from these products and their accessories; its marketers continue to examine customers' perceptions of value because of the effect on demand.

CUSTOMER PERCEPTIONS AND DEMAND

When customers act on the basis of their perceptions of price and benefits, their purchases create demand for a product. If customers perceive the price too high in relation to the benefits, they simply won't buy, which lowers demand; if they perceive the price as too low for the expected benefits or quality, demand also will suffer. On the other hand, if the total perceived benefits outweigh the total perceived price, customers are more likely to buy, raising demand. When P&G introduced Swiffer, customers perceived the total benefits as worth the price of buying the mop and replacement cleaning cloths, which boosted demand. Over time, so many customers switched to wipe-type products (higher demand) that rival Rubbermaid saw sales of its traditional brooms and mops drop by 20% (lower demand).

Research can help marketers determine customers' sensitivity to pricing and the level of demand for a product at different price points. This sensitivity is shown by the **price elasticity of demand**, calculated by dividing the percentage change in unit sales demanded by the percentage change in price. When a small price change significantly increases or decreases the number of units demanded, demand is *elastic;* when a price change does not significantly change the number of units

EXHIBIT 8.2 How Pricing Affects Demand		
Change in Price	*Under Inelastic Demand*	*Under Elastic Demand*
Small increase	Demand drops slightly	Demand drops significantly
Small reduction	Demand rises slightly	Demand rises significantly

demanded, demand is *inelastic*. Exhibit 8.2 indicates how different price changes affect demand under elastic and inelastic demand conditions.

In general, customers tend to be less sensitive to a product's price when they[3]:

- are unaware of or can't easily compare substitutes and prices;
- would incur costs or difficulties in switching products;
- perceive that the product's quality, status, or another benefit justifies the price;
- are spending a relatively small amount or are sharing the cost;
- perceive the price as fair.

Consider the inelastic demand for upscale children's apparel, as illustrated by Japan's Narumiya International:

> **Narumiya International.** When Narumiya introduced expensive fashions for preteen girls in Japan 10 years ago, department stores would not carry the line because of the high prices. Another challenge was wringing profits from a market that has been shrinking as the Japanese birth rate declines year after year. The founder persisted, saying: "Many older people don't spend a lot on themselves, but there's almost no limit to how much they'll spend on their grandchildren." His assessment of the market's lack of price sensitivity proved correct. After a popular singing group started wearing Narumiya's styles, the company became the market leader amid a wave of strong demand for high-end preteen clothing. Narumiya can charge the equivalent of $80 for a blouse because customers perceive no substitute and value the prestige of wearing the latest styles.[4]

Customers' price sensitivity and perceptions of value also can be used to deal with imbalances of supply and demand. For example, U.S. steel mills recently experienced unusually strong demand while simultaneously coping with raw materials shortages; in response to the imbalance, some added surcharges to the price per ton. Construction firms that had to meet their deadlines saw no alternative to paying the higher prices and even then, some had to wait longer than usual for their orders.[5] As another example, many airlines price flights lower during off-peak periods to stimulate demand. Price-sensitive travelers can save money by flying during off-peak periods, while travelers who are less price-sensitive (valuing the perceived benefits more than the perceived price) can opt to fly during peak periods despite the higher fares. The idea of managing rush-hour traffic through pricing is catching on in some municipalities:

> **Pricing Roadway Access.** To more effectively handle highway congestion, Orange County and San Diego charge drivers $6 or more for access to express

lanes. Those drivers who perceive value in the benefit of arriving at their destinations more quickly can choose to pay the express-lane charge; those who believe the price outweighs the benefit will not. As another example, London charges drivers £5 (more than $8) to enter certain parts of the city during peak periods. These examples of pricing to balance supply and demand during busy periods help municipalities avoid traffic tie-ups, move vehicles along, and minimize air pollution. London has not only reduced downtown traffic by 20%, its pricing has generated revenue for public transportation projects.[6]

VALUE-BASED PRICING

Researching and analyzing how customers perceive the value of a product should be the first step in formulating an appropriate pricing strategy to build demand and meet internal objectives. Nagle and Holden note that this is not the typical approach to pricing. The most common way is to start with the product and its cost, set a price that covers the cost, and then communicate the value to customers (see Exhibit 8.3). In contrast, the starting point for **value-based pricing** is research about customers' perceptions of value and the price they are willing to pay. Then the company finds ways of making the product at a reasonable cost (**target costing**) to return a reasonable profit or achieve other marketing plan objectives based on the value price.[7] P&G does this with products to be sold through Dollar General discount stores: By packaging products such as Dawn dishwashing liquid in smaller sizes, P&G achieves lower cost targets and can market to consumers through Dollar General stores at the value-based retail price of $1.[8]

Apex, which specializes in manufacturing DVD players, is another good example:

> **Apex.** This California-based company confers with channel partners about shoppers' price sensitivity, then designs a product using target costing in accordance with customers' perceptions of value and price. "Some partners—and Wal-Mart might be an example—are going to want what we call a 'door-buster,'" explains an Apex official. In response, the company manufactures a basic DVD player (without high-cost features) that can be priced well below $100. Bargain-hunting shoppers swarm into the store to buy the low-priced model, the store benefits from higher traffic, and Apex meets its unit sales and revenue objectives.[9]

Practical Planning Tip

Understand customers' perceptions and product costs so you can use target costing to best advantage.

EXHIBIT 8.3   Cost-Based Versus Value-Based Pricing

Cost-Based Pricing

PRODUCT ⟶ COST ⟶ PRICE ⟶ VALUE ⟶ CUSTOMERS

Value-Based Pricing

CUSTOMERS ⟶ VALUE ⟶ PRICE ⟶ COST ⟶ PRODUCT

Planning Pricing Decisions

When planning pricing, marketers first must determine what this strategy is intended to achieve, given the marketing, financial, and societal objectives they have set. They also need to investigate the various external influences (customers; competitors; channel members; legal, regulatory, and ethical concerns) and internal influences (costs and break-even; targeting and positioning strategy; product strategy; and other marketing decisions) that can affect pricing decisions.

PRICING OBJECTIVES

Because a product's price is the organization's source of revenue, marketers should establish specific objectives for all pricing decisions (see Exhibit 8.4). These objectives must be consistent with each other and with the overall mission, direction, goals, and marketing plan objectives. Due to market realities, organizations may have to trade off one pricing objective for another. Rarely can a company boost profitability while simultaneously raising its market share to a much higher level, for example. Ford faces this issue when pricing its vehicles:

Ford. Share or profit? "I've seen us in eras where we blindly chased share and created all kinds of problems," Ford's CEO recently observed. In the early 1990s, Ford used pricing to achieve its objective of gaining market share for the Taurus. By offering discounts of up to $2,600 per car, Ford made the Taurus the best-selling U.S. car in 1993 (beating out the Honda Accord). Today, Ford is using pricing more to improve profits than to generate higher revenues and increase market share. One result is that the company is deemphasizing low-price, low-margin volume sales of cars to rental companies. Strong competition remains a threat, so Ford's marketers will be carefully balancing pricing objectives to reach the CEO's near-term goal of boosting annual pretax profits to $7 billion.[10]

EXHIBIT 8.4   Sample Pricing Objectives

Type of Objective	*Sample Pricing Objectives*
Financial	• For profitability: Set prices to achieve gross profit margin of 40% on this year's sales • For return on investment: Set prices to achieve full-year ROI of 18%.
Marketing	• For higher market share: Set prices to achieve a market share increase of 5% within 6 months. • For customer acquisition: Set prices to attract 1,500 new customers from January to June.
Societal	• For philanthropy: Set prices to raise $10,000 for charity during second quarter of year. • For energy conservation: Set prices to sell 500 hybrid gas-electric vehicles nationwide during August.

Even one additional percentage point of market share can translate into millions of dollars in higher sales, which is why companies sometimes put share ahead of profit when setting pricing objectives. Hewlett-Packard has done this in PCs, where it is willing to set prices that return little or no profits as a way of pressuring archrival Dell. Its computer division earned profit margins of 1% or less for the 2 years following H-P's acquisition of Compaq because the main pricing objective was to win share. CEO Carly Fiorina points out that selling PCs at attractive prices helps H-P sell more printers, accessories, and consulting services.[11]

EXTERNAL PRICING INFLUENCES

Practical Planning Tip
Analyze these influences for each geographic region if you plan to price market by market.

Many factors outside the organization—and outside its control—come into play when marketers make decisions about pricing. In addition to customers, pricing can be influenced by competitors (as in the H-P example), channel members (as in the Apex example), and legal, regulatory, and ethical considerations. Because not every external influence is equally important for each product, targeted segment, or market, marketers should analyze each within the context of other marketing plan decisions and the organization's situation.

Customers

Perceptions of value, behavior, and attitudes all affect a customer's reaction to pricing. In consumer markets, research shows that customers are willing to buy a good or service if the price falls within a range they view as acceptable for that type of product.[12] This suggests that consumer marketers have some pricing latitude if they stay within the accepted range or change the product to change its perceived value. However, it is important to remember that today's price is a big factor in customers' decisions to continue the relationship and buy again tomorrow, as the auto repair chain Monro Muffler knows. The company is using pricing to build customer loyalty for long-term profit, rather than pricing for short-term gain. The CEO explains: "We're lower priced on oil changes, but we're not lower priced on everything. Once you build up trust with the customer, price becomes less important in the equation." In fact, Monro Muffler's results show that new customers satisfied with the cheap oil changes are returning for different repairs, lifting both sales and profits.[13]

In business markets, customers frequently search for the lowest price to minimize their organizational costs, and some switch suppliers constantly to pay less for parts, materials, components, or services. Globalization has only increased customers' choices and opportunities to obtain better prices. Consider the situation of ArvinMeritor, which feels intense pressure to price its car and truck parts as low as possible for automakers that, in turn, feel pressure to keep vehicle prices low. Thus, "when DaimlerChrysler or Volvo negotiates a 5- to 7-year deal, you don't want to lose, because when you do, you're out for 5 to 7 years," notes one of its executives. With this behavior in mind, ArvinMeritor uses continuous improvement to increase efficiency so it can keep prices low, offer new products, and win multiyear contracts.[14]

Rather than offering the lowest price, many B2B marketers stress specific benefits such as how the product saves customers money or how it adds value in some other way. Differentiating the product on the basis of something other than price and clearly demonstrating the value will help strengthen customer relationships. For instance, some B2B consultants prove the value of their services by tying some or all of the price to the achievement of specific objectives, such as helping the customer cut costs by a certain percentage. This kind of pricing arrangement convinced Texas Petrochemicals to hire Celerant Consulting. "If we didn't see savings, they didn't get paid," states Texas Petrochemicals' CEO.[15]

Even where free alternatives are available—as on the Internet—savvy marketers have been able to attract loyal paying customers. Consider the Wall Street Journal Online, which has nearly 700,000 subscribers paying $79 per year ($39 for those who also subscribe to the print version). Why pay for news that can be found elsewhere for free? Customers trust the *Wall Street Journal* brand, appreciate the exclusive columns and intraday updates, like customizing the publication's home page, and find value in innovations such as industry-specific news pages.[16]

Competitors

Customer behavior is one external clue to an acceptable price range (the ceiling, in particular). The competitive situation provides another external clue. By analyzing the prices, special deals, and probable costs of competing products, a company can get a better sense of the alternatives that are available to customers and competitors' pricing objectives and strategies. Home Depot, for instance, electronically compares the prices of key products to the prices charged by competitors. Its marketing managers look at these comparisons, plus internal records, sales trends, and other information, when setting prices by product, by store, and by market.[17]

Pricing is a highly visible competitive tool in many industries, often exerting downward pressure on profits and limiting pricing options. However, because no two companies have exactly the same objectives, resources, costs, and situations, competitors cannot simply copy each other's pricing. Consider the dilemma of US Airways, which faces ever-higher competition due to expansion of low-price carriers such as Southwest and AirTran. US Airways knows that travelers can easily compare prices and shop for the lowest fares. Therefore, to remain competitive and regain profitability, US Airways must rethink its pricing structure and simultaneously lower its costs, which are the industry's highest.[18] As another example, because of strong and direct competition in the United States, Coca-Cola and Pepsi-Cola soft drinks remain close in price—nor have their prices risen much in two decades.[19]

Marketers need not always match or beat competitors' prices but they do have to ensure that their product's price fits into the value equation as perceived by customers. Here is how Mylan Laboratory handles pricing for its generic prescription drugs:

Mylan Laboratories. After a branded drug's patent expires, any company can apply for FDA approval to market it in generic form. As generic versions of a drug come on the market, prices and margins tend to drop; according to a recent study, the average branded drug price is $76.29, compared with an average generic drug cost of $22.79. Mylan Laboratories earns higher profit margins by focusing on generics that are more difficult to manufacture, such as time-release oral tablets and drugs delivered through adhesive skin patches. There is less competition in these segments, Mylan can charge a bit more because its products are differentiated, and customers still save money.[20]

Channel Members

Companies that reach customers through wholesalers or retailers must take into account these intermediaries' pricing expectations and marketing objectives. As an example, more than half of the shoppers who buy at Family Dollar and Dollar General stores have household income below $30,000, so those retailers aim to keep most prices at or below $10. Thus, to achieve their profit and market share objectives, dollar store retailers must keep merchandise costs and prices within certain limits.[21] In turn, P&G and other manufacturers that sell to dollar stores set prices that accommodate both channel and customer expectations.

A sample progression of how a consumer product might be priced by the producer, wholesaler, and retailer is in Exhibit 8.5. In this sample, the producer charges the wholesaler $20 for the product and the wholesaler sells it to the retailer for $24, 20% above the producer's price. The retailer sells the product to the consumer for $36, which is 50% above the price paid by the retailer and 80% above the price paid by the wholesaler. Of course, the actual number of participants in the outbound side of the value chain will vary according to product, industry, market, and segment, affecting the prices paid by intermediaries and the ultimate customer. Note that when a participant performs more functions or enhances the product in a unique way, it may be able to set a higher price (and make more profit) because its immediate customers perceive more value in the offering.

In pricing a product, also consider that the Internet is bringing wholesale and retail prices down in many categories, thanks to more efficient transaction capabilities, convenient price comparisons, and higher competition—sometimes from unexpected sources. For instance, Amazon.com, which started out as an online book retailer, recently began marketing fine jewelry. Its transactional technology is already in place, so it can easily offer a wider range of products to the millions of shoppers who browse the site every year. Amazon can buy a pair of gem-studded earrings at wholesale for $850 and retail them for $1,000. In contrast, a traditional jewelry store might price the same earrings at $1,700. Amazon is counting on price-

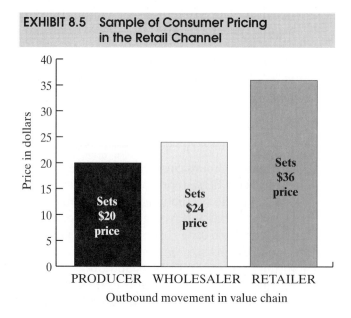

EXHIBIT 8.5   Sample of Consumer Pricing in the Retail Channel

sensitive customers to compare jewelry prices and value before buying. "We believe over time, customers figure these things out," observes its chief financial officer.[22]

Legal, Regulatory, and Ethical Concerns

Whether planning for domestic or international marketing, all companies need to comply with a variety of pricing laws and regulations. Some of these include:

- *No price collusion.* In the United States, the European Union, and many other areas, competing firms are not allowed to collaborate in setting prices and cannot take other pricing actions that reduce competition.
- *No minimum retail price.* In the United States, United Kingdom, and some other countries, companies are not permitted to enforce a minimum retail price among channel members (although in some cases, a "suggested" retail price may appear on the package or price tag).
- *No price discrimination.* In the United States, a company usually cannot charge different prices for essentially the same product at the same time in the same market unless the lower price(s) are available through discounts or allowances that are open to all. However, there are exceptions; for example, different prices may be allowed if the company has different costs, is responding to competition, or is clearing outdated merchandise.[23]
- *No predatory pricing.* The United States outlaws the aggressive use of low pricing to damage a competitor or reduce competition.
- *Price limits.* Some nations set an upper limit on the price that can be charged for certain products, as Canada does with prescription drugs.

Practical Planning Tip
Be sure your pricing strategy complies with your company's ethical code.

Apart from applicable laws and regulations, marketers must make decisions about ethic dilemmas in pricing. Is it ethical for a company to raise prices during an emergency, when products may be scarce or especially valuable? Should a company set a high price for an indispensable product knowing that certain customers will be unable to pay? What are a company's ethical responsibilities regarding full disclosure of prices for upkeep, updates, or replacement parts? How far in advance should customers be notified of planned price increases, and what form should notification take? The chief information officer of Hyundai Motor America recently complained about technology companies that attempt to "slip in surprise increases for maintenance, licensing, or other services."[24] As difficult as the ethical aspects of pricing may be, marketers must carefully think through the consequences on customer relationships and company image.

INTERNAL PRICING INFLUENCES

Within the organization, costs and break-even are critical influences on pricing. Targeting and positioning strategy, product strategy, and other marketing decisions must also be factored into pricing plans.

Costs and Break-even

Costs typically establish the theoretical floor of the pricing range, the lowest price at which the organization will avoid losing money. Even the largest company cannot afford to price products below cost for an extended period, although (where legal) it may do so to combat a competitive threat or achieve another objective over a limited period. Therefore, companies need to understand their costs and the **break-even point**—the sales level at which revenue covers costs. Costs and break-even are more easily calculated for existing products in existing market segments, where marketers can use historical results as a basis for future projections. For new products and segments, marketers must rely on research-based forecasts and expert estimates of costs and sales volume (see Chapter 10). When detailed or timely information is unavailable, marketers often make educated guesses about costs for planning purposes.

The total cost of a product consists of *fixed costs*—overhead expenses such as rent and payroll, which do not vary with volume—plus *variable costs*—expenses such as raw materials, which do vary with volume. As one example, corporate rent is a fixed cost and jet fuel is a variable cost for airlines; to keep ticket prices low and avoid unexpected cost spikes, Southwest and JetBlue use "hedging" techniques that lock in low fuel costs for months.[25] As another example, consider the costs for Bronco Wine's Charles Shaw brand. The company buys huge quantities of surplus grapes directly from vineyards at extremely low prices (minimizing variable costs) and maintains a highly efficient bottling and distribution system (keeping fixed costs low). It sells the wines to the gourmet grocery chain Trader Joe's, which sets a retail price of just over $2 per bottle. Because customers perceive the value, they buy by the caseload, giving Charles Shaw—nicknamed "Two-Buck Chuck"—a 15% share of the California wine market.[26]

Once marketers know a product's total costs, they can calculate the average cost of producing a single item (total costs divided by production) at various output levels, corresponding to different assumptions about demand. This reveals cost changes at a number of output levels and indicates how low the company might price the product at each level to at least cover its costs.

Now the marketer calculates the break-even point to see how a price will affect revenues and profits at different sales levels. The formula for calculating the break-even volume is:

$$\text{Break-even volume} = \frac{\text{fixed cost}}{\text{price} - \text{variable cost}}$$

Exhibit 8.6 illustrates a sample break-even analysis for a company that manufactures specialized software for dentists. In this example, the price (unit revenue) is $995, the variable cost is $45 per unit, and the fixed cost totals $40,550. Thus, the calculation is:

$$\text{Break-even volume} = \frac{40{,}550}{995-45} = \frac{40{,}550}{950} = 42.6 \text{ units (rounded up to 43)}$$

Practical Planning Tip
If you don't know your costs, estimate for now and start tracking costs for next year's plan.

The break-even charting function in *Marketing Plan Pro* visually indicates this point and shows how profits rise as unit sales and revenues increase. The chart is linked to appropriate tables in the marketing plan, so any changes made to unit or dollar figures will be reflected in the break-even chart.

Cost containment is a high priority for many companies today, not just to achieve quarterly profit targets but to prepare for future market conditions. Deluxe, the U.S. market leader in printing checks for consumers and businesses, is a good example:

EXHIBIT 8.6   Break-Even Analysis

Fixed Costs		
Creation of printed material graphics and text	$	3,200
Creation of CD-ROM graphics	$	650
Initial set up fee for CD	$	1,600
Initial set up fee for printed materials	$	1,250
Production of 2,000 demo units	$	30,750
Estimated Fixed Costs	$	40,550
Per–unit variable costs (to fulfill orders sold)	$	45
Per–unit revenue	$	995
Break-even (in Units)		43

Break-Even Analysis:		
Assumptions:		
Average Per–Unit Revenue	$	995
Average Per–Unit Variable Cost	$	45
Estimated Fixed Costs	$	40,550
Units Break–even		43
Sales Break–even	$	42,471

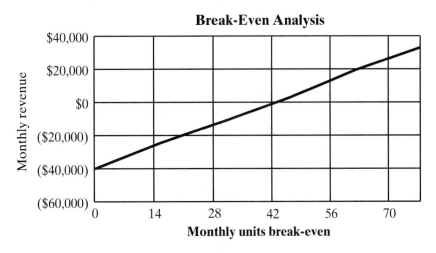

Units break-even point = where line intersects with $0

Deluxe. Checks are a mature industry: usage is declining 3–5% yearly as electronic transactions become more commonplace. Yet 90% of Deluxe's revenue comes from printing checks, which explains its determination to defend against other check printers and electronic payment methods. Meanwhile, mergers among financial institutions are giving big banks more power to negotiate lower prices with Deluxe. To prevent significant deterioration of profit margins, Deluxe has cut costs by closing some facilities and concentrating on higher efficiency. However, cost-cutting is only one part of Deluxe's plan for the future; it also is investing in new product lines as part of its growth strategy.[27]

Targeting and Positioning Strategy

A product's price must be appropriate for the organization's targeting and positioning strategy. To illustrate, because Southwest Airlines targets the segment of price-sensitive travelers and positions itself as affordable and no-frills, charging high fares would be inconsistent (and would confuse customers). Conversely, if the luxury goods manufacturer Louis Vuitton put low price tags on its handbags and accessories, the target segment of affluent consumers would question the products' positioning as symbols of status, style, and quality. In fact, Vuitton refuses to mark down its handbags for clearance, because low pricing would conflict with the positioning.[28]

Product Strategy

Marketers should not only examine every pricing decision in the context of costs, targeting, and positioning, they should set prices in line with their product strategy. In particular, pricing can be used to manage the product's movement through the life cycle:

- *Introduction.* Some companies use **skimming pricing** during the introduction stage of the life cycle, pricing a new product high to establish a top-quality image or highlight unique value and more quickly recover development costs in line with profitability objectives. Intel does this when introducing powerful new computer chips, which customers value for their speed and other benefits. Other marketers prefer **penetration pricing**, pricing products relatively low to gain market share (penetrate the market) in a short period. Toyota used penetration pricing to build sales of its feature-packed Yaris subcompact car in Europe.[29]
- *Growth.* Pricing is important for competitive strategy during the growth stage, when rival products challenge the new product. As an example, P&G cut the price of its WetJet mop to counter Clorox's entry into the market. During growth, companies also use pricing to stimulate demand while moving toward the break-even point.
- *Maturity.* With sales growth slowing, companies can use pricing to defend market share, retain customers, pursue profitability, or expand into additional channels. The Snow King Resort Hotel in Jackson Hole, Wyoming, offers low prices through the Travelocity Web site as a way to attract visitors in a crowded and mature market. Vacationers pay less, Travelocity earns revenue, and the hotel fills rooms that might otherwise sit empty.[30]

- *Decline.* Pricing can help clear older or outdated products to make way for new ones, stimulate sales to prevent or at least slow a product's decline, or maximize profits. To illustrate, makers of cell phones and other tech products often cut prices to sell off older models when they introduce new models. Yet prices do not necessarily drop during decline: scarcity may make a product more valuable to certain customers and therefore justify a higher price.

Moreover, pricing is vital for managing the strategy of products in a single line and in the overall mix. For instance, marketers may set different prices to signal the value of the features and benefits of different products in one line. Bombay Company, a U.S. retailer, learned through research that its product-line pricing was too complex for shoppers. Now the stores price the products within a line at three tiers, corresponding to "good, better, best" quality. The dollars-and-cents prices have changed as well: "You would walk into a store and see a product for $62.50," says a Bombay executive. "Well, that didn't make any sense. It should be $59."[31]

Sometimes marketers plan to price one product in order to encourage purchases of other products in the line or mix, as Gillette does with razors and blades. Every 8 years, the company introduces an entirely new type of razor, priced higher than current models. Then, over time, it gradually increases the price of blades that fit older razor models to encourage customers to trade up to the new model.[32]

Other Marketing Decisions

The marketing plan's direction will strongly influence the organization's pricing strategy. For survival, the organization's prices should cover costs at the very least; for bankruptcy, organizations can use pricing to liquidate stock and raise

Practical Planning Tip

Price multiple products in the context of achieving your plan's overall objectives.

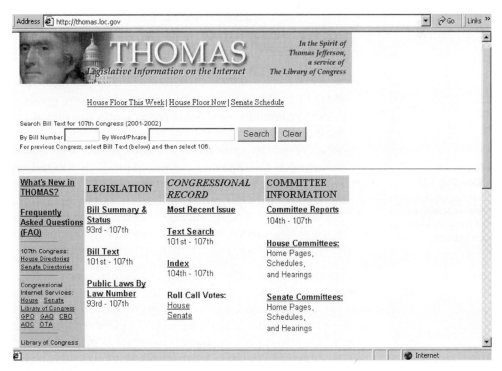

Marketers can check the U.S. Congress Thomas Web site for information on new legislative initiatives that may affect pricing.

money quickly. For aggressive growth, the company may decide to set prices that return slim or no profit margins in the short run. The online DVD rental service Netflix, for instance, wants to grow rapidly and has been spending about $35 to acquire each new customer. However, as a publicly owned company, it feels pressure to report profits, which is why it recently raised the monthly subscription fee by 10% to offset acquisition costs and other marketing expenses.[33]

In addition to the influence of channel members, pricing is influenced by decisions about suppliers and logistics. In terms of promotion strategy, higher-priced products aimed at higher-income customer segments are often promoted in different media and with different messages than lower-priced products aimed at lower-income segments. Pricing is a big challenge for companies that market through personal selling—especially when customers expect to negotiate prices with salespeople. For this reason, the Swiss pharmaceutical firm Roche has equipped its salespeople with software to check the profitability of different prices before finalizing sales to medical institutions or other customers.[34]

ADAPTING PRICES

If internal factors suggest the price floor and external factors suggest the price ceiling, price adaptation helps companies modify and fine-tune prices within an acceptable range—or even beyond. Marketers may use price adaptation to make changes in support of their objectives:

- *Discounts.* Many companies offer quantity discounts for buying in volume and seasonal discounts for buying out of season. Business customers also may earn a cash discount for prompt payment; intermediaries may earn a functional discount when they perform specific channel functions for a producer.
- *Allowances.* Wholesalers and retailers may receive discounts, extra payments, or extra product allocations for participating in special promotions. Some companies offer trade-in allowances for businesses or consumers who bring in older products and buy newer ones.
- *Bundling or unbundling.* The company may enhance customer perceptions of value by bundling one product with one or more goods or services at a single price. McDonald's meal deals, for example, are priced lower than the sum of the individual menu items but help the firm sell more soft drinks and fries, boosting overall profit margin. Unbundling can be used if the bundle price is perceived as too high and individual products will sell well on their own.
- *Product enhancement.* Enhancing the product to raise its perceived value can help the company maintain the current price or perhaps increase the price.
- *Segment pricing.* Pricing may be adapted for certain customer segments, such as a children's menu (segmenting by family composition), a senior discount (segmenting by age), or a delivery charge (segmenting by need for service).

Practical Planning Tip
Consider which adaptations are traditional—and nontraditional—in your industry or channel.

Specific pricing tactics can help marketers achieve specific marketing or financial objectives. Loss-leader pricing, for instance, with popular or new items priced near cost, is a common way to build store or Web site traffic; as mentioned earlier, a retailer might offer Apex's basic DVD players as a "doorbuster" to attract customers. Objectives for customer acquisition might be supported by short-term pricing cuts or tactics that temporarily enhance value, such as low interest rates during select periods. The chosen adaptation depends on the company's resources and capabilities, its goals and strategic direction, and its marketing plan objectives.

EXHIBIT 8.7	Alternative Reactions to Competitive Price Cuts	
Strategic Options	*Reasoning*	*Consequences*
1. Maintain price and perceived quality. Engage in selective customer pruning.	Firm has higher customer loyalty. It is willing to lose poorer customers to competitors.	Smaller market share Lowered profitability
2. Raise price and perceived quality.	Raise price to cover rising costs. Improve quality to justify higher prices.	Smaller market share Maintained profitability
3. Maintain price and raise perceived quality.	It is cheaper to maintain price and raise perceived quality.	Smaller market share Short-term decline in profitability Long-term increase in profitability
4. Cut price partly and raise perceived quality.	Must give customers some price reduction but stress higher value of offer.	Maintained market share Short-term decline in profitability Long-term maintained profitability
5. Cut price fully and maintain perceived quality.	Discipline and discourage price competition.	Maintained market share Short-term decline in profitability
6. Cut price fully and reduce perceived quality.	Discipline and discourage price competition and maintain profit margin.	Maintained market share Maintained margin Reduced long-term profitability
7. Maintain price and reduce perceived quality.	Cut marketing expense to combat rising costs.	Smaller market share Maintained margin Reduced long-term profitability
8. Introduce an economy model.	Give the market what it wants.	Some cannibalization but higher total volume

Marketers also should plan for the short-term and long-term effects of price competition. If every company matches or beats the price of its rivals and a price war ensues, customers will soon perceive few if any differences and be less brand-loyal. In fact, research shows that in more than 2 dozen product categories, customers give more weight to price than to brand because they perceive few differences among the brands. In contrast, they give more weight to brand than to price when buying automobiles and alcoholic beverages, which have more perceived differences.[35] See Exhibit 8.7 for some alternative reactions to competitive price cuts. Stressing product, promotion, or channel differentiation, along with value-based pricing, will confer the strongest advantage, given that prices are easily matched but non-price-related points of difference are not.

Summary

From a customer's perspective, value is the difference between the total perceived benefits and the total perceived price of a product. Marketers care about customers' price perceptions because they influence the number of units demanded. Price elasticity, which indicates customers' price sensitivity, is calculated by dividing the percentage change in unit sales demanded by the percentage change in price. Marketers should use value-based pricing rather than cost-based pricing to formulate a strategy that will drive demand and satisfy company objectives.

As they plan pricing strategy, marketers first must determine what they want to achieve in the context of the marketing plan's marketing, financial, and societal objectives. Next, they need to factor in key external influences (customers; competitors; channel members; legal, regulatory, and ethical concerns) and key internal influences (costs and break-even; targeting and positioning strategy; product strategy; and other marketing decisions) when making pricing decisions. Finally, they have to consider when and how to adapt prices as appropriate.

CHAPTER 9

Developing Integrated Marketing Communication Strategy

In this chapter:

- Preview
- Planning for Integrated Marketing Communication
    - Choose the Target Audience
    - Set Objectives and Budget
    - Examine Issues
    - Choose IMC Tools
    - Plan Research
- Using IMC Tools
    - Advertising
    - Sales Promotion
    - Public Relations
    - Direct Marketing
    - Personal Selling
- Summary

Preview

Every marketing plan anticipates the use of marketing messages, whether as commercials or coupons, personal selling or public relations—perhaps all of these and more. This chapter discusses planning for the five primary communication tools, starting with the concept of integrated marketing communication to coordinate messages and media. Next, the chapter explores how to choose the target audience, set the objectives and budget, examine relevant issues, select one or more tools, and prepare for research before and after a promotion or campaign. The chapter closes with a closer look at planning for the five tools that marketers use to communicate with their audiences.

Once you have completed this chapter and made your IMC choices, record them with *Marketing Plan Pro* software or in a written plan. See the checklist below for a summary of key questions to ask when planning IMC strategy.

Planning for Integrated Marketing Communication

The fourth component of the marketing mix is integrated marketing communication (promotion) strategy, which covers five basic tools: advertising, sales promotion, public relations, direct marketing, and personal selling. Although promotion

---

CHAPTER 9 CHECKLIST   Planning IMC Strategy

Audience Analysis
- ✔ What is the profile of a typical audience member?
- ✔ How do the audience's demographic, geographic, psychographic, and behavioral characteristics affect media and message choices?
- ✔ What are the audience's media usage habits?
- ✔ Which IMC tools are most appropriate for the target audience?

Objectives and Budget
- ✔ What is the IMC strategy intended to achieve?
- ✔ How do the IMC objectives support the marketing plan's objectives?
- ✔ Is the budget sufficient to achieve the objectives with the chosen tools?

Issues
- ✔ What legal, regulatory, and ethical issues must be considered for the audience, geographic region, or IMC tool?
- ✔ What social and cultural issues must be considered?
- ✔ What competitive issues must be considered?

Research
- ✔ What does research reveal about the market, audience, and communication preferences?
- ✔ How can research be used to pretest messages or media and evaluate IMC effectiveness?

**Practical
Planning Tip**
Strive to maintain a dia-
logue with customers
for feedback and open
communication.

was traditionally a monologue initiated by the organization, today marketers are encouraging dialogues through messages and media that invite interaction. For maximum effect, marketers should coordinate the content and delivery of all marketing communications for a particular product and brand (and for the organization) to ensure consistency and support the positioning and direction, an approach known as **integrated marketing communication.**

Consider the level of integration in American Express's multimedia promotion of its Blue credit card:

American Express. American Express has used a variety of coordinated messages and media to market its Blue card to young, tech-savvy customers. The card was launched at a free Sheryl Crow concert in New York City and promoted in major markets with newspaper, magazine, television, and transit advertising plus free concerts and other activities. AmEx also arranged a week of blue-themed prizes on the popular game show *Wheel of Fortune.* Online, it created contests keyed to the card's cash-back benefits and invited people to subscribe for e-mail updates after watching a video of Jerry Seinfeld talking up the AmEx brand to Superman (a video that later aired on network television). The result: Blue exceeded AmEx's objectives, attracting 1.5 million cardholders in less than a year.[1]

AmEx knows the importance of controlling the look and content of every message to convey the right impression of the Blue card. Integration not only avoids confusion about the brand and the benefits, it reinforces the connection with the color blue and therefore sparks instant recognition when people in the target audience are exposed to a Blue card communication. The total effect of all AmEx's local and national IMC activities differentiates the card and communicates its value in a crowded competitive arena.

IMC strategy involves defining the target audience, establishing objectives and a budget, analyzing pertinent issues, selecting appropriate IMC tools, and planning pre- and post-implementation research to evaluate effectiveness. These decisions draw on the SWOT analysis conducted earlier in the planning process and are closely related to the product's movement through the life cycle.

CHOOSE THE TARGET AUDIENCE

The target audience might consist of customers and prospects or, when image-building is part of the marketing plan, may consist of employees, community leaders, local officials, and a number of other key stakeholders. Some IMC strategies used to achieve market share and sales objectives can be characterized in terms of "push" or "pull" (see Exhibit 9.1). In a **push strategy**, the company targets intermediaries, encouraging them to carry and promote (push) the product to business customers or consumers. In a **pull strategy**, the company encourages consumers or business customers to ask intermediaries for the product, building demand to pull the product through the channel. The decision to use push or pull must fit with channel decisions and be appropriate for the product, its pricing, and its positioning.

EXHIBIT 9.1   Push and Pull Strategies

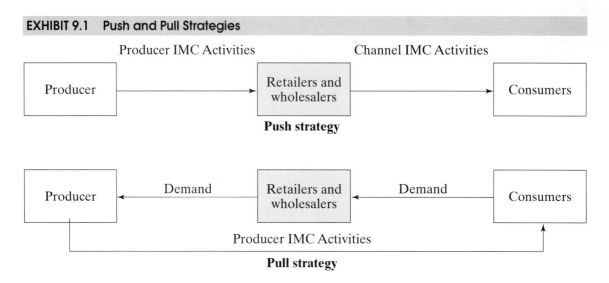

Many companies combine push and pull. Heineken, for example, focuses on Latino consumers in the United States by sponsoring the televised Latin Grammy Awards and the Billboard Latin Music Awards, among other IMC activities, to build demand (pull) for its beers. Targeting retailers and restaurants, the company provides point-of-purchase materials and a special Web site for distribution information and orders (push). This combination has helped Heineken beers attain wider distribution and higher sales in U.S. markets with large Latino populations.[2]

Marketers need to look beyond generalities and develop a profile of the typical member of the target audience in as much detail as possible, including gender; age; lifestyle; media, product, and payment preferences; attitudes; timing of buying decisions; and so on. This level of detail reveals nuances to help shape what the communication should say and how, when, and where to say it. Here's how Dr Pepper supported a new product by understanding the target audience's interests and media usage:

> **Dr Pepper.** When Dr Pepper launched its Raging Cow flavored milk drinks, the company targeted young adults, aged 18 to 24, using a funny but fake blog—a kind of personal journal posted online—written from a cow's perspective. Within 3 weeks, the blog was drawing 21,000 visitors daily. Dr Pepper's marketers stopped posting new blog entries after 4 months because "we achieved buzz and the awareness of the core consumers we were trying to reach," according to Dr Pepper's director of corporate communications. The company then shifted from the objective of brand building to the objective of stimulating purchases, accomplished through sampling, store displays, and other IMC activities.[3]

It is important to rethink decisions about the target audience whenever a new marketing plan is being prepared, or more often as the environment evolves. For example, after a grapefruit drink was featured on *Sex and the City,* the Florida Department of Citrus decided to invest more than $1 million promoting grapefruit

**Practical
Planning Tip**
Review the market and
customer analyses for
clues to communicating
with your audience.

juice to young, urban, professional women. Despite this IMC support, grapefruit juice sales fell for 4 consecutive growing seasons. Then the department reexamined the market and discovered that men were drinking more grapefruit juice than women, which prompted changes in the target audience and choice of IMC tools.[4]

SET OBJECTIVES AND BUDGET

IMC can be used to move the target audience through a series of responses corresponding to beliefs, behavior, and feelings about the product or brand. As Exhibit 9.2 shows, marketers of low-involvement products such as inexpensive items first want to influence the audience's beliefs, then the audience's actions, and, finally, its feelings. If a consumer sees value in a certain type of pen (beliefs), she may buy one and try it (behavior) and then decide whether she likes it (feelings). Marketers of high-involvement products such as cars also start by influencing the audience's beliefs; then they strive to influence feelings and behavior. In contrast, marketers who emphasize the consumption experience initially try to influence the audience's feelings, followed by actions and then beliefs. Clearly, these are simplified response models; in reality, target audiences are exposed to multiple messages in multiple media—often simultaneously, as when someone listens to the radio while surfing the Web.[5] Thus, marketers should understand the response model for a given product or category when setting objectives tied to the marketing plan's objectives.

If a company wants to acquire new customers, it must ensure that the audience knows about the offer (influencing beliefs). One IMC objective might be to "achieve 25% awareness of Product A among the target audience within 4 months," with the exact percentage and timing dependent on the marketing objective, the promotion investment, and knowledge of the customer's buying process. Related objectives might be to "have 900 prospects request an information package about Product D before June 30" and "generate 300 qualified leads for the sales staff by March 15."

If research shows that the segment is aware of the product but has no strong preference for it (feelings), the objective might be to "achieve 18% preference for Product E among the target audience within 3 months." If research indicates that customers like the product enough to try it (behavior), the aim might be to "achieve 9% trial of Product C among the target audience within 6 months" or "have 200 customers request samples of Product B during January." Using IMC to enhance image, the objective might be to "make 55% of the target audience aware

EXHIBIT 9.2   Models for Audience Response to IMC

Low involvement model:

IMC activities ⟶ Influence beliefs ⟶ Influence behavior ⟶ Influence feelings

High involvement model:

IMC activities ⟶ Influence beliefs ⟶ Influence feelings ⟶ Influence behavior

Experiential model:

IMC activities ⟶ Influence feelings ⟶ Influence behavior ⟶ Influence beliefs of the corporation's philanthropic donations by December 31" or to "double the percentage of the target audience having positive attitudes toward the corporation within 12 months."

A number of factors should be considered when devising an IMC budget, including the overall marketing budget, the objectives to be achieved, the choice of advertising or other tool(s), the number of markets to be covered, the competitive circumstances, the potential return on investment, and so on. Because organizational resources are finite, marketers need to be realistic about the situation, have definite short- and long-term objectives in mind, and budget creatively. See Chapter 10 for more about budgeting.

EXAMINE ISSUES

IMC strategy can be affected by a variety of legal, regulatory, ethical, cultural, and competitive issues. For example, it is illegal for companies in the United States, United Kingdom, and some other nations to make false claims for a product or describe a food as "low fat" if it does not meet certain criteria.[6] Communications for products such as prescription drugs must comply with strict rules; sometimes messages must include health or product use warnings and the company must be prepared to safeguard customer privacy in particular ways. Moreover, if companies communicate ethically and, where possible, follow voluntary industry ethics guidelines, they are more likely to build trust with target audiences and polish their image.

Practical Planning Tip
Look beyond legalities to plan ethical communications that will earn your audience's trust.

Although any specific social issues affecting communication will vary from product to product, all marketers should understand the public's perception of promotions. In a recent U.S. survey, 60% of the respondents said their view of advertising was "much more negative than just a few years ago," and 54% said they "avoid buying products that overwhelm them with advertising and marketing."[7] Negative attitudes toward promotion can cause a backlash, as Columbia Pictures found out during the controversy over part of its prerelease promotion for *Spider-Man 2*:

Columbia Pictures. With *Spider-Man 2* just weeks away from its debut, Columbia planned to put the movie name and spider-web graphics on bases during a weekend of Major League Baseball games. It also wanted to put signs up inside stadiums and give away Spider-Man merchandise. When the promotion was announced, however, fans expressed dismay at the idea of branding the bases. Columbia monitored the results of online polls by ESPN and AOL, realized that public opinion was overwhelmingly negative, and quickly dropped that part of the promotion. "It's disappointing, in that we thought it would be a fun aspect and not harmful," said the president of worldwide marketing. "But we realize in retrospect that a lot of people are very upset about it."[8]

Competitive issues also should be considered. How can the company use IMC to play up a meaningful point of difference setting its product apart from rival products? How are competitors using IMC? How can the company counter campaigns from competitors with much larger budgets and better-established brands or products? How can the company use IMC to attract attention despite a cluttered marketing environment?

CHOOSE IMC TOOLS

Marketers can choose among a wide variety of techniques in the five basic categories of IMC tools, as shown in Exhibit 9.3. Here is a brief overview; highlights of planning for each will be examined later in the chapter:

- *Advertising.* Advertising is cost-effective for communicating with a large audience, with the marketer in complete control of message and media. Marketers often use advertising to introduce and differentiate a product, build a brand, polish the organization's image, communicate competitive superiority, or convey an idea. Nonprofits have found advertising to be effective as well: the Baltimore Symphony Orchestra recently used it to reach out to new audience segments when opening its second Maryland concert hall.[9]
- *Sales promotion.* This marketer-controlled tool can be used to target consumers, businesses, or channel members and sales representatives. It is particularly useful for accelerating short-term sales results; combating competitive pressure; provoking product trial; building awareness and reinforcing other IMC activities; encouraging continued buying and usage; and increasing the offer's perceived value. When Columbia Pictures gave away movie-themed merchandise before the debut of *Spider-Man 2,* it was using sales promotion to build awareness and pull people into local theaters when the movie opened.
- *Public relations.* Public relations has more credibility than other promotion tools because the audience receives the message through media channels perceived

EXHIBIT 9.3   Major Promotion Tools

Tool	*Use*	*Examples*
Advertising	Efficiently get messages to large audience	Television and radio commercials; Internet banner ads; magazine and newspaper ads; product and company brochures; billboards; CD- and video-based ads
Sales promotion	Stimulate immediate purchase, reward repeat purchases, motivate sales personnel	Samples; coupons; premiums; contests, games, sweepstakes; displays; demonstrations; trade shows; trade incentives
Public relations	Build positive image and strengthen ties with stakeholders	Event sponsorship; news releases and briefings; speeches; public appearances
Direct marketing	Reach targeted audiences and encourage direct response	E-mail campaigns; printed and online catalogs; telemarketing; direct mail letters and brochures; direct response television
Personal selling	Reach customers one-to-one to make sales, strengthen relationships	Sales appointments; sales meetings and presentations

to be more objective than sources controlled by the organization. However, the outcome is unpredictable: marketers cannot control what the media will report, nor guarantee that the company or product will actually get any media coverage at all. Marketers use public relations when they want to present the product and company in a positive light; build goodwill and trust; and inform customers, channel members, and other stakeholders about the product and its benefits.

- *Direct marketing.* A highly focused, organization-controlled tool, direct marketing facilitates two-way interaction with a specific audience, allows for pinpoint targeting, and accommodates offers tailored to individual needs and behavior. Marketers can easily measure the outcome and compare it with objectives to determine effectiveness and efficiency. Direct marketing helps organizations start, strengthen, or renew customer relationships; increase sales of particular products; test the appeal of new or repositioned products; or test alternate marketing tactics such as different prices.
- *Personal selling.* Personal selling is an excellent organization-controlled tool for reaching business customers and consumers on a personal basis to open a dialogue; learn more about needs; present complex or customized information; or obtain feedback. Companies selling expensive goods or services or customizing products for individual customers frequently rely on personal selling. However, it is labor intensive and expensive, which is why many products are not marketed in this way. On the other hand, a number of consumer products are being successfully marketed through personal selling at home parties. Southern Living at Home, owned by the publisher of *Southern Living* magazine, has 25,000 independent representatives selling its cookbooks, candles, and home decor items in U.S. homes.[10]

When possible, marketers want to spark positive **word-of-mouth (WOM) communication**, encouraging people to tell other people about a company, a product, a brand, or some clever marketing they noticed. Information spread by WOM (or *word-of-mouse* online) has more credibility because it comes from a personal source rather than being controlled by the organization. The earlier example of Dr Pepper generating "buzz" for its Raging Cow beverages shows WOM in action: people who read the cow's blog told other people, building brand awareness and setting the stage for product trial. The outcome of WOM is unpredictable and often cannot even be accurately measured.

PLAN RESEARCH

If time and money are available, the marketing plan should allow for pretesting and post-implementation research to evaluate IMC activities. Marketers often pretest to find out whether the target audience understands the message and retains information about the brand or product. They also want to see whether the audience responds as expected: do beliefs, attitudes, or behavior change as a result of the communication? Such results help in fine-tuning the format, content, delivery, and context of a communication before the bulk of the campaign is implemented.

Practical Planning Tip

When pretesting, allow time for testing any changes before launching the campaign.

Post-implementation research will show whether the IMC strategy accomplished its objectives and which activities were particularly effective. For example, the U.S. unit of Amsterdam's ING Group conducts extensive post-implementation research of messages designed to attract new customers:

> **ING Direct.** ING Direct, the largest Web-based bank in the United States, analyzes the results of every Internet ad and direct-mail campaign so it can improve future IMC programs. The company's target audience is Web-savvy middle-class people in urban areas, aged 30 to 50 years old, who have about $14,000 in savings and want a convenient banking experience plus a high interest rate. The company boosts brand awareness with media advertising and uses Internet ads and direct-mail packages to bring in new business. Based on ING's research, the most effective of its IMC activities has been a mailing offering a $25 incentive to open a new account.[11]

Using IMC Tools

Marketing plans usually cover the use of various tools in one or more campaigns (with the details and explanations shown in an appendix or other documents). In line with the principle of integration, marketers should consider the overall effect when planning for any combination of advertising, sales promotion, public relations, direct marketing, and personal selling. Careful coordination of content and delivery across messages and media is essential for consistency; otherwise, the target audience could become confused and the results of the IMC strategy might easily fall short of expectations.

ADVERTISING

For the purposes of developing a marketing plan, advertising's two basic decisions concern the message (what content will be communicated?) and the media (what vehicle or vehicles will deliver the message, and when, where, and how?). These decisions must be in keeping with the target audience's characteristics, needs, behavior, and receptivity; the budget allocated for advertising; relevant issues affecting IMC strategy; and the objectives set (e.g., awareness or purchase of the product). Moreover, the message and media have to work together: If, for example, the plan calls for product demonstration, a visual medium like the Internet or television will be the best choice—but only if the budget allows and the chosen vehicle reaches the target audience.

The ad's wording, format and design, graphics, sound, and other medium-specific elements will communicate the message appeal. Some messages rely on a **rational appeal**, using facts and logic to stimulate response by showing how the product solves a problem or satisfies a need. Many B2B ads, in particular, are based on rational appeals linked to the specific benefits that business buyers seek. As an example, paper manufacturer MeadWestvaco used a rational appeal when advertising its Tango paper for commercial printers. After research revealed that printers want paper to perform the same on job after job, the company put the tagline "Always Performing" in its print ads to convey the benefit of consistency.[12] A message with an **emotional appeal** relies on feelings (fear, love, anger, happiness, or another emotion) to motivate audience response. For instance, a magazine ad for Ford Quality Certified pre-owned vehicles appeals to the fear of buying an unsafe used car: it pictures a safe and adds the words, "It's really the safe choice. If it's not certified, it's just used."[13]

heavily moisturized hair without the heavily part. new Dove® shampoos and conditioners are made with a unique formula of weightless moisturizers that leave hair soft and smooth but not weighed down. moisture and lift — the best of both worlds.

This ad cites "moisture and lift" as two specific reasons why women should buy Dove Shampoo.

Practical Planning Tip
Be sure the creative execution of a message will work in each medium under consideration.

Each medium has characteristics that convey the message in a different way; the Internet offers sight, sound, motion, and interactivity, whereas print ads can offer color, longer life, and the ability to communicate more details. To achieve IMC objectives, even the most creative message must be presented in a specific medium or vehicle (such as a certain magazine or Web site) that will reach the target audience. In particular, in-store television is becoming a medium of choice for consumer packaged goods because the message reaches shoppers when and where they buy. Unilever has been so successful promoting products such as Axe deodorant on Wal-Mart's television network that it now creates 7 campaigns yearly for this medium.[14]

Two key decisions in planning media choices are how many people to reach during a certain period (known as **reach**) and how often to repeat the message during that period (known as **frequency**). Reaching more people is costly, as is repeating the message multiple times. Thus, the marketer must determine how to allocate the budget by balancing reach with frequency, based on knowledge of the target audience. The choice of where to advertise—in geographic terms—depends on where the product is available or will be introduced during the course of the marketing plan (see Exhibit 9.4). In terms of timing, a message or campaign might run continuously (reminding the audience of benefits or availability), during periods of seasonal or peak demand (when the audience is interested in buying), or steadily but with sporadic intensity (along with sales promotions or other marketing activities).

Consider Monster.com's experience in timing its advertising:

Monster.com. Knowing that many people start to think about changing jobs in January, the career site Monster.com plans a major IMC push early each year with the objective of bringing in résumés from more job-seekers. Sometimes its marketing plan includes Super Bowl commercials, which are costly to produce and air but get Monster's messages to the right people at the right time. "Our target audience is men and women aged 18 to 49," explains Monster's senior vice president of marketing, "and we can get really quick reach and frequency against that audience with the Super Bowl buy." The company is also testing ad campaigns in several local markets to determine where it will get the best return on its IMC budget.[15]

EXHIBIT 9.4   The Media Mix

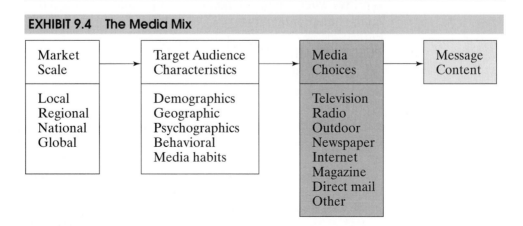

SALES PROMOTION

It takes time to build a brand, cultivate customer loyalty, or reinforce commitment among channel members, but sales promotion can help by reducing perceived price or enhancing perceived value for a limited time. Among the sales promotion techniques that marketers can use when targeting customers and prospects are sampling, couponing, rebates and refunds, premiums, sweepstakes and contests, bonus packs, and loyalty programs. Among the techniques that marketers can use when targeting channel members and salespeople are allowances and incentives, sales contests, training and support, and point-of-purchase materials. Exhibit 9.5 describes the purpose of each and highlights issues to be considered during planning.

Objectives for sales promotion activities targeting customers and prospects may include building awareness; encouraging product trial or usage; encouraging speedy response; reinforcing loyalty; supporting advertising or other IMC activities; or defending against competitors. Objectives for sales promotion activities targeting channel members and sales representatives may include enhancing product knowledge; building commitment; reinforcing focus and loyalty; encouraging speedy response; supporting channel and other IMC activities; or defending against competitors.

Here's a good example of sampling in action:

Ralph Lauren. For its launch of the fragrance Polo Blue in the United Kingdom, the fashion firm Ralph Lauren targeted affluent, professional men aged 20 to 35. The company had two objectives: to build awareness and to encourage trial of the new fragrance. During a brief and intense campaign, samplers visited 100 preselected offices in London to give away tiny trial-size tubes of Polo Blue along with brand-emblazoned adhesive notes and postcards. The personal interaction between the target audience and Lauren's samplers added a human touch to the promotion and fostered two-way communication about the new fragrance.[16]

Many marketers include sales promotion in their marketing plans as a way of accelerating response over a set period, with clearly measurable results (such as counting the number of coupons redeemed and the number of units sold). However, overuse can lead customers or channel members to be more price-sensitive when buying certain types of products, posing a potential threat to brand equity and profitability.[17]

PUBLIC RELATIONS

The purpose of public relations (PR) is to open the lines of communication and develop positive relationships with one or more of the organization's stakeholder groups. Target audiences (the *public* in public relations) usually include some combination of customers and prospects, employees and job applicants, channel members, suppliers, government officials, local community groups, special interest groups, and the financial community. As an example, Atlanta's Home-Banc Mortgage directs PR at four target audiences. For home buyers and homeowners, it emphasizes superior customer service; for local communities, it emphasizes involvement in nearby Habitat for Humanity projects; for the financial community,

EXHIBIT 9.5 Sales Promotion Techniques

Technique and Purpose	*Issues*
Sampling — Allow prospects to examine and experience product without risk.	• Does the budget allow for sampling? • How, when, and where will samples be distributed?
Couponing — Reduce the perceived price of a product.	• Will coupons be redeemed by loyal customers rather than prospects? • Will coupons be redeemed properly?
Rebates and Refunds — Reduce the perceived price and lower the perceived risk.	• Is the organization prepared for the mechanics? • How will returning money to customers affect financial objectives?
Premiums — Offer something extra free or for a small price to enhance product's value.	• How will the premium affect the plan's financial objectives? • Will the premium be unattractive or too attractive?
Sweepstakes, contests, and games — Attract attention and build excitement about a product or brand.	• What legal and regulatory rules apply? • Does the budget allow for prizes, operational mechanics, and IMC support?
Bonus packs — Bundle two or more products together for a special price, lowering the perceived price.	• Does the budget allow for special packaging? • Will customers perceive sufficient added value?
Allowances and incentives — Give retailer or wholesaler financial reasons to support the product.	• Will intermediaries offer their customers special prices as a result? • Will intermediaries overorder now, reducing orders in later periods?
Contests — Reward salespeople for selling a certain product.	• Will the product receive adequate attention after a contest is over? • Will the budget cover the cost of prizes and administration?
Training and support — Educate salespeople about product and support the sales effort.	• How often is training needed? • How much support does a product or channel member need?
Point-of-purchase materials — Use signs, other methods of in-store promotion.	• Will retailers use the materials? • Does the budget allow for providing different intermediaries with different materials?

it emphasizes its rapid expansion and innovation; and for job applicants, it emphasizes its attractiveness as an employer.[18]

Some of the objectives that marketers may set for PR are:

- *Understanding stakeholders' perceptions and attitudes.* PR can help take the public's pulse and identify concerns about products and operations, social responsibility, or other issues. Whether feedback comes in through letters, e-mails, phone calls, or interaction with company personnel, the organization can learn what its audiences care about and see itself through the public's eyes—then plan to respond.

- *Enhancing image.* Shaping and maintaining the organization's image generates goodwill and sets the stage for positive long-term relations with target audiences. One way organizations do this is by having management and employees participate in community events, charitable causes, and other local activities.

- *Communicating views and information.* Sometimes PR is used to correct public misperceptions or clarify a company's stand or action on a particular issue. After accusations that The Gap's clothing is made in overseas factories that operate like sweatshops, the company investigated and started reporting about conditions at its 3,000 factories. The first report said that The Gap dropped 136 factories because of violations but also candidly noted that "few factories, if any, are in full compliance all of the time" with the retailer's code of labor practices. This honesty strengthened trust among key target audiences such as investors and union officials.[19]

- *Building brand and product awareness.* Through news conferences, special events, and other techniques, PR can spotlight a brand or a product line. Germany's Siemens uses PR to demonstrate its technological savvy in B2B products such as medical diagnostic equipment. The company recently sent a 14-car train on a world tour, filled to capacity with Siemens products, specialists, and multimedia kiosks. Thousands came aboard, increasing brand awareness, stimulating new orders, and boosting market share—returns far outweighing the $16 million cost of outfitting the train.[20]

Practical Planning Tip
Identify the specific audience to be targeted for each public relations objective you set.

Southwest Airlines recently achieved a number of objectives through PR related to its participation in the A&E *Airline* television series:

Southwest Airlines. "The first question I am always asked when discussing this project is, 'Why would Southwest Airlines—or any other company, for that matter—agree to open itself up to a camera crew?'" says President Colleen Barrett. Her answer: "I had faith that the viewing public would quickly see why Southwest has ranked number 1 in terms of customer satisfaction, per Department of Transportation statistics, for the last 12 consecutive years." Southwest employees were filmed as they checked passengers in, worked in flight, and coped with blackouts and other problems. The airline paid nothing and had no control over what aired, although it could correct errors. The series reached millions of potential and current customers, delighted employees, and drew a flood of job applications.[21]

DIRECT MARKETING

In direct marketing, the organization reaches out to customers and prospects through mail, broadcast and print media, the Internet, and other media. This IMC tool is cost-effective for precise targeting and the use of customized messages, offers, and timing, even one recipient at a time if enough information is available about each individual's needs and characteristics. Because the audience responds directly to the organization, marketers can easily measure results and see whether objectives have been met—and change the message or medium fairly quickly if necessary. The marketing plan should summarize the objectives, the expected response, how results will be measured, any use of research, relevant issues, and the connection with other IMC objectives.

Many direct marketing programs aim for an immediate sale; other objectives may be building awareness, influencing perceptions and attitudes, continuing customer relationships, obtaining leads for sales staff, or encouraging prospects to take the next step toward buying. Nonprofits typically set objectives such as generating contributions, signing up volunteers, and selling products to benefit the cause. Heifer International, for example, uses its Web site, fundraising letters, and printed catalogs to bring in donations. In turn, Heifer uses the money to give livestock or bees to families in poor areas so they can make a living in an environmentally sustainable way. Because the organization's Web site is easy to navigate and clearly communicates the benefits of giving as well as where the money goes, Heifer now receives more online donations than any other nonprofit—$8 million-plus during one recent year.[22]

To be effective, the direct marketing message must be relevant to the target audience and not be perceived as junk mail or spam. The Cosmetique Beauty Club handled this challenge by inviting prospects to opt in for e-mail offers. It clearly marked e-mails as containing cosmetics offers from Cosmetique and allowed recipients to opt out at any time. By sending e-mails only to people who elected to receive them, the company was able to attract more than 100,000 new members in just 9 months.[23]

PERSONAL SELLING

Personal selling is appropriate if the target audience requires customized goods or services, needs assistance assessing needs, makes large purchases, or requires individual attention for other reasons. This is an important IMC tool for pharmaceutical firms, equipment manufacturers, and many other B2B marketers, as well as for some marketers that target consumers. The one-to-one nature of personal selling (in person or by phone) supports strong customer relationships; therefore, the emphasis may not be on making an instant sale but on building connections for the future. "Focus on developing a win–win relationship for both the company and the customer," advises Larry Panattoni, a sales representative for Servatron in Spokane, Washington, and "orders will follow."[24]

Practical Planning Tip

Support the personal selling effort with IMC activities that help build awareness and demand.

Decisions that marketers face in planning for personal selling are whether to hire salespeople or work with an outside sales agency; how to recruit, train, manage, motivate, and compensate sales staff; how many salespeople are needed and how they will be organized (e.g., by product, by market, by type of customer). A number of decisions about structuring the sales process itself draw input directly from the marketing plan:

- *Identifying and qualifying prospects.* Based on earlier segmentation and targeting decisions, management identifies the audience for personal selling activities and determines how prospects will be qualified for sales contact.
- *Planning the presales approach.* Data from earlier market and customer analyses informs the approach that a salesperson plans in contacting prospects.
- *Making sales contact.* Based on the prospect's needs and the firm's positioning, the salesperson explains the value added by product features and their associated benefits.

- *Handling objections.* Using knowledge of the product, the prospect's needs, and the competition, the salesperson addresses specific concerns and questions.
- *Closing the sale.* The salesperson completes the sale, arranges payment, and schedules delivery with an understanding of pricing and logistics strategies.
- *Following up after the sale.* To continue building the relationship, the salesperson must understand the customer service strategy, the customer's needs, and applicable IMC support, such as frequent-buyer programs.

Summary

Integrated marketing communication is an approach that coordinates the content and delivery of all marketing communications for a brand, product, or organization to ensure consistency and support the chosen positioning and direction. IMC strategy covers advertising, sales promotion, public relations, direct marketing, and personal selling. Some IMC strategies push products by addressing the channel as the target audience; others pull products through the channel by addressing customers as the target audience; and some combine push and pull, targeting both customers and the channel.

Depending on the plan's overall objectives, IMC may be used to move the target audience through responses corresponding to beliefs, behavior, and feelings about the product or brand. In planning IMC strategy, marketers should look at legal, regulatory, ethical, social, cultural, and competitive issues before selecting appropriate IMC tools. Ideally, the marketing plan should allow for pretesting and post-implementation research to evaluate the IMC strategy. Planning for each IMC tool entails decisions that link back to the overall objectives and strategies set during the marketing planning process.

CHAPTER

Planning Performance Measurement and Implementation Control

In this chapter:

Preview

The final step in formulating a marketing plan is preparing to check the organization's progress toward performance targets after implementation. Because macro- or microenvironmental changes are inevitable, marketers will be better able to cope if they define procedures and standards for tracking results and are prepared to address significant problems. This chapter discusses four tools for checking marketing performance: forecasts of future sales and costs, budgets allocating financial resources, schedules identifying the timing of marketing tasks, and metrics to gauge movement toward achieving objectives. The second part of the chapter looks at how marketing control is used to identify, analyze, and correct variations from expected results.

After reading this chapter and planning your forecasts, budgets, schedules, and metrics, record them with *Marketing Plan Pro* software or in a written plan. Also document any contingency plans you have developed. Think about the questions in the checklist below when planning a marketing audit.

CHAPTER 10 CHECKLIST   Planning a Marketing Audit

Marketing Strategy

✔ Does the mission focus on market and customer needs, and is it used to guide marketing planning?

✔ Are marketing-mix strategies appropriate in light of the situation analysis?

✔ Do all marketing objectives support the strategies, goals, and mission?

✔ Do marketing personnel understand the marketing plan and have the skills and resources to implement it?

Marketing Operations and Results

✔ Does the organization have effective systems for tracking and reporting marketing results and external trends to marketing decision makers?

✔ Does the organization have effective systems for managing marketing-mix activities?

✔ Does the organization have effective systems for managing relationships with channel members, salespeople, suppliers, and partners?

✔ Can the organization benchmark operations and results against industry or world-class standards, adjusting for individual factors?

✔ How does management analyze performance problems and follow up with corrective action and contingency plans?

✔ Is the organization achieving its desired financial, marketing, and societal objectives?

Stakeholder Relations

✔ How are stakeholders' comments, feedback, and priorities obtained, analyzed, and incorporated into organizational decisions?

✔ How do customers and other stakeholders perceive the brand/product/company and how have perceptions changed over time?

Measuring Marketing Performance

Before implementing the marketing plan, marketers need to be able to predict the probable outcomes of their programs; after implementation, they must periodically measure progress toward achieving objectives. The time to establish checkpoints and rules for measuring performance is during the planning process, so the organization is ready to check interim results regularly. Once implementation is underway, marketers can monitor these measures and analyze progress over time to diagnose any variations and make any changes needed to get back on track.

Marketing plans typically include four main tools for measuring performance progress: forecasts, budgets, schedules, and metrics (see Exhibit 10.1).

FORECASTING SALES AND COSTS

Practical Planning Tip
You can't manage what you don't measure, so plan to track the progress of your marketing plan.

Forecasts are future projections of what sales and costs are likely to be in the months and years covered by the plan. To do a good job of forecasting, companies must weigh external factors like demand, threats, and opportunities as well as internal factors like goals, capabilities, and constraints. Many companies prepare forecasts for the best-case, the worst-case, and the most likely scenario. Nonprofit organizations may prepare forecasts of future contributions, overall need for services, and projected service utilization, along with future estimates of associated costs. Forecasts can never be more than good estimates, and in fact marketers must allow for some forecast error because these are only projections. Still, forecasts should be as accurate as possible, because the organization relies on them when developing strategies and planning the resources needed to implement the marketing plan.

Here's how McDonald's uses forecasting:

McDonald's. Like other fast-food chains, McDonald's forecasts sales for each location at different times of the day and days of the week so it can project costs, plan staffing levels, and order food and other supplies. Its forecasts also allow for the effect of holidays, seasonality, economic conditions, competitive actions, and other elements that influence demand. The McDonald's on Broadway near busy Times Square in New York City checks the dates of movie premieres because the restaurant is within walking distance of 35 cinemas and dinner sales can spike by as much as 25% when a blockbuster opens.[1]

EXHIBIT 10.1 Tools for Measuring Marketing Progress

Tool	*Application*
Forecasts	Used to predict future sales and costs as checkpoints for measuring progress
Budgets	Used to allocate funding across programs in specified periods and then track expenditures during implementation
Schedules	Used to plan and coordinate the timing of tasks and programs
Metrics	Used to establish measures for specific performance-related outcomes and activities and then track results against measures

Clearly, marketers need to review forecasts often, especially in light of internal or external shifts that can influence sales, costs, and marketing performance. To illustrate, Ford's marketers constantly scan the environment for signs that their sales forecasts need to be updated. Having felt the effects of sudden and dramatic economic downturns, they not only look at daily vehicle sales but also check informal sources such as Internet chat rooms to get a sense of consumer confidence. "When you have this month-to-month volatility, it creates a certain level of anxiety," says Ford's director of sales analysis. "You've got to really pay attention."[2]

Forecasting must account for the effect that marketing activities will have on the direction and velocity of sales. For example, the company will probably forecast higher sales for a new product if it plans to use penetration pricing to encourage rapid adoption. On the other hand, if it uses skimming pricing to skim profits from the market, the forecast for introductory sales volume will probably be lower than with penetration pricing. Why does this matter? Relying on a forecast that underestimates sales could leave a company with insufficient inventory or staffing to satisfy demand; on the other hand, relying on an overestimate could lead to overproduction and other costly problems.

Even when forecasts come very close to reality, unanticipated events can change everything, as United Technologies well knows:

United Technologies. With a product mix as diverse as air conditioners, elevators, aircraft engines, and maintenance services, United Technologies Corp. (UTC) prepares its B2B global forecasts based on geography, politics, economic trends, and many other factors. However, no one could have predicted the precipitous drop in demand for air travel after the 2001 terrorist attacks, which prompted airlines to postpone or reduce aircraft purchases and hurt UTC's engine sales for several years. On the other hand, demand for elevators and air conditioning equipment soared so high due to Asia's construction boom that UTC actually raised its yearly sales forecast by $1 billion in mid-2004.[3]

Types of Forecasts

McDonald's, United Technology, and Ford all use sales and cost forecasts as they develop their marketing plans. The most commonly used types of forecasts are:

- *Forecasts of market and segment sales.* The company starts by projecting a market's overall industrywide sales for up to 5 years, using the definition created during the market analysis. This helps size the entire market so managers can set share objectives and estimate the share competitors will have in future years. If possible, the company also should forecast year-by-year sales in each targeted segment.
- *Forecasts of company product sales.* Based on market and segment forecasts, market and customer analysis, direction decisions, and marketing strategies, the company now projects the number and dollar amount of product (or product line) sales for each market or segment. These are usually presented month by month for a year or for the period covered by the marketing plan. Some companies create separate forecasts for each new product so these can be tracked more closely.

- *Forecasts of cost of sales.* Here, management forecasts the costs associated with company product sales forecasts, based on data gathered for the analysis of the current situation and on data about cost trends. These forecasts may be adjusted after marketing budgets have been prepared.
- *Forecasts of sales and costs by channel.* When companies sell through more than one channel level or intermediary, they may want to project monthly unit and dollar sales by product by channel and, if feasible, costs per channel. These forecasts focus attention on channel cost-efficiency and provide a yardstick for measuring and analyzing actual channel results and expenses.

Practical Planning Tip
The specific forecasts you prepare depend on your organization and its priorities.

Creating this series of forecasts is only part of the task. Next, the marketer calculates the month-to-month and year-to-year change for the figures in each forecast to examine trends (such as how much growth in sales is being projected for the coming 12 months) and rate of change (such as how quickly costs are rising). Forecast projections and trend calculations can be used to check on target markets, review objectives, reallocate resources, and measure actual against expected results. Given the rapid rate of change in many markets, many companies update forecasts monthly or more often to reflect current conditions; many also collaborate with key suppliers and channel members for more precise forecasting. Wal-Mart, for instance, provides sales data for forecasting to more than 3,500 suppliers on a weekly basis.[4]

Sources and Tools for Forecasting Data

Just as Wal-Mart shares sales data with its suppliers, many companies obtain data for forecasting purposes from their value-chain partners. Marketers can also tap primary research sources such as studies of buying patterns and buying intentions that suggest demand levels by market, segment, category, or product. However, marketers must use judgment, remembering that customers may not buy in the future as they have in the past, nor will they necessarily make future purchases even though they told researchers they would do so.[5] Trade associations, government statistics, and industry analysts' reports can be valuable secondary sources of data.

Some marketers predict future sales by applying causal analysis methods such as regression analysis, econometric models, and neural networks; or using time series methods such as smoothing and decomposition. They may also apply judgmental forecasting tools such as sales force estimates, executive opinion, and the Delphi method, as shown in Exhibit 10.2. Because these tools may be subject to human error or bias, marketers generally use a combination of judgment and statistical analysis updated with estimates from knowledgeable sources for increased accuracy.

As difficult as forecasting can be for existing products, planners face even more challenges in forecasting for new products. Some companies use the Bass model for forecasting initial purchases of new products; this is appropriate when (1) the company has been able to collect sales data for even a brief period, or (2) the product is similar to an existing product or technology with a known sales history.[6] When a product is so innovative that it establishes a new product category—such as digital music players—marketers have no historical or industry data to factor into their forecasts. Instead, some predict sales using the results of simulated test marketing research, while others look at sales patterns of products with similar market behavior for clues to the new product's future sales. Once forecasts are in place, marketers create budgets to allocate resources and prepare to track expenses.

EXHIBIT 10.2 Judgmental Tools for Forecasting

Forecasting Tool	*Use*
Sales force estimates	Composite projection based on estimates made by sales personnel; convenient but accuracy depends on instincts, experience, and objectivity of salespeople.
Executive opinion	Composite projection based on estimates made by managers; convenient but accuracy depends on instincts, experience, and objectivity of managers.
Delphi method	Composite projection based on successive rounds of input from outside experts, who ultimately come to consensus on estimates; time consuming but sometimes helpful when forecasting sales of new products or new markets.

BUDGETING TO PLAN AND TRACK EXPENSES

Budgets are time-defined allocations of financial outlays for specific functions, programs, customer segments, or geographic region. Budgeting enables marketing managers to allocate expenses by program or activity over specific periods and compare these with actual expenditures. Some organizations insist that budget preparation follow internal financial calendars; some specify profit hurdles or particular assumptions about expenses and allocation; some mandate particular formats or supporting documentation; and some require budgets based on best-case, worst-case, and most likely scenarios. A growing number of businesses are no longer fixing budgets annually but instead are adjusting budgets monthly based on market realities or tying budgets to longer-term performance.[7]

Practical Planning Tip
Combine bottom-up and top-down budget input when allocating marketing funds.

Budgeting Methods for Marketing Spending

How much money should be budgeted for marketing programs? Smaller companies often deal with this question using **affordability budgeting**, simply budgeting what they believe they can afford, given other urgent expenses:

> **Cincinnati Custom Cleaning.** When Dave and Christine McAdams founded Cincinnati Custom Cleaning, they phased in a direct-mail campaign to acquire new customers, targeting medical offices as their first segment. As they grew, they continued to prospect by mail every month; "every time we had a little extra money, we spent it on postage," says Christine McAdams. By bootstrapping, the company was able to build monthly revenues to $30,000 and expand into more segments of the corporate market.[8]

Affordability budgeting worked for Cincinnati Custom Cleaning in its early days, when the cofounders had very little to spend. However, this is generally not a good way to set budgets, because it doesn't allow for the kind of significant, ongoing investments often needed to launch major new products or enter intensely competitive markets. In effect, budgeting based on affordability ignores the profit payback that comes from spending on marketing to build sales.

Ideally, the size of the marketing budget should be based on careful analysis of the link between spending and sales (or, for nonprofits, donations). By building a sophisticated model of how sales actually react to different spending levels, the company can determine exactly how big the marketing budget must be to achieve its sales targets. Companies without such models tend to rely on rule-of-thumb budgeting methods that do not directly correlate spending with sales, such as the percentage-of-sales method, the competitive-parity method, and the objective-and-task method.

With **percentage-of-sales budgeting**, management sets aside a certain percentage of dollar sales to fund marketing programs, based on internal budgeting guidelines or previous marketing experience. Although this is simple to implement, one disadvantage is that sales are seen as the source of marketing funding, rather than as the result of budget investments. Another is that the company may have no justification (other than tradition) for choosing the percentage devoted to marketing. Finally, if the budget is continually adjusted based on month-by-month sales, lower sales may lead to a lower marketing budget—just when the company needs to maintain or even increase the budget to stimulate higher sales.

When companies use **competitive-parity budgeting**, they fund marketing by matching what competitors spend (as a percentage of sales or specific dollar amount). Again, this is a simple method, but it ignores differences between companies and doesn't allow for adjustments to find the best spending level for achieving marketing plan objectives. Imagine if competitors of the software company Salesforce.com matched its $33 million marketing and sales budget as a percentage of revenues. Salesforce.com currently spends 65% of revenues on marketing and sales, whereas Oracle spends 22% and Microsoft spends 18% on marketing.[9]

Practical Planning Tip
Don't match what competitors spend, but do be aware of their budget priorities.

With the widely used **objective-and-task budgeting method**, marketers add up the cost of completing all the marketing tasks needed to achieve their marketing plan objectives. In the absence of a proven model showing how sales levels respond to marketing spending, the objective-and-task method provides a reasonable way to build a budget by examining the cost of the individual programs that contribute to marketing performance—as long as the appropriate objectives have been set.

Budgets within the Marketing Budget

Once the overall budget has been established, marketers start to allocate marketing funding across the various activities in the time period covered by the marketing plan. Then, when they implement the marketing plan, they can input actual expenditures for comparison with planned expenditures. The marketing plan usually includes:

- *Budgets for each marketing-mix program.* These budgets list costs for each program's tasks or expense items, presented month by month and with year-end totals. Depending on the company's preferred format, marketing-mix budgets also may show expected sales, gross or net margins, and other objectives and profitability measures. Tracking expenses by program reinforces accountability and helps management weigh expected costs against actual costs—and results.
- *Budgets for each brand, segment, or market.* Creating these types of budgets forces companies to understand their costs and returns relative to individual brands, segments, and markets. Sara Lee, for instance, budgets by brand categories, as defined by forecast growth and expected return. High-growth brands such as Champion receive higher budgets to yield more return than slower-growth brands such as Playtex.[10]

- *Budgets for each region or geographic division.* Budgeting by region or geography focuses attention on the cost of marketing by location and allows easy comparisons between outlays and returns.
- *Budgets for each division or product manager.* These budgets help divisional and product managers track costs for which they are responsible, compare spending with results achieved, and pinpoint problems or opportunities for further investigation.
- *Budget summarizing overall marketing expenses.* This summary budget may be arranged by marketing program or tool, by segment or region, or by using another appropriate organizing pattern. Typically, this budget shows month-by-month spending and full-year totals; in some cases, companies may project spending for multiple years in one summary budget. And this budget may include expected gross or net margins and other calculations based on sales and expenditures.

All these budgets serve as checkpoints against which actual spending can be measured. In this way, marketers can quickly spot overspending and calculate margins and other profitability measures to check on progress toward financial objectives. The next step is to coordinate the timing of each activity through scheduling.

SCHEDULING MARKETING PLAN PROGRAMS

Schedules are time-defined plans for completing a series of tasks or activities (milestones) related to a specific program or objective. Scheduling helps the company define the timing of these tasks and coordinate implementation to avoid conflicts and measure progress toward completion. To create a detailed program-by-program schedule, marketing managers list the main tasks and activities for one program at a time and, through research or experience, assign each a projected start and end date. Some companies create a series of schedules, based on best-case, worst-case, and most likely scenarios for timing. Schedules also identify who is responsible for supervising or completing each task in each program.

Practical Planning Tip
Include the timing and progress of ongoing programs or activities in your situation analysis.

Marketing plans typically include a summary schedule showing the timing and responsibility for each planned program; the appendix or separate documents may show detailed schedules for each program along with Gantt charts, critical path schedules, or other project management tools. The point is to make the timing as concrete as possible so managers can quickly determine whether they are on schedule. Then they use metrics to monitor key performance-related activities and outcomes.

MEASURING WHAT MATTERS: METRICS

Metrics are numerical measures of specific performance-related activities and outcomes used to see whether the organization is moving closer to its objectives and goals. Metrics focus employees on activities that make a difference; set up performance expectations that can be objectively measured; and lay a foundation for internal accountability and pride in accomplishments. The marketing plan need not include metrics for all activities, just those that significantly affect performance. For example, Nationwide Financial monitors customer retention and 11 other metrics to measure progress toward objectives; to reinforce the importance of this system, the firm links management compensation to achieving preset metrics levels.[11]

Practical Planning Tip
Review recent and previous year's metrics measurements when analyzing the current situation.

Metrics must cover activities that are relevant to the mission, as the nonprofit Nature Conservancy found when it reevaluated what it was measuring:

The Nature Conservancy. The mission of the Nature Conservancy is to pre-serve the global diversity of animals and plants by protecting rare species habitats. For decades, the organization measured progress using two metrics: (1) the amount of money raised and (2) the number of acres preserved. By these standards, the Conservancy was performing well: it had increased paid memberships from 28,000 to more than 1 million in less than 30 years, was raising $750 million-plus yearly, and was protecting more than 66 million acres worldwide. Yet these metrics did not reflect progress toward biodiver-sity. After testing dozens of potential metrics, the Conservancy established new measures related to effectiveness in (1) halting extinction threats and preserving biodiversity, (2) launching programs and reaching goals for preservation, and (3) developing the resources and capabilities to carry out its mission. Later it added metrics for good nonprofit governance, in response to questions raised about its finances and transactions.[12]

All kinds of organizations use metrics to track progress toward meeting objec-tives and satisfying external and internal customers. Rear Admiral David Antanitus uses metrics to determine whether U.S. Navy personnel are installing new shipboard computer and communication systems on time, within budget, and in fully functioning condition. Simply tracking the accuracy of system installation drawings, he says, reduced error rates by up to 50%. Today's metrics may not be appropriate for tomorrow, however. "Good metrics also evolve, and by continually measuring the same things, you may be missing new opportunities to improve," he stresses.[13] This illustrates another important point: results should be evaluated using metrics that make sense in the current situation, even if these are not the same metrics chosen during the planning process.[14]

Identifying Metrics

The Nature Conservancy identified its key metrics by working backward from its mission and long-term goals to find specific outcomes and activities that signal progress. Many businesses follow the same reasoning, matching their metrics to long- and short-term objectives. For example, companies pursuing growth need metrics to measure changes in customer relationships and sales. Such metrics might include measurements of customer acquisition, customer retention, cus-tomer defection, customer satisfaction, customer lifetime value, and sales trends by customer or segment.[15]

Consider McDonald's, which knows that the majority of its U.S. restaurant sales come from drive-through orders. Cutting even 6 seconds from drivers' wait-ing time can boost sales by a full percentage point. Although McDonald's recently lowered waiting time to about 157 seconds—a one-year improvement of 6 sec-onds—this metric remains important because the average drivers' wait at rival Wendy's is about 116 seconds.[16]

Metrics that reveal increases in the customer base and customer satisfaction serve as early indicators of future sales performance. Conversely, lower scores on these metrics are warning signs of problems that must be addressed, as Toyota found out:

> **Toyota.** Japan-based Toyota sold 10% more Scion cars in the United States than it forecast for the model's first year. However, according to satisfaction surveys conducted by J.D. Power & Associates, Scion customers lodged 158 complaints per 100 cars—far higher than the industry average of 119 complaints per 100 cars. Although the complaints were minor, Toyota needed to bring the score down as it drove toward its second-year objective of selling 8,000 Scions monthly and, looking ahead, reaching its 2010 goal of capturing 15% of the global car market (with little or no growth in car sales within its home country).[17]

Practical Planning Tip

Remember to include metrics for any programs that span marketing plan periods.

Good performance as measured by customer satisfaction, market share, social responsibility targets, and other nonfinancial metrics sometimes means accepting the trade-off of lower short-term financial performance.[18] In terms of financial outcomes, common metrics are gross or net profit margins for each product and product line, channel, promotion, and price adjustment, among other measures. Exhibit 10.3 shows some sample metrics for a number of marketing plan objectives.

Nonprofits frequently work backward from their objectives to create metrics that quantify periodic results and trends for:

- donations received (metrics such as donations by source and productivity of fundraising by program or source)
- number of people being helped (metrics such as utilization of service by segment or location)
- public image (metrics such as awareness by stakeholder segment and attitude by stakeholder segment)

EXHIBIT 10.3   Sample Metrics for Marketing Plan Objectives

Type of Objective	Sample Metrics
Marketing	• To acquire new customers: Measure number or percentage of new customers acquired by month, quarter, year. • To retain current customers: Measure number or percentage of customers who continue purchasing during a set period. • To increase market share: Measure dollar or unit sales divided by total industry sales during a set period. • To accelerate product development: Measure the time needed to bring a new product to market.
Financial	• To increase sales revenue by product: Measure product sales in dollars per week, month, quarter, or year. • To improve profitability: Measure gross or net margin for a set period by product, line, channel, marketing program, or customer. • To reach break-even: Measure the number of weeks or months until a product's revenue equals and begins to exceed costs.
Societal	• To make products more environmentally-friendly: Measure the proportion of each product's parts that are recyclable or have been recycled during a set period. • To build awareness of a social issue: Research awareness among the target audience after the program or a set period. • To conserve electricity or fuel: Measure amount used by month, quarter, year.

A second way to identify metrics is by looking for key components or activities related to customer buying behavior, using research gathered during the analysis of markets and customers. This means finding measurements that signal customer movement toward a purchase. Once customers start buying, the company can use metrics to measure sales by transaction or by segment, customer or segment purchase frequency, sales by channel or intermediary, and so forth. Exhibit 10.4 presents sample metrics keyed to some basic stages in the buying process (compare with the audience response models in Exhibit 9.2 on page 135).

Businesses that rely on personal selling usually set up metrics to measure the sales pipeline, such as number of prospect inquiries, number of qualified leads generated, number of meetings with qualified leads, number of bids accepted, percentage of prospects converted to customers, and number of orders received. Channel productivity may be judged using metrics such as number or percentage of customers or sales generated per channel or intermediary; cost and profits per sale by channel or intermediary; speed of order fulfillment; and percentage of stock-outs. Of course, the exact metrics depend on each organization's situation and priorities.

Using Metrics

Marketers must find practical ways to measure meaningful outcomes and activities. Not every outcome or activity can be measured, nor is every possible metric actually meaningful. If a company lacks the budget to conduct valid attitudinal research, it cannot use customer attitudes as a metric, for example. Another potential problem is that marketers will simply aim to meet each metrics target without watching the overall effect on strategic outcomes.[19]

EXHIBIT 10.4   Metrics Based on Customer Buying Behavior

Behavior	*Sample Metrics*
Customer becomes aware of a product.	Measure customer awareness of product and competing products, by segment.
Customer learns more about the product.	Measure number of information packets or catalogs requested; number of hits on Web site; number of people who visit store; number who subscribe to e-mail newsletter.
Customer has a positive attitude toward the product.	Measure customer attitudes toward the product and competing products, by segment; feedback from hotlines, letters and e-mail, channel and sales sources, etc.
Customer tries the product.	Measure number of people who receive free samples; number who redeem coupons for trial sizes.
Customer buys the product.	Measure sales by transaction, segment, product, channel, payment method; conversion from trials and information requests.
Customer is satisfied.	Measure customer satisfaction by product and by segment; satisfaction feedback from hotlines, letters and e-mails, channel sources, etc.
Customer becomes loyal.	Measure customer retention; size and frequency of repeat purchases; utilization of frequent buyer program.

The U.S. Small Business Administration Web site offers ideas for start-ups and growing businesses that are planning and implementing marketing plans.

Although metrics start with periodic measurements of marketing plan activities and outcomes, they are most valuable to marketers when viewed in the context of:

- *Expected outcomes.* How do the outcomes measured by metrics compare with the expected outcomes in the marketing plan? If the metric is dollar sales by segment, the marketer will compare actual segment sales over a given period with expected segment sales for that period to evaluate progress.
- *Historical results.* How do the outcomes measured by metrics compare with the actual outcomes in previous periods? Because marketers review previous results as part of their internal environmental analysis, they have the data to weigh current outcomes against previous outcomes, which can reveal unusual trends and suggest possible problems that could affect performance.
- *Competitive or industry outcomes.* How do the outcomes measured by metrics compare with competitors' outcomes or average outcomes for the industry? When comparable competitive or industry information is available, marketers can check these against their own organization's outcomes to gauge relative

performance and reveal strengths and weaknesses. However, marketers must remember that competitors operate under different circumstances and have very different goals, costs, and outcomes, so competitive comparisons are only useful in relative terms.

- *Environmental influences.* How do the outcomes measured by metrics appear in relation to environmental trends, such as an economic boom or a parts shortage? Marketers need to interpret metrics in the context of everything else affecting the organization. If metrics indicate that sales objectives are barely being achieved when an economic boom has dramatically boosted demand, the organization should reevaluate its metrics or create new ones to find out why sales aren't higher still.

Many companies check performance metrics on a monthly basis, although some check weekly and some daily—or more often, when they have access to fresh data and know they can gain or lose a sale at the click of a mouse. Americanas.com, a Brazilian dot-com retailer of electronics and appliances, checks sales data every 20 minutes. If sales are lower than the day's objectives, managers find out which products are selling the slowest, then change some aspect of their marketing—such as posting a new photo of the product or e-mailing customers with a special offer—to boost sales.[20] Remember that metrics are merely tools to track the progress of programs after implementation, nothing more. Management must make decisions and take action when metrics show that the expected results are not being achieved.

Controlling Marketing Plan Implementation

In preparing a marketing plan, marketers need to plan for four types of marketing control: annual plan, profitability, productivity, and strategic control (see Exhibit 10.5). Because marketers generally formulate new marketing plans every year, they need **annual plan** control to assess the progress of the current year's marketing plan. This type of control covers broad performance measures, performance toward meeting marketing plan objectives, and performance toward meeting marketing strategy and program objectives.

EXHIBIT 10.5 Types of Marketing Plan Control

Control	Use
Annual plan control	Gauge the organization's progress toward achieving overall marketing plan objectives and individual program objectives.
Profitability control	Gauge the organization's performance in achieving profit-related objectives through measures such as return on investment, return on equity, return on assets, contribution margin, gross/net profit margin.
Productivity control	Gauge the organization's efficiency in managing the sales force, channels, marketing communications, and products.
Strategic control	Gauge the organization's effectiveness in managing marketing, customer relationships, and social responsibility and ethics.

**Practical
Planning Tip**
You may want to control performance on other financial measures, including costs.

Profitability control assesses the organization's progress and performance based on key profitability measures. The exact measures differ from organization to organization, but often include return on investment (or other return measures), contribution margin, and gross or net profit margin. Many companies measure the monthly and yearly profit-and-loss results of each product, line, and category, as well as each market or segment and each channel. By comparing profitability results over time, marketers can spot significant strengths, weaknesses, threats, and opportunities early enough to make appropriate changes.

Productivity control assesses the organization's performance and progress in managing the efficiency of key marketing areas. Closely related to profitability control, productivity control usually covers the efficiency of the sales force, promotions, channels and logistics, and product management. Productivity is so important to the bottom line that some companies appoint marketing controllers to establish standards, measure performance, and boost marketing efficiency without compromising customer satisfaction or other objectives. Moreover, some companies measure the productivity of their product development and manufacturing activities as well as order fulfillment and other tasks, knowing that behind-the-scenes inefficiencies can damage customer relationships. GlaxoSmithKline applies this type of control to its product development process, bringing new drugs into the pipeline more quickly and screening out low-potential drugs much earlier than in the past.[21]

Strategic control assesses the organization's effectiveness in managing the marketing function, customer relationships, and social responsibility and ethics issues—three areas of strategic importance. Whereas other types of control are applied monthly or more often, strategic control may be applied once or twice a year, or as needed to clarify the organization's performance in these strategic areas. To assess the effectiveness of the marketing function, companies should conduct a yearly **marketing audit**—a detailed, systematic analysis of marketing capabilities and performance (see this chapter's checklist). Auditing the marketing function helps management gauge its strengths, pinpoint areas for improvement, and hold marketing personnel accountable for performance. After an audit is conducted, a summary of the findings should be included in the internal environmental analysis section of the marketing plan.

APPLYING CONTROL

The control process, introduced in Chapter 1, is essential for guiding the implementation of any marketing plan to determine whether programs are working out as planned and give marketers information to make decisions about changing, continuing, or abandoning marketing programs. This assumes that the organization is willing to make changes; despite today's volatile business environment, fewer than 25% of companies responding to a recent survey said they always develop plans for corrective action.[22]

After setting the marketing plan's objectives, marketers set standards and measurement intervals (drawn from marketing plan budgets, forecasts, metrics, and schedules) to measure interim progress. For example, assume that the forecast calls for selling 1,000 units of Product A and the budget assumes an average price of $40. The next step is to periodically measure actual results, then compare them with preset standards to diagnose any variances. In this example, the company might compare actual monthly sales and price results with the forecast and budget standards. It can be helpful to diagnose results in the context of historic, competitive, or industrywide results and research the macro- and microenvironmental issues affecting performance.

The final step is to take corrective action, if necessary, by making adjustments or implementing a contingency plan formulated in advance. One approach is to change the program, the strategy, or the implementation in a bid to achieve the planned results. A second approach is to change the standards or objectives by which performance is measured, appropriate when the variance is not a one-time occurrence and the company understands the underlying influence(s) on performance. Although corrective action is the last step in marketing control, its outcome becomes input for setting or reevaluating objectives at the start of the next control or marketing planning cycle.

PREPARING CONTINGENCY PLANS

Contingency plans are plans that organizations have ready to implement if one (or more) of their original strategies or programs is disrupted by significant, unexpected changes. Hospitals, banks, telecommunications firms, and other organizations that must operate without interruption are especially meticulous about contingency planning. Even so, flexibility and ingenuity are needed, as in PatriotNet's experience:

PatriotNet. This small Internet service provider in Fairfax, Virginia, had a contingency plan for keeping customers informed during emergencies. After a hurricane knocked out power and telephone lines, however, staff members were barred from the office for safety reasons—a development the contingency plan did not anticipate. Nonetheless, the company's systems allowed for off-site operations, so the CEO and her 13 employees all worked from home that day, using cell phones and Web-based phone technology to reroute incoming customer calls and notify customers about the status of their connections. PatriotNet not only maintained good relations with customers during the outage, it fielded a number of sales calls to establish good relations with prospects.[23]

Marketers usually prepare contingency plans showing how their organization will respond in the case of emergencies such as:

- computer systems outages
- prolonged power or telecommunications interruptions
- natural disasters
- sudden bankruptcy of a major customer or supplier
- contamination or other environmental disasters
- sudden technological breakthrough by a competitor
- major failure of a program or strategy
- price war or other extreme competitive development
- significant criminal, sabotage, or terrorist activities

Marketers should formulate contingency plans as they develop their marketing plans, then periodically review and update these plans to be sure they are ready to deal with emergencies. When preparing a contingency plan, think creatively about the organization's options, priorities, and resources to come up with alternatives that minimize the impact of the disruption and allow the organization to recover as quickly as possible. And use the lessons learned from dealing with the emergency as input for analyzing the current situation when preparing the next marketing plan.

Summary

As preparation for implementation, marketing plans typically specify four main tools for measuring performance progress: forecasts, budgets, schedules, and metrics. A forecast is a future projection of what sales and costs are likely to be in the months and years covered by the plan. Most companies forecast by market, segment, product, and channel. Budgets are time-defined allocations of financial outlays for specific functions, programs, customer segments, or geographic region; four budgeting methods are affordability, percentage-of-sales, competitive-parity, and objective-and-task. Schedules are time-defined plans for completing a series of tasks or activities (milestones) related to a program or objective, used to manage marketing plan implementation.

Metrics are numerical measures of performance-related activities and outcomes that marketers apply to determine whether they are moving closer to their objectives. Metrics focus employees on activities that make a difference, set up performance expectations that can be objectively measured, and lay a foundation for internal accountability and pride in accomplishments. Metrics should be examined in the context of expected outcomes, previous results, competitive/industry outcomes, and environmental influences. Organizations use four types of marketing control: annual plan, profitability, productivity, and strategic control (including the marketing audit). If results are disrupted by significant, unexpected changes, the organization should have contingency plans ready for implementation.

Sample Marketing Plan: SonicSuperphone

Sonic, a hypothetical start-up company, is about to introduce a new multifunction cell (mobile) phone handset with unique features and functions. This product is entering a U.S. market crowded with offerings from Nokia, Motorola, Samsung, and numerous other rivals. The following sample marketing plan shows how Sonic is preparing to launch its first product.

Executive Summary

Early next year, Sonic will introduce a new product in the fast-growing but pressured U.S. market for "smart" cell phones. Competing against well-established multinational rivals, we plan to launch a high-quality handset combining a number of useful, innovative features that eliminate the need for users to carry multiple devices. We are targeting specific segments in the consumer and business markets, taking advantage of forecasts indicating accelerated demand for multifunction smart phones.

We will differentiate this first product, the SonicSuperphone, on the basis of innovation and versatile communication, organization, and entertainment capabilities, supported by skimming pricing to emphasize high quality. Among our marketing priorities are building brand awareness among affluent consumers and targeted business customers; reaching specific sales levels; breaking even early in the second year; and operating in an environmentally friendly manner. Sonic's core competencies of technical expertise and efficient assembly procedures will minimize variable costs and enable us to react quickly to market trends and technological advances. For the product's introduction, we will use a push strategy aimed at channel members combined with a pull strategy aimed at customer segments.

Situation Analysis

Sonic was founded 18 months ago by two entrepreneurs with extensive high-tech experience and a creative design for a new smart phone, to be introduced as the SonicSuperphone. The cofounders hold an industry-exclusive license for voice recognition software to manage files, applications, and communication. They also have designed a handset that is compatible with major satellite radio and television systems, another industry breakthrough. As a result, our product's features and functions deliver significantly more benefits than typical camera phones,

FIGURE A1.1 SonicSuperphone Features, Functions, and Benefits	
Feature or Function	*Benefit*
Receive and record broadcasts from satellite radio and TV	Enjoy radio and TV programs anywhere, anytime, without carrying separate gadgets
Take and transmit photos, record 10-minute video snippets	Instantly, easily take and send photos and video on the go
Display live Web cam video input	Monitor home, children, pets in real time through live Web cam video
Voice-activated software and file exchange	Access basic programs and send or receive files using voice commands
Expansion slots for more storage, future functions, third-party devices	Meet individual needs by adding peripherals, video game accessories, storage capacity, more

Web-enabled cell phones, or personal digital assistants (PDAs) with phones (see Figure A1.1).

We will face strong competition: Nokia, Motorola, and Samsung together account for more than 55% of the units sold in the global handset market. Nonetheless, our core competencies in technology and production should provide an important edge (see the SWOT analysis). Moreover, as the following sections explain, the product's launch will be based on favorable market trends; advanced technology; skimming pricing; selective distribution; extensive knowledge of our markets, customers, and competitors; and tight marketing control.

Market Needs and Trends

The SonicSuperphone can meet a wide variety of customer needs, replacing multiple gadgets and enabling consumers and businesspeople to carry only one device. These needs include:

- *Communication.* Stay in touch on the go by voice, e-mail, text messaging, and digital and video images.
- *Manage information.* Receive and access documents and files, make changes or record data, store files, and transmit to home or office systems.
- *Capture images.* Take photos or make video recordings on the spot, to save or transmit to home or office.
- *Receive/record radio and TV.* Listen to the radio, watch television, and record 60 minutes of radio (10 minutes of video) for later playback.
- *Monitor from a remote location.* Watch and listen to what happens in a child's room, at the front or back door, in a pet's enclosure, or in an office without being there.

Within the consumer market, our primary target segment is middle- to upper-income professionals who want one portable device to coordinate their busy schedules, communicate with family and colleagues, monitor home or family security, and occasionally access radio or television. Consumers in this segment are well educated (attended or completed college or graduate school), and have annual household incomes above $75,000. A secondary target segment is young adults, aged 18 to 30, who are early adopters of (and can afford to buy) electronics; this segment will be particularly interested in the SonicSuperphone's entertainment and digital imaging features and the ability to attach video game units or other gadgets.

Within the business market, our primary target segment consists of executives, entrepreneurs, and small business owners who travel, want to access company files and use basic software without a keyboard, need to stay in touch with customers and coworkers, and sometimes need to take photographs or videos on the spur of the moment. Business customers will be particularly interested in the voice-activated software and file exchange feature, although they also may be attracted by the ability to connect a printer or expand functionality with other peripherals. An additional business segment being considered for second-year entry: medical users, doctors and nurses who want to access and update patients' medical records; photograph, video, or remotely monitor patients; and consult reference materials stored in expanded memory.

Sales projections for enhanced handsets show continued increases, with camera phones outpacing all other types (see Figure A1.2). Overall, the market for cell phones is quickly maturing: global sales are expected to increase by slightly more than 7% from 2005 to 2006 and less than 5% from 2006 to 2007. Camera phones remain in the growth stage: global sales are expected to increase by 24% from 2005 to 2006 and by nearly 23% from 2006 to 2007. In contrast, sales of PDA phones are much smaller in absolute terms and projected to grow more slowly. For example, Nokia estimates that business-oriented PDA phones and services will become a $43 billion industry by 2007, yet its own Communicator model has sold only slightly more than 400,000 units since being introduced several years ago.

Other market trends point to positive acceptance of our SonicSuperphone. Digital photo-messaging is extremely popular, with nearly 30 million camera phones sold in the United States during 2004. In general, sales of handsets with digital imaging capabilities exceed sales of conventional digital cameras, encouraging the development of new camera phone accessories, image transfer and exchange services, image storage and organization devices, and other products.

Although we are targeting only the U.S. market at this time, we recognize that global trends may foreshadow domestic trends. For example, in Japan, 80% of the cell phones purchased include cameras, a growing number can record a few minutes of video, and the replacement market is very strong. One new Sony-Ericsson camera phone sold 40,000 units on its first day. If our prelaunch marketing can generate excitement and clearly differentiate the SonicSuperphone from competing handsets, its novelty may very well stimulate similar enthusiasm among consumers and businesspeople here.

FIGURE A1.2	Projected Worldwide Mobile Handset Sales		
	2005	*2006*	*2007*
All cell phones	610 million units	655 million units	685 million units
Camera phones	250 million units	310 million units	380 million units
PDA phones	10 million units	10.5 million units	11 million units

SWOT Analysis

In taking advantage of growth opportunities in the U.S. market, Sonic can build on several powerful strengths, including our license for voice-recognition software (a feature unmatched by competitors at this time), our expertise in video and audio functionality, and our high production efficiency. We expect that some competitors will have voice-recognition systems and television/radio reception/recording systems for handsets within 6 to 12 months; still, our head start should provoke positive brand associations and contribute to strong sales.

Our major weakness is the lack of brand awareness and image; we also lack the financial resources and global sourcing contacts of the largest handset manufacturers. Moreover, the SonicSuperphone will be heavier and larger than competing handsets because of its multifunction capabilities (which we will counter by emphasizing the convenience of a single phone replacing multiple devices). We see opportunities in higher demand for smart phones, wider availability of peripherals and applications, and frequent media coverage of technologies for personal and business use. We see potential threats from intense competition, pressure to keep prices low, and slow adoption of satellite radio, Internet radio, and Web cams (possible clues to acceptance patterns for our SonicSuperphone). Figure A1.3 summarizes these strengths, weaknesses, opportunities, and threats.

Competition

On the broadest level, our SonicSuperphone will compete with all handsets available in the United States. In particular, our main competitors will be the three industry giants (see Figure A1.4 for market share analysis), plus other well-known multinationals that make camera phones and smart phones for U.S. markets. These competitors have formidable global resources, high brand recognition, and extensive experience in product development and management. Nokia and Motorola introduce as many as 40 new handsets every year; Samsung has launched up to 150 new handsets in a year, with an average price perhaps 30% higher than Motorola's average handset price. Moreover, major competitors benefit from their economies

FIGURE A1.3   SWOT Analysis for SonicSuperphone

Strengths (internal capabilities that support achievement of objectives)	Weaknesses (internal factors that might prevent achievement of objectives)
• Exclusive license for voice recognition • Expertise in TV and radio compatibility • Production quality, efficiency	• Lack of brand awareness and image • Heavier, larger unit than competing models • More limited resources than competitors
Opportunities (external circumstances that may be exploited to achieve objectives)	Threats (external circumstances that might interfere with achievement of objectives)
• Increasing demand for smart phones • Availability of peripherals, applications • Media interest in technologies for everyday use	• Intense competition • Downward pricing pressure • Low penetration of satellite radio, Web cams

FIGURE A1.4 Estimated Market Share Analysis	
Competitor	*Current Share (estimated by units)*
Nokia	30%
Motorola	15%
Samsung	11%

of scale: Nokia's gross profit margin is above 20%, Samsung's is about 18%, and Motorola's is below 10%.

The SonicSuperphone will be the first U.S. handset equipped for radio and television reception and recording. This competitive advantage will help establish our brand and support an image of innovation. We estimate that competitors will add entertainment features to their U.S. handsets within the next 12 months. Nokia, Motorola, and Siemens are currently working to incorporate licensed technology for compressing television signals for handset viewing; a new Samsung handset in Asia can tune into 40 satellite television stations. Some handsets allow voice-recognition dialing but none offers voice-activated file access, storage, and transmission—a feature of our handset that should appeal to business customers in particular.

Critical Issues and Environmental Factors

One issue critical to our success is proper promotion of the voice-recognition system that Sonic has licensed. Potential buyers may be skeptical that a handset can recognize and act on their verbal commands to access, open, change, save, and send files. Therefore, we will join with the software firm to demonstrate the benefits of voice activation through a public relations campaign. Also, we will launch a product-specific radio advertising campaign featuring celebrities voicing a variety of commands as the SonicSuperphone responds. Our magazine campaign will show how quickly SonicSuperphone users can accomplish tasks using voice recognition. Finally, we will give SonicSuperphones to certain opinion leaders as a way of stimulating positive word-of-mouth communication.

Another critical issue is how quickly the SonicSuperphone's radio/television reception and recording features will gain acceptance, in light of the slow growth of satellite and Internet radio. Satellite radio gained approximately 2 million subscribers in its first 3 years but rapid growth is expected as additional content becomes available, in part because federal regulations governing satellite radio differ from those governing broadcast radio. The Internet radio audience is also relatively small, with an estimated 38 million listeners tuning in at least once a month. Variety is one draw; the ability to tune to out-of-town stations is another. We will research the attitudes, motivations, and behavior of these audiences and apply the insights to smart phone marketing.

Macroenvironmental factors likely to affect Sonic include demographics (such as trends in household income); economic issues (such as the purchasing power of targeted segments); technology (such as faster development of portable entertainment systems); laws and regulations (such as government rules governing telecommunications, radio, and television); ecological concerns (such as being able to recycle product parts); and cultural trends (including the popularity of mobile entertainment electronics).

Microenvironmental factors likely to affect Sonic include suppliers (especially our industry-exclusive license for voice recognition); marketing intermediaries (such as relations with retailers and with phone, television, and radio service providers); competitors (mainly from the big three firms); and customers (including their perceptions of the SonicSuperphone and voice-activated information management).

Marketing Strategy

SonicSuperphone's positioning will be based on superior innovation, high quality, and status. We will segment our consumer and business markets using demographic factors such as income, behavior, and benefits sought. Through differentiated marketing, we will target selected segments for initial entry and add secondary segments (such as medical users) later.

Using all elements of the marketing mix, supported by service and internal marketing, we will educate the market about our product's features and benefits to motivate purchases by first-time users as well as consumers and businesspeople who switch from competing handsets. Although television advertising is not affordable in our start-up situation, we will use creative radio, magazine, online, and other media to reach targeted segments. Skimming pricing will reflect our positioning consistent with the high-end brand image we seek to create.

MISSION, DIRECTION, AND OBJECTIVES

Sonic's mission is to make innovative electronics that help consumers and businesspeople become more productive, connected, informed, and entertained in their daily lives. We will pursue rapid growth through the achievement of the following objectives:

- *Marketing objectives:* to achieve first-year unit sales volume of 240,000; to gain 40% brand awareness among targeted consumer segments and 50% among targeted business segments by the end of next year; to establish strong channel relationships with upscale retailers and major phone service carriers within 90 days.
- *Financial objectives:* to restrict first-year losses on the SonicSuperphone to less than $10 million; to reach the break-even point within 18 months of introduction; to earn an annual ROI of 15% within the first 4 years.
- *Societal objectives:* to earn the U.S. government's Energy Star designation for power efficiency by the time of introduction; to recycle 25% of the product's parts after its useful life is over; to build community relations by offering deeply discounted SonicSuperphones to nonprofit organizations and charitable groups.

PRODUCT STRATEGY

As shown in Figure A1.1, our product will have features and functions that deliver a number of benefits highly valued by the targeted segments. Some of these features are exclusive to our initial model, although competitors may be able to match this offering within 6–12 months. We are partnering with a major accessories manufacturer to provide a full line of SonicSuperphone branded accessories. All products carrying our brand must meet rigorous quality and technical standards, as verified by an independent testing laboratory. Moreover, power supply components will have to be more efficient than competing models, offering the dual benefits of longer use when charged and minimal environmental impact.

Depending on market needs, competitive pressure, and demand, we will lengthen the product line by introducing a GPS-enabled model within 18 months of launching our first model. This new product will reinforce our innovation positioning, retain customers (especially businesspeople) who want to trade up to more features, and support longer-term market-share objectives. It also will solidify channel relationships and satisfy additional needs of certain targeted segments. In addition, we are interviewing designers as we decide whether to create limited-edition fashion handsets soon after our first model is introduced.

The SonicSuperphone brand name will be presented in lettering suggesting speed, linked with a stylized, iridescent lightning bolt logo on the product and all accessories, store displays, Web pages, and other communications. We will co-brand models sold through our phone service providers, to show channel support and reinforce customer recognition. All brand elements will be carefully coordinated to contribute to salience, distinctiveness, and image.

(In an actual marketing plan, the product strategy section would include more information about branding, product design and features, packaging and labeling, product compatibility, and other details. Such information is not included in this sample plan.)

PRICING STRATEGY

Our financial pricing objectives are to achieve profitability within 18 months of introducing the new product and achieve second year ROI of 12%. We aim to hold first-year losses at $10 million or less, including product development and production expenses as well as IMC and channel costs related to the introduction. We will use a skimming pricing strategy to support an image of innovation and high quality: the first SonicSuperphone model will carry an average wholesale price of $375 and an average retail price of $500. Thus, first-year revenues are projected to be $90 million based on sales of 240,000 units.

Typically, multifunction phones are priced above $300; customers perceive high value in the additional benefits of these full-featured products and our targeted segments are less price-sensitive with regard to leading-edge technology. Still, product prices and features vary widely, as this brief competitive sample indicates:

- *Nokia 6600* ($450 retail) features 2x zoom digital camera, video recording and video streaming, color display, PDA functionality, wireless Web browsing.
- *Samsung i500* ($600 retail) has Palm-compatible PDA features, separate touch-screen and pad for handwriting recognition, wireless Web browsing, color display.
- *Motorola MPx200* ($300 retail) is a flip-phone with PDA organizing features, e-mail and Web browsing capabilities, audio and video player, and long battery life.
- *Sony P900* ($800 retail) is a flip-phone with large screen, PDA organizing features, Web browser, video and audio players, wireless connections but no camera flash.

- *Toshiba PCS Vision Video Phone VM4050* ($330 retail) has excellent screen resolution, built-in camera with flash, 15 seconds of video recording, and speakerphone functions.

Our research shows that customers who pay for a smart phone with service bundle are more likely to remain loyal. Therefore, we are researching optimal price points for bundling the SonicSuperphone with subscriptions to satellite radio services, satellite television services, and various phone/wireless services.

(In an actual marketing plan, the pricing strategy section would include more information about the expected break-even volume, fixed and variable costs, pricing by channel, promotional pricing, segment price sensitivity, competitive pricing, and other details. Such information is not shown in this sample plan.)

PROMOTION STRATEGY

Two marketing objectives for our promotion strategy are to generate 40% brand awareness within the consumer target market and 50% brand awareness within the business target market by the end of next year. To achieve these objectives, we will create a multimedia brand-building campaign that differentiates the product from competing handsets. We also will use trade sales promotion to support our distribution strategy and hold high-profile launch events to generate publicity and media coverage in consumer media. Through our catalog partners, we will deliver customized direct marketing packages to prospects with a specific demographic and behavioral profile. Highlights of our initial 6-month promotion activities are shown in Figure A1.5.

We will soon begin pretesting message and creative elements for specific target audiences. During the launch period, we will advertise in magazines such as *Forbes FYI* to reach high-income consumers and business segments and use cooperative advertising to have the SonicSuperphone featured in upscale catalogs and on retailers' Web sites. We are fine-tuning our media plan to deal with clutter, competitive advertising, and audience fragmentation. In addition, we are working with channel partners to develop policies for communicating pricing by market.

(In an actual marketing plan, the promotion strategy section would include more information about integrating messages and media, specific tools to be used, and communication programs. Such information is not shown in this sample plan.)

CHANNEL STRATEGY

Consistent with skimming pricing and our high-quality image, we are using selective distribution to market the SonicSuperphone through two main channels. The first consists of upscale catalog/online/store retailers such as Hammacher Schlemmer, Brookstone, Sharper Image, and Skymall. These retailers have extensive customer databases that we can leverage for customized, product-specific direct marketing promotions; they also are known for good customer service and speedy order fulfillment.

The second channel consists of cell phone service providers. We have reached agreement to offer the initial model through Verizon, which gives us access to their stores in major markets and opportunities for co-branded promotions. Soon we expect to have agreements with two other phone service providers and with radio and television satellite services.

Although channel costs are a factor, we have decided to emphasize customer service and logistical efficiency. Channel partners will access a secure extranet to

FIGURE A1.5	Highlights of IMC Activities
Month	*Activity*
January	• Start trade campaign to educate channel partners for push strategy supporting product launch. • Give SonicSuperphones to selected product reviewers, opinion leaders, media representatives, and celebrities as part of public relations strategy. • Train sales personnel to explain Sonic's features, benefits, and competitive advantages. • Post product preview information on company and retailer Web sites. • With phone service providers, plan sales activities targeting businesspeople. • With satellite radio and television firms, plan sales activities targeting consumers.
February	• Begin integrated print/radio/Internet push campaign targeting professionals, businesspeople, affluent consumers. • Distribute point-of-sale materials and schedule in-store demonstrations. • Through catalog retailers, send direct mail packages to high-potential prospects. • Hold a launch party to spark media coverage and buzz.
March	• Rotate messages as consumer advertising campaign continues. • Add sales promotions such as discounting accessories to encourage switching from competing handsets. • Distribute new in-store displays. • Arrange targeted e-mail promotions through retail partners.
April	• Announce trade sales contest for May-June. • Launch a trade campaign focusing on May-June sales opportunities. • Temporarily reduce frequency of consumer ad messages.
May	• Roll out new radio commercials and print ads featuring celebrities using the SonicSuperphone. • Send retailers display blow-ups of new print ads.
June	• Exhibit at semiannual electronics industry show. • Provide channel partners with new feature/benefit sales aids. • With retailers, plan year-end holiday promotions and sales contests.

place orders, track shipments, and handle other functions. Our suppliers will have sufficient parts and components ready for peak production periods, and our flow of goods will ensure proper inventory levels during the introduction. On the other hand, we cannot have excess inventory due to the threat of technological obsolescence.

(An actual marketing plan would include more information about channel functions, criteria for selection and evaluation, customer requirements, competitors' channel strategies, and other details. Such information is not shown in this sample plan.)

SERVICE AND INTERNAL MARKETING

As part of our customer service strategy, the SonicSuperphone will carry a 1-year warranty on parts and labor. Repairs will be handled by a nationwide firm whose technicians have been trained by our engineers. We will receive weekly reports so we can pinpoint any problems to be addressed through manufacturing or design adjustments. To ensure that customers receive the expected level of warranty service, we will conduct quarterly customer satisfaction surveys.

Sonic will provide comprehensive training and point-of-sale service for channel partners. Customers and retailers will be able to obtain service support 24 hours a day, 7 days a week, on the Web, on a toll-free hotline, or by pressing the "Service" button on the SonicSuperphone. Because we are establishing a new brand, we have high service standards and will measure results to ensure that we consistently meet those standards. We will survey a sample of customers monthly and annually to track satisfaction and plan improvements. To build internal support and improve product and customer knowledge, our internal marketing activities will include monthly staff meetings; weekly e-mail bulletins; beta-testing by staff and channel members; coordination of marketing and production schedules; and recognition rewards for meeting sales and customer satisfaction objectives.

Marketing Research

Sonic's use of marketing research includes:

- *Product development.* Through concept testing, surveys, focus groups, and market tests, we have identified the features and benefits that targeted segments most value in enhanced phones and related electronics. We are collecting additional data on usability, quality and value perceptions, and new features of interest to medical users.
- *Integrated marketing communication.* We plan to measure brand awareness before, during, and after our campaigns to determine the effectiveness of each medium in reaching the targeted audience and stimulating the desired response. We also want to analyze customers' attitudes toward competitors' campaigns and learn how customers receive and interpret our messages so we can refine promotions for more impact.
- *Customer satisfaction.* We are planning comprehensive studies to gauge customer satisfaction and identify product defects or other issues that require immediate attention. We will also solicit feedback from retail partners and phone service providers.

Financials and Forecasts

Total first-year revenue for the SonicSuperphone is projected at $90 million, based on sales of 240,000 units at an average wholesale price of $375. We anticipate first-quarter sales of $18 million, second-quarter sales of $22 million, third-quarter sales of $21 million, and fourth-quarter sales of $29 million. These projections assume cumulatively higher business sales and a spike in year-end consumer sales. Figure A1.6 shows unit forecasts by market and channel.

Heavy investments in product development, promotion, and channel support will mean a first-year loss of up to $10 million. However, we should reach the break-even point of 267,500 units early in the second year, a realistic objective given the narrow margins in this market. Once we introduce a second model, we plan to lower the wholesale price of the first model—in line with standard industry practice—to lower the retail price and increase sales volume. Our first-year marketing budgets cover advertising, sales materials, point-of-purchase displays, con-

FIGURE A1.6 First-Year Sales Forecasts	
By Market	*Unit Sales*
Consumer	88,000
Business	152,000
Total	240,000
By Channel	*Unit Sales*
Catalog/online/store retailers	180,000
Phone service carrier(s)	60,000
Total	240,000

sumer and trade sales promotions, public relations, online marketing, channel costs, travel, marketing research, sales training and support, shipping, and customer service support.

(In an actual marketing plan, each action program would carry its own financial assumptions, management assignments, and schedules. The full marketing plan also would include a detailed profit and loss analysis; month-by-month forecasts by product and channel; and summary and detailed budgets by program and activity, market/segment, region, and manager. None of these are shown in this sample plan.)

Performance and Control

We plan stringent control activities to monitor quality and customer service satisfaction so we can respond immediately to any problems. We also are monitoring customer service communications to detect any early signs of customer concern or confusion. Other metrics to be monitored include monthly sales (to gauge progress toward revenue and unit sales objectives), monthly costs (to gauge progress toward the break-even point), quarterly awareness levels (to gauge progress toward brand awareness targets), monthly sales by channel (to gauge progress in channel relationships), and the number of nonprofits making special purchases (to gauge progress toward community relations objectives). In addition, we are tightly controlling schedules to ensure timely implementation.

A contingency plan also has been developed to deal with severe downward pricing pressure on enhanced handsets. This may occur if a major competitor initiates a price war or develops a lower-cost technology. Our contingency plan calls for introducing a significant but short-term price promotion such as a rebate to remain competitive while gauging the price sensitivity of different segments. Based on the outcome of this short-term promotion, we would revise the marketing plan as necessary to defend market share while retaining a minimally acceptable level of profitability.

(An actual marketing plan would include detailed schedules and management assignments by program and activity. For control purposes, the plan also would allow for month-by-month comparison of actual versus projected sales and expenses; it would also summarize any contingency plans. None of these are shown in this sample plan.)

Sources for Appendix 1

Some background information for the fictional sample plan was adapted from: Brad Stone, "Your Next Computer," *Newsweek,* June 7, 2004, pp. 51+; Andy Reinhardt, "Can Nokia Get the Wow Back?" *BusinessWeek,* Mary 31, 2004, pp. 48–50; "A Few Who Got Us Here," *Newsweek,* June 7, 2004, pp. 74+; "Mobile Snaps," *The Economist,* July 5, 2003, p. 59; Leigh Gallagher, "Pix Populi," *Forbes,* March 15, 2004, pp. 156–157; Andy Reinhardt, "The Camera Phone Revolution," *BusinessWeek,* April 12, 2004, p. 52; Clive Thompson, "Remote Possibilities," *New York Times Magazine,* November 16, 2003, pp. 80–82; Andy Reinhardt, "Can Nokia Capture Mobile Workers?" *BusinessWeek,* February 9, 2004, p. 80; Cindy Kano, "Office Noa," *Fortune,* May 17, 2004, p. 148; Peter Lewis, "The PDA Ain't Dead Yet," *Fortune,* May 17, 2004, p. 56; Jonathan Roubini, "The Best Phone on the Market?" and "Sony's Pricey PDA/Phone Combo," *PC Magazine,* May 4, 2004, p. 45; "Battling for the Palm of Your Hand," *The Economist,* May 1, 2004, pp. 71–74; Peter Kafka, "Buy My Internet Radio, Please," *Forbes.com,* June 3, 2004, www.forbes.com; Lisa Haarlander, "Satellite Radio in Cars May Be Next Big Must-Have Technology," *Buffalo News,* May 17, 2004, www.buffalonews.com; Barbara Rose, "Samsung Gains Ground on Motorola in Cell Phone Sales," *Chicago Tribune,* March 7, 2004, www.chicago.tribune.com.

2

Documenting a Marketing Plan with *Marketing Plan Pro* Software

Introduction to *Marketing Plan Pro*

The *Marketing Plan Pro* software bundled with this handbook helps you document your marketing plan through a structured yet flexible framework for customizing both contents and presentation. As you set up a new plan, the software asks a series of questions about your product, organization, and planning needs. Based on your responses, it selects and presents appropriate sections for you to complete. You can take advantage of built-in templates to create spreadsheets, tables, and charts; import images or insert hyperlinks; adjust page formats; and add color. When the plan is complete, you can print it, translate it into a read-only document, export it to other programs, or export it for posting on the Web.

In addition, you can use *Marketing Plan Pro* to examine dozens of sample marketing plans showing how manufacturers, service businesses, consulting firms, startups, and nonprofit groups approach the wide variety of issues, opportunities, threats, and choices they face. Each plan follows a similar structure, so you can easily compare and contrast their contents to see how marketing priorities, strategies, activities, and budgets differ from one organization to another. Simply browsing these samples may spark new avenues to explore while formulating your own marketing plan.

Using *Marketing Plan Pro*

If you establish the basic structure of your marketing plan before you finish Chapter 2, you'll be ready to document the results of your environmental scanning and analysis. Launch the software, click to create a new plan, and answer the questions to tailor the plan's setup. Your responses will prompt *Marketing Plan Pro* to include the specific sections you'll need and eliminate those that are unnecessary for your marketing circumstances.

Now you're ready to begin writing. Here are the sections to complete as you read each chapter in this handbook:

- *Chapter 2.* Your company; SWOT analysis; situation summary.
- *Chapter 3.* Market analysis; growth and share analysis; market research.
- *Chapter 4.* Market analysis; target marketing; positioning.
- *Chapter 5.* Objectives; service.
- *Chapter 6.* What you're selling; product strategy; Strategy Pyramid.
- *Chapter 7.* Channels; place strategy; Strategy Pyramid.
- *Chapter 8.* Pricing strategy; break-even analysis; Strategy Pyramid.
- *Chapter 9.* Promotion strategy; Strategy Pyramid.
- *Chapter 10.* Sales forecast; budgets analysis; implementation and controls.

While formulating your plan, you may need to insert additional topics as well as explanatory tables, charts, spreadsheets, and other extras, depending on your product and organization. Once you've drafted the body of the plan, the last sections you'll write are the summaries, ending with the executive summary. Finally, take time to review your plan, check the information on the cover page and table of contents, and then print or export it.

For more information and technical support, see the Prentice Hall page on Palo Alto Software's Web site (www.paloalto.com/prenticehall) or the *Marketing Plan Pro* support page (http://www.paloalto.com/su/mp).

Glossary

affordability budgeting Method in which companies budget for marketing based on what they believe they can afford. (Chapter 10)

annual plan control Type of marketing control used to assess the progress and performance of the current year's marketing plan. (Chapter 10)

attitudes An individual's lasting evaluations of and feelings toward something. (Chapter 3)

B2B marketing Business-to-business marketing (Chapter 1)

benefits Need–satisfaction outcomes customers desire from the product. (Chapter 6)

brand equity Extra value perceived in a brand that enhances long-term loyalty among customers. (Chapter 6)

brand extension Putting an established brand on a new product in a different category, aimed at a new customer segment; also known as *category extension*. (Chapter 6)

branding Using words, designs, or symbols to give a product a distinct identity and differentiate it from competing products. (Chapter 6)

break-even point Point at which revenues cover costs and beyond which the product becomes profitable. (Chapter 8)

budget Time-defined allocation of financial outlays for a specific function or program. (Chapter 10)

business market Companies, nonprofit organizations, and institutions that buy products for operations or as supplies for production; also known as the *organizational market.* (Chapter 3)

cannibalization Allowing a new product to cut into sales of one or more existing products. (Chapter 6)

cause-related marketing Marketing a product or brand through a link to benefiting a charitable cause. (Chapter 5)

channel The set of functions and structure of organizations performing them outbound on the value chain to make a particular good or service available to customers in each market; also known as the *distribution channel.* (Chapter 7)

competitive-parity budgeting Method in which company creates a budget by matching what competitors spend, as a percentage of sales or a specific dollar amount. (Chapter 10)

concentrated marketing Focusing one marketing strategy on one attractive market segment. (Chapter 4)

consumer market Individuals and families that buy products for themselves. (Chapter 3)

contingency plan Plan that is ready to implement if significant, unexpected changes in the situation disrupt one (or more) of the organization's strategies or programs. (Chapter 10)

core competencies The set of skills, technologies, and processes that allow a company to effectively and efficiently satisfy its customers. (Chapter 1)

cost leadership strategy Generic competitive strategy in which the company seeks to become the lowest-cost producer in its industry. (Chapter 2)

customer churn Turnover in customers during a specific period; often expressed as a percentage of the organization's total customer base. (Chapter 6)

customer lifetime value Total amount a customer spends with a company over the course of a long-term relationship. (Chapter 6)

derived demand In B2B marketing, the principle that demand for a business product is based on demand for a related consumer product. (Chapter 3)

differentiated marketing Creating a separate marketing strategy for each targeted segment. (Chapter 4)

differentiation strategy Generic competitive strategy in which the company creates a unique differentiation for itself or its product based on some factor prized by the target market. (Chapter 2)

diversification Growth strategy of offering new products to new markets through internal product development capabilities or by starting (or buying) a business for diversification purposes. (Chapter 5)

dynamic pricing Prices vary from customer to customer or situation to situation. (Chapter 8)

emotional appeal Message strategy that relies on feelings rather than facts to motivate audience response. (Chapter 9)

ethnographic research Type of marketing research in which customers are observed in actual product purchase or usage situations (Chapter 3)

features Specific attributes that enable the product to perform its function. (Chapter 6)

financial objectives Targets for performance in managing specific financial results. (Chapter 5)

fixed pricing Pricing that does not vary; the customer pays the price set by the marketer. (Chapter 8)

focus strategy Generic competitive strategy in which the company narrows its competitive scope to achieve a competitive advantage in its chosen segments. (Chapter 2)

forecast Future projection of what sales and costs are likely to be in the period covered by the plan. (Chapter 10)

frequency How many times, on average, the target audience is exposed to the message during a given period. (Chapter 9)

goals Longer-term performance targets for the organization or a particular unit. (Chapter 1)

integrated marketing communication Coordinating content and delivery so all marketing messages are consistent and support the positioning and direction in the marketing plan. (Chapter 9)

internal marketing Marketing that targets managers and employees inside the organization to support the marketing mix in the marketing plan. (Chapter 5)

lifestyle The pattern of living that an individual exhibits through activities and interests. (Chapter 3)

line extension Putting an established brand on a new product added to the existing product line. (Chapter 6)

logistics Managing the movement of goods, services, and related information from the point of origin to the point of sale or consumption and balancing the level of service with the cost. (Chapter 7)

macroenvironment Largely uncontrollable external elements that can potentially influence the ability to reach goals; these include demographic, economic, ecological, technological, political-legal, and social-cultural forces. (Chapter 2)

market All the potential buyers for a particular product. (Chapter 3)

market development Growth strategy in which the company identifies and taps new segments or markets for existing products. (Chapter 5)

market penetration Growth strategy in which the company sells more of its existing products to customers in existing markets or segments. (Chapter 5)

market segmentation Grouping customers within a market according to similar needs, habits, or attitudes that can be addressed through marketing. (Chapter 4)

market share The percentage of sales in a given market held by a particular company, brand, or product; can be calculated in dollars or units. (Chapter 3)

marketing audit A detailed, systematic analysis of an organization's marketing capabilities and performance. (Chapter 10)

marketing control The process of setting goals and standards, measuring and diagnosing results, and taking corrective action when needed to keep marketing plan performance on track. (Chapter 1)

marketing objectives Targets for performance in managing specific marketing relationships and activities. (Chapter 5)

marketing plan A document that summarizes marketplace knowledge and the strategies and steps to be taken in achieving the objectives set by marketing managers for a particular period. (Chapter 1)

marketing planning The process of researching and analyzing the market and situation and developing marketing objectives, goals, strategies, and plans that are appropriate for the organization's resources, competencies, mission, and objectives. (Chapter 1)

mass customization Creating products, on a large scale, with features tailored to individual customers. (Chapter 6)

metrics Numerical measures of specific performance-related activities and outcomes. (Chapter 10)

microenvironment Groups that have a more direct effect on the organization's ability to reach its goals: customers, competitors, channel members, partners, suppliers, and employees. (Chapter 2)

mission Statement of the organization's fundamental purpose, its focus, and how it will add value for customers and other stakeholders. (Chapter 2)

motivation   What drives the consumer to satisfy needs and wants. (Chapter 3)

niche   Smaller segment within a market that exhibits distinct needs or benefit requirements. (Chapter 4)

objective-and-task budgeting   Method in which budget is determined by totaling the cost of all marketing tasks needed to achieve the marketing mix objectives and marketing plan objectives. (Chapter 10)

objectives   Shorter-term performance targets that support the achievement of an organization's or unit's goals. (Chapter 1)

penetration pricing   Pricing a product relatively low to gain market share rapidly. (Chapter 8)

percentage-of-sales budgeting   Method in which company allocates a certain percentage of sales revenues to fund marketing programs. (Chapter 10)

perception   How the individual organizes environmental inputs such as ads and derives meaning from the data. (Chapter 3)

positioning   Using marketing to create a distinctive place or image for a brand or product in the mind of customers. (Chapter 1)

price elasticity of demand   Percentage change in unit sales of demand divided by the percentage change in price; where customers are price-sensitive and demand changes considerably due to small price changes, the demand is elastic. (Chapter 8)

primary research   Research conducted specifically to address a certain situation or answer a particular question. (Chapter 3)

product development   Growth strategy in which the company sells new products to customers in existing markets or segments. (Chapter 5)

product life cycle   The stages of introduction, growth, maturity, and decline through which a product moves in the marketplace. (Chapter 6)

product line   Group of products made by one company that are related in some way. (Chapter 6)

product mix   Assortment of all the product lines marketed by one company. (Chapter 6)

productivity control   Type of marketing control used to assess the organization's performance and progress in managing the efficiency of key marketing areas. (Chapter 10)

profitability control   Type of marketing control used to assess the organization's progress and performance based on profitability measures. (Chapter 10)

psychographic characteristics   Variables used to analyze consumer lifestyle patterns. (Chapter 3)

pull strategy   Using marketing to encourage customers to ask intermediaries for the product, thereby pulling it through the channel. (Chapter 9)

push strategy   Using marketing to encourage channel members to stock the product, thereby pushing it through the channel to customers. (Chapter 9)

quality   How well the product satisfies customer needs. (Chapter 6)

rational appeal   Message strategy that relies on facts or logic to motivate audience response. (Chapter 9)

reach   How many people in the target audience are exposed to the message during a particular period. (Chapter 9)

schedule   Time-defined plan for completing work that relates to a specific purpose or program. (Chapter 10)

secondary research   Research data already gathered for another purpose. (Chapter 3)

segments   Groups within a market having distinct needs or characteristics that can be effectively addressed by specific marketing offers and programs. (Chapter 1)

service recovery   How an organization plans to recover from a service lapse and satisfy its customers (Chapter 5)

skimming pricing   Pricing a new product high to establish an image and more quickly recover development costs in line with profitability objectives. (Chapter 8)

societal objectives   Targets for achieving specific results in social responsibility. (Chapter 5)

stakeholders   People and organizations that are influenced by or that can influence an organization's performance. (Chapter 1)

strategic control   Type of marketing control used to assess the organization's performance and progress in the strategic areas of marketing effectiveness, customer relationship management, and social responsibility and ethics. (Chapter 10)

subcultures   Distinct groups within a larger culture that exhibit and preserve distinct cultural identities through a common religion, nationality, ethnic background, or lifestyle. (Chapter 3)

sustainable marketing   Forming, maintaining, and enhancing customer relationships to meet all parties' objectives without compromising the achievement of future generations' objectives. (Chapter 1)

SWOT analysis   Summary of an organization's strengths, weaknesses, opportunities, and threats in preparation for marketing planning. (Chapter 2)

target costing   Using research to determine what customers want in a product and the price they will pay, then finding ways of producing the product at a cost that will accommodate that price and return a profit. (Chapter 8)

target market   Segment of the overall market that a company chooses to pursue. (Chapter 4)

targeting   Decisions about which market segments to enter and in what order, and how to use marketing in each. (Chapter 1)

undifferentiated marketing   Targeting all market segments with the same marketing strategy. (Chapter 4)

value   The difference between total benefits and total costs, as perceived by customers. (Chapter 1)

value chain   The series of interrelated, value-added functions and the structure of organizations that perform these functions to get the right product to the right markets and customers at the right time, place, and price; also known as *supply chain.* (Chapter 7)

value-based pricing   Setting prices by starting with customers' perspective of the product's value and the price they are willing to pay, then working backward to make the product at a cost that will also meet the company's objectives. (Chapter 8)

word-of-mouth communication   People telling other people about an organization, a brand, a product, or a marketing message. (Chapter 9)

References

CHAPTER 1

1. Tara Weiss, "Netflix Online Rental Service Gains Popularity . . ." *Hartford Courant,* February 23, 2004, www.ctnow.com; Paul Sweeting, "Netflix Out to Conquer New Worlds," *Video Business,* January 26, 2004, pp. 1+; Christopher Null, "How Netflix Is Fixing Hollywood," *Business 2.0,* July 2003, pp. 41–43.
2. "Nestlé's Marketing Crisis," *Marketing,* February 19, 2004, pp. 24+; "Selling to the Developing World," *The Economist,* December 13, 2003, p. 8; Amie Smith Hughes, "Home Improvement," *Promo,* September 1, 2003, n.p.; "Nestlé: A Dedicated Enemy of Fashion," *The Economist,* August 31, 2002, pp. 47–48.
3. Sir George Bull, "What Does the Term Marketing Really Stand for?" *Marketing,* November 30, 2000, p. 30.
4. David Pringle, "Nokia Takes Leap into Wi-Fi Arena with New Phone," *Wall Street Journal,* February 23, 2004, p. B4; Justin Fox, "Nokia's Secret Code," *Fortune,* May 1, 2000, pp. 160+.
5. Jerry Flint, "Fallacy of the Niche Car," *Forbes,* March 1, 2004, p. 76; David Wethe, "Car Dealerships Face the Great Homogenization," *New York Times,* January 11, 2004, Sec. 3, p. 4.
6. Stanley Holmes, "Starbucks Waltzes Into Music," *BusinessWeek,* March 22, 2004, p. 13; Andy Serwer, "Starbucks: Hot to Go," *Fortune,* January 26, 2004, pp. 60+; Cora Daniels, "Mr. Coffee," *Fortune,* April 14, 2003, pp. 139+.
7. Wailin Wong, "Coke Takes Swig of Argentine Drink," *Wall Street Journal,* November 26, 2003, p. B3B; Julie Creswell and Julie Schlosser, "Has Coke Lost Its Fizz?" *Fortune,* November 10, 2003, pp. 215+; Gerry Khermouch and Diane Brady, "Brands in an Age of Anti-Americanism," *BusinessWeek,* August 4, 2003, pp. 69+.
8. "Sony Corp.," *Wall Street Journal,* May 20, 2004, p. 1; Ken Belson, "As Newcomers Swarm, Sony Girds for a Fight," *New York Times,* February 8, 2004, Sec. 3, p. 4; Bolaji Ojo, "Sony, Matsushita Slash Supply Base to Cut Costs," *EBN,* August 23, 2003, p. 1.
9. Stephanie Balzer, "Suns Search for Fan Rebound," *Phoenix Business Journal,* May 4, 2001, p. 3.
10. Kate Murphy, "Catering to a Love Affair with the Past," *New York Times,* December 28, 2003, Sec. 3, p. 4.
11. Martin Fackler, "Will Ratatouille Bring Japanese to McDonald's?" *Wall Street Journal,* August 14, 2003, pp. B1, B5; Khermouch and Brady, "Brands in an Age of Anti-Americanism."
12. Jeanette Borzo, "Get the Picture," *Wall Street Journal Europe,* January 16, 2004, pp. R2+; George Anders, "Why Real-Time Business Takes Real Time," *Fast Company,* July 2001, pp. 158–161.

13. Kevin J. Clancy and Peter C. Krieg, *Counterintuitive Marketing* (New York: Free Press, 2000), pp. 199–201.

14. Gail Edmondson, "Toyota's New Traction in Europe," *BusinessWeek,* June 7, 2004, p. 64; Robert Salladay, "Hybrids Move Closer to Using Carpool Lanes," *Los Angeles Times,* May 7, 2004, p. B1; David Welch, "Not Your Father's . . . Whatever," *BusinessWeek,* March 15, 2004, pp. 82–83.

15. Elizabeth Olson, "Dot-Com Survivor Hits on Right Plan," *New York Times,* February 5, 2004, p. C6.

16. Susan Chandler, "Designers Find Their Target," *News-Times* (Danbury, CT), September 4, 2001, p. C8; www.target.com.

17. See Philip Kotler and Kevin Lane Keller, *Marketing Management* 12e (Upper Saddle River, N.J.: Prentice Hall, 2006), Chapter 2; and Alan R. Andreasen and Philip Kotler, *Strategic Marketing for Non-Profit Organizations,* 6e (Upper Saddle River, N.J.: Prentice Hall, 2003), pp. 80–82.

18. "Nestlé's Marketing Crisis."

19. George S. Day, "Feeding the Growth Strategy," *Marketing Management,* November–December 2003, pp. 15+.

20. Frances Brassington and Stephen Pettitt, *Principles of Marketing 3e* (Harlow, Essex, UK: Financial Times Prentice Hall, 2003), p. 19.

21. "FedEx Delivers Cleaner Air," *Hartford Courant,* April 6, 2004, p. A8; Charles Haddad, "FedEx and Brown Are Going Green," *BusinessWeek,* August 11, 2003, pp. 60–62.

22. John S. McClenahen, "Rare Beauty," *Industry Week,* January 2004, p. 67.

23. Saul Hansell, "Amazon Reports First Full-Year Profit," *New York Times,* January 28, 2004, p. C3; Griff Witte, "Amazon's Year of the Money," *Washington Post,* January 28, 2004, p. E1; Robert D. Hof, "Amazon's Go-Go Growth? Gone," *BusinessWeek,* February 12, 2001, 39.

24. Holly Vanscoy, "Life After Living.com," *Smart Business,* February 2001, pp. 68–70.

25. U.S. Census Bureau, "State and County QuickFacts," www.quickfacts.census.gov/cgi-bin/usa.

26. Ralph A. Oliva, "Seeds of Growth," *Marketing Management,* November–December 2003, pp. 39–41.

27. See "Model of Exchange Shifts Towards Services," *Marketing News,* January 15, 2004, p. 25.

28. Bret Begun, "The Italian Stallion," *Newsweek,* December 1, 2003, p. 12.

29. Matthew Boyle, "Brand Killers," *Fortune,* August 11, 2003, pp. 88+.

30. Julie Schlosser, "Markdown Lowdown," *Fortune,* January 12, 2004, p. 40; "Zilliant," *Fortune,* November 24, 2003, p. 210.

31. Phred Dvorak, "Nintendo Steers Away from the Pack," *Wall Street Journal,* May 11, 2004, p. B10; Phred Dvorak, "Nintendo's GameCube Sales Surge After Price Cut," *Wall Street Journal,* November 4, 2003, p. B4.

32. Dean Foust, "Coke: Wooing the TiVo Generation," *BusinessWeek,* March 1, 2004, pp. 77–80.

33. Jane Spencer, "Cases of 'Customer Rage' Mount as Bad Service Prompts Venting," *Wall Street Journal,* September 17, 2003, pp. D4+.

34. "Federal Government Makes Improvements to Customer Service," *Wall Street Journal,* July 31, 2003, p. D2.

35. Susan Greco, "The Best Little Grocery Store in America," *Inc.,* June 2001, pp. 54–61.

36. Cecilie Rohwedder, "Style & Substance: Making Fashion Faster," *Wall Street Journal,* February 24, 2004, p. B1.

37. Patrick Dillon, "Peerless Leader," *Christian Science Monitor,* March 10, 2004, p. 11.

38. Irene M. Kunii, "Websmart 50: Shiseido," *BusinessWeek,* November 24, 2003, p. 100.

39. See Kotler and Keller, *Marketing Management* 12e, Chapter 1.

40. Day, "Feeding the Growth Strategy."

41. John S. McClenahan, "New World Leader," *Industry Week,* January 2004, pp. 36+; Bob Donath, "Irritations Lead Users to Innovations," *Marketing News,* October 9, 2000, p. 16; Michael Arndt, "3M: A Lab for Growth?" *BusinessWeek,* January 21, 2002, pp. 50–51.
42. Michelle Conlin and Jessi Hempel, "The Corporate Donors," *BusinessWeek,* December 1, 2003, pp. 92–96.
43. R. S. Flinn, "Big Bank Mergers Create Space for the Little Guy," *New York Times,* December 21, 2003, Sec. 14, p. 17.
44. Timothy J. Mullaney, "Deck the Halls with High-Speed Access," *BusinessWeek,* December 8, 2003, pp. 54–56.
45. Timothy J. Mullaney, "Jewelry Heist," *BusinessWeek,* May 10, 2004, pp. 82+; "Niche Internet Retailers Hit Their Stride," *News-Times* (Danbury, CT), February 5, 2004, p. B8; Mullaney, "Deck the Halls with High-Speed Access."
46. "Ben & Jerry's Coffee for a Change," *Specialty Coffee Retailer,* January 2004, p. 6; Andy Serwer, "Economic Crunch," *Fortune,* December 8, 2003, pp. 64+.

CHAPTER 2

1. Don E. Schultz, "Others' Benchmarks Overlook *Your* Brand," *Marketing News,* March 15, 2004, p. 7.
2. "Eastman Kodak Co.," *Photo Marketing,* February 2004, pp. 17+; Joseph Nocera, "Kodak: The CEO vs. the Gadfly," *Fortune,* January 12, 2004, pp. 84–92.
3. Personal communication with Dr. Kevin Lane Keller, coauthor with Philip Kotler, *Marketing Management* 12e (Upper Saddle River, N.J.: Prentice Hall, 2006).
4. James C. Collins and Jerry I. Porras, *Built to Last* (New York: HarperBusiness, 1994), pp. 220–221.
5. Morgan Stanley Annual Report 2003, p. 9.
6. Médecins Sans Frontières Web site, www.msf.org.
7. Paul Sweeting, "Netflix Out to Conquer New Worlds," *Video Business,* January 26, 2004, pp. 1+; Calmetta Coleman, "Pruning Costs," *Wall Street Journal,* February 12, 2001, p. R30.
8. "Procter & Gamble's A.G. Lafley on Design," *Journal of Business & Design,* Fall 2003, pp. 2–5; Sarah Ellison, "Crest Spices Up Toothpaste War with New Tastes," *Wall Street Journal,* September 15, 2003, pp. B1, B10.
9. Sarah McBride, "Riding the Coattails," *Wall Street Journal,* September 22, 2003, p. R5.
10. Jeffrey E. Garten, "Wal-Mart Gives Globalism a Bad Name," *BusinessWeek,* March 8, 2004, p. 24.
11. Lisa M. Keefe, "P&G's Multiculti Marketing DNA," *Marketing News,* March 1, 2004, pp. 13+.
12. Mark Tatge, "Cat's in the Bag," *Forbes,* March 15, 2004, p. 178; James B. Arndorfer, "Cat Looking to Make Inroads in Asia," *Crain's Chicago Business,* November 10, 2003, p. 24; James B. Arndorfer, "Cat Is Set to Dig Deeper in China," *Crain's Chicago Business,* June 30, 2003, p. 4.
13. Robert Johnson, "Incognito, Polyester Boogies Onto the Playing Field," *New York Times,* March 21, 2004, Sec. 4, p. 5.
14. Thea Singer, "Can Business Still Save the World?" *Inc.,* April 2001, pp. 58–72.
15. Eric Torbenson, "With Low Fares and Glitzy Features, JetBlue Posts Impressive Results," *Dallas Morning News,* March 4, 2004, www.dallasnews.com; Wendy Zellner, "WebSmart 50: JetBlue," *BusinessWeek,* November 24, 2003, p. 92.
16. Cliff Edwards, "On Desktops, Flat Is Where It's At," *BusinessWeek,* March 29, 2004, p. 14.
17. Eric J. Savitz, "Bull Market for Red Tape," *Smart Money,* May 2004, pp. 56+.
18. Kerry Capell, "Richard Branson's Next Big Adventure," *BusinessWeek,* March 8, 2004, pp. 44–45.

19. Jim Kerstetter, Peter Burrows, Steve Hamm, and Spencer E. Ante, "Microsoft's Midlife Crisis," *BusinessWeek,* April 19, 2004, pp. 88+; Jay Greene and Andy Reinhardt, "Microsoft: First Europe, Then . . .?" *BusinessWeek,* March 22, 2004, pp. 86–87; Steve Lohr, "Musical Chairs with the Big Boys," *New York Times,* March 21, 2004, Sec. 3, pp. 1+.

20. Krissana Parnsoonthorn, "Thai-Owned Producer of Food Business Set for Rapid Expansion in Scandinavia," *Bangkok Post,* 20 February 2003, www.bangkokpost.com; Sofia Javed, "Ethnic E-Tailer Builds Expertise in Untapped Market," *Marketing News,* October 9, 2000, p. 24.

21. "U.K. Insurance Firm Asks Customers to Help Prioritize Its Socially Responsible Investments," *Financial Times,* March 1, 2004, www.ft.com.

22. Nanette Byrnes, "Toys 'R' Us: Beaten At Its Own Game," *BusinessWeek,* March 29, 2004, pp. 89–90.

23. Discussion is based on Michael Porter, *Competitive Advantage* (New York: Free Press, 1985), pp. 11–26.

24. Robert Berner, "Coach's Driver Picks Up the Pace," *BusinessWeek,* March 29, 2004, pp. 98–100.

CHAPTER 3

1. David Welch, "Not Your Father's . . . Whatever," *BusinessWeek,* March 15, 2004, pp. 82–83.

2. Based on Gary L. Lilien and Arvind Rangaswamy, *Marketing Engineering* 2e (Upper Saddle River, N.J.: Prentice Hall, 2003), p. 159.

3. Jonathan Fahey, "Lord of the Rigs," *Forbes,* March 29, 2004, pp. 67–72.

4. Steve Hamm, "Tech Comes Out Swinging," *BusinessWeek,* June 23, 2003, pp. 62–66.

5. Fahey, "Lord of the Rigs."

6. "Kodak Beats Fujifilm in China's Film Market," *Asia Africa Intelligence Wire,* February 24, 2004, n.p..

7. Michael Arndt, "Factories: The Gears Are Turning," *BusinessWeek,* March 15, 2004, pp. 40+.

8. "More than 50% of Consumers Buy Fairtrade Goods," *Marketing,* March 4, 2003, p. 3.

9. Mara Der Hovanesian, "Websmart 50: Wells Fargo," *BusinessWeek,* November 24, 2003, p. 96.

10. Leon Erlanger, "Should You Trust TrustE?" *PC Magazine,* February 17, 2004, p. 59.

11. Rob Walker, "Whirlpool Is Pushing a Whole Suite of Products Tied to the Idea of the Laundry Room as 'Family Studio,'" *New York Times Magazine,* January 11, 2004, p. 16; Pete Engardio, "Smart Globalization," *BusinessWeek,* August 27, 2001, pp. 132–136.

12. Philip Kotler, *Marketing Management 11e* (Upper Saddle River, NJ: Prentice Hall, 2003), p. 11.

13. "Hering's World-Class Harmonicas," *Music Trades,* February 2004, pp. 222+; Tony Smith, "Resurrected Harp-Maker Plays to Win," *Marketing News,* February 26, 2001, p. 47.

14. Brian Grow, "Hispanic Nation," *BusinessWeek,* March 15, 2004, pp. 58+.

15. Keven T. Higgins, "Competition Can't Ketchup to Heinz," *Marketing Management,* January/February 2004, pp. 22+; "The Latest Crazy Color from Heinz in Its Kid-Targeted EZ Squirt Condiment Line Is Stellar Blue," *DSN Retailing Today,* May 5, 2003, p. S12.

16. Rob Walker, "The Drink Is Not About Loyalty to a Consistent Taste But to a Consistent Idea about Taste," *New York Times Magazine,* March 28, 2004, p. 24; Hollis Ashman and Jacqueline Beckley, "The Spin on Sprite Remix," *Food Processing,* September 2003, pp. 18+.

17. Lawrence Kudlow and Jim Kramer, "Carnival Cruise Lines: VC and COO Interview," *America's Intelligence Wire,* March 2, 2004, n.p.; Rebecca Tobin, "In the Hot Seat: Bob Dickinson," *Travel Weekly,* December 29, 2003, p. 9.

18. Steven Levy, "All Eyes on Google," *Newsweek,* March 29, 2004, pp. 48–58.
19. Rob Walker, "The Right-Hand Diamond Ring," *New York Times Magazine,* January 4, 2004, p. 16; Blythe Yee, "Ads Remind Women They Have *Two* Hands," *Wall Street Journal,* August 14, 2003, pp. B1, B5.
20. Tobias Mayer, "The Breaker and the Box," *New York Times,* March 14, 2004, Sec. 3, p. 8.
21. Peter Kafka, "Apple Seed," *Forbes,* February 16, 2004, p. 50.
22. Jerry Useem, "Another Boss, Another Revolution," *Fortune,* April 5, 2004, pp. 112+.
23. Bruce Einhorn, "The Net's Second Superpower," *BusinessWeek,* March 15, 2004, pp. 54+.
24. Arndt, "Factories: The Gears Are Turning."
25. Todd Wasserman, "Sharpening the Focus," *Brandweek,* November 3, 2003, pp. 28+.

CHAPTER 4

1. Jim Rendon, "Now, a Man's World Is at the Spa or Salon," *New York Times,* March 28, 2004, Sec. 3, p. 3; Laura Klepacki, "Nivea Carves Out Distinct Position," *WWD,* March 19, 2004, p. 9.
2. James Brooke, "Topple the Queen! Enthrone Yourself on a Stamp," *New York Times,* June 27, 2000, p. A4; Alicia Henry, "You Oughta Be In . . . Stamps?" *BusinessWeek,* August 25, 2003, p. 14.
3. Monica Roman, "Avon Looks Fabulous," *BusinessWeek,* February 16, 2004, p. 44; Jill Jusko, "Avon Calling—On Russia," *Industry Week,* December 2003, p. 48.
4. "Dollar General Corp.," *BusinessWeek,* April 5, 2004, p. 116.
5. Hassan Fattah, "The Rising Tide," *American Demographics,* April 2001, www.americandemographics.com.
6. Louise Lee, "Courting the 'Mass Affluent,'" *BusinessWeek,* March 8, 2004, pp. 68–69.
7. Brian Grow, "Hola, Amigo! You're Approved," *BusinessWeek,* April 12, 2004, p. 84.
8. "It's a Children's Party," *Grocer,* February 14, 2004, pp. 48+.
9. "Tesco Merges Its C-Store Ops," *Grocer,* March 13, 2004, p. 5; "Taste the Differences," *Grocer,* January 20, 2001, S10+.
10. "Taste the Differences."
11. Fara Warner, "Yes, Women Spend (and Saw and Sand)," *New York Times,* February 29, 2004, Sec. 3, p. 3; Peg Tyre, "Trading Spaces, and Jabs," *Newsweek,* April 5, 2004, p. 46.
12. Kevin T. Higgins, "Competition Can't Ketchup to Heinz," *Marketing Management,* January–February 2004, pp. 22+.
13. "Guangzhou Mobile Strives to Strengthen Customer Loyalty," *Asia Africa Intelligence Wire,* January 7, 2004, n.p.
14. Scott Van Camp, "Esselte in Supplies Strategy," *Brandweek,* February 9, 2004, p. 18.
15. Marcus Lillkvist, "Macromedia Plans to Branch into Web-Based Conferencing," *Wall Street Journal,* February 9, 2004, p. B8; "Success Story: Countrywide," WebEx site, www.webex.com/webex_customer-wholesale.html.
16. Michael Arndt, "3M's Rising Star," *BusinessWeek,* April 12, 2004, pp. 62+.
17. John Tagliabue, "Sniffing and Tasting with Metal and Wire," *New York Times,* February 17, 2002, Sec. 3, p. 6.
18. Anne Kadet, "Don't Skimp on That Auction," *Smart Money,* May 2004, p. 115; Michael Krauss, "eBay 'Bids' on Small-Biz Firms to Sustain Growth," *Marketing News,* December 8, 2003, pp. 6+; "eBay Courts Small Business," *Promo,* February 1, 2004, www.promo.com.
19. Julie Schlosser, "Teacher's Bet," *Fortune,* March 8, 2004, pp. 158+.
20. Will Wade, "A Game of Phone Catch-Up on the Net," *New York Times,* December 18, 2003, pp. G1, G8.
21. Michael Arndt, "Flying Budget, But in Style," *BusinessWeek,* March 15, 2004, pp. 114–115; Micheline Maynard, "Are Peanuts No Longer Enough?" *New York Times,* March 7, 2003, Sec. 3, pp. 1, 9.

22. Dana James, "Play It Straight," *Marketing News,* May 21, 2001, p. 15; "Agfa's Second Crack at Cracking Digital," *Print Week,* January 15, 2004, p. 17.
23. Jim Farrell, "Marketing Their Way to a Better Image," *Hartford Courant,* November 14, 2003, p. B3.

CHAPTER 5

1. "Office Depot to Acquire 124 Kids 'R' Us Units," *DSN Retail Fax,* March 8, 2004, p. 1.
2. H. Igor Ansoff, "Strategies for Diversification," *Harvard Business Review,* September–October 1957, pp. 113–124; Philip Kotler, *Kotler on Marketing* (New York: The Free Press, 1999), pp. 46–48.
3. Leon Harris, "HSBC Targets More Than 20 pc Growth," *Business Times,* August 18, 2003, n.p.
4. Hasbro 2003 Annual Report, pp. 2–3.
5. Tommy Fernandez, "Small Business: Union Square Businesses Cell Themselves," *Crain's New York Business,* December 15, 2003, p. 17.
6. Julee Greenberg, "Barbie's Dream Line Goes Global," *WWD,* February 12, 2004, p. 18.
7. Peter Burrows, "Cisco's Comeback," *BusinessWeek,* November 24, 2003, pp. 116+.
8. Julia Boorstin, "Yum Isn't Chicken of China—Or Atkins," *Fortune,* March 8, 2004, p. 50.
9. "Turnaround Candidates: Rallis India," *Asia Africa Intelligence Wire,* March 7, 2004, n.p.
10. "Expansion Plans for Cable & Wireless in India," *India Telecom,* February 2004, p. 7; Tony Gover, "Cable & Wireless' Exit from U.S. Business Lets It Focus on U.K. Operations," *Sunday Business,* December 14, 2003, www.sundaybusiness.co.uk.
11. "New Metrics for Tracking a CRM Program's Success," *Report on Customer Relationship Management,* February 2002, p. 1.
12. Adam Lashinsky: "Ten Tech Trends: There's No Stopping eBay," *Fortune,* February 23, 2004, pp. 78–79.
13. Kathleen Kerwin, "When the Factory Is a Theme Park," *BusinessWeek,* May 3, 2004, p. 94.
14. Jon Gertner, "Newman's Own," *New York Times,* November 16, 2003, Sec. 3, p. 4.
15. Personal communication with Judy Strauss.
16. Ross Goodwin and Brad Ball, "What Marketing Wants the CEO to Know," *Marketing Management,* September–October 2003, pp. 18+.
17. Tom Pope, "Fundraising Ideas from North of the Border," *The Non-Profit Times,* January 15, 2003, pp. 1+.
18. Joann Muller, "Playing Hard to Get," *Forbes,* April 19, 2004, p. 65.
19. Pope, "Fundraising Ideas from North of the Border."
20. Shawn Young, "AT&T, MCI Revenue Is Still Falling," *Wall Street Journal,* January 23, 2004, p. A5.
21. Susan Adams, "Bush Baby," *Forbes,* March 15, 2004, pp. 190+.
22. Jack Hayes, "Industry, Communities Profit with Cause-Related Marketing," *Nation's Restaurant News,* March 3, 2003, p. 98.
23. Brian Ellsworth, "The Oil Company as Social Worker," *New York Times,* March 11, 2004, pp. W1, W7.
24. Charles Keenan, "Translating Customer Service to the Front Lines," *American Banker,* May 7, 2001, pp. 18A+.
25. David Rynecki, "Putting the Muscle Back in the Bull," *Fortune,* April 5, 2004, pp. 162–170.
26. Rod Stiefbold, "Dissatisfied Customers Require Recovery Plans," *Marketing News,* October 27, 2003, pp. 44–46.
27. Bruce Orwall and Emily Nelson, "Small World: Hidden Wall Shields Disney's Kingdom," *Wall Street Journal,* February 13, 2004, p. A1; "Working Their Magic: Disney

Culture Molds Happy Employees," *Employee Benefit News,* September 1, 2003, www.benefitnews.com.

28. James R. Peterson, "A Bank Where the Customer Is Always Right," *ABA Banking Journal,* March 2001, pp. S16+.

CHAPTER 6

1. Vivian Marino, "From Cereal to Juice, a Year of Innovation," *New York Times,* January 4, 2004, Sec. 3, p. 7.
2. Allison Fass, "Unplanned Obsolescence," *Forbes,* April 12, 2004, p. 64.
3. Faith Keenan, "A Mass Market of One," *BusinessWeek,* December 2, 2002, pp. 68+.
4. Keenan, "A Mass Market of One;" "Customerizing Chinos," *USA Today Magazine,* July 2003, pp. 78+.
5. David Kirkpatrick, "Why 'Bottom Up' Is on Its Way Up," *Fortune,* January 26, 2004, p. 54.
6. Steve Lohr, "Big Blue's Big Bet: Less Tech, More Touch," *New York Times,* January 25, 2004, Sec. 3, p. 1.
7. Janet Guyon, "Will Godzilla Defeat King Kong?" *Fortune,* March 8, 2004, p. 46.
8. Peter Landers, "Hospital Chic: The ER Gets a Makeover,"*Wall Street Journal,* July 8, 2003, pp. D1, D3.
9. Gail Edmondson, "Designer Cars," *BusinessWeek,* February 16, 2004, pp. 56+.
10. Adam Aston, "This Volvo Is Not a Guy Thing," *BusinessWeek,* March 15, 2004, pp. 84–86; Keith Naughton, "Detroit's Hot Buttons," *Newsweek,* January 12, 2004, pp. 38–39.
11. Deborah L. Vence, "The Lowdown on Trans Fats," *Marketing News,* March 15, 2004, pp. 13–14.
12. Kate Murphy, "Thinking Outside the Can," *New York Times,* March 14, 2004, Sec. 3, p. 3.
13. Catherine Arnold, "Way Outside the Box," *Marketing News,* June 23, 2003, pp. 13+.
14. K.C. Crain, "Last Olds Will Roll Off the Line in June," *Automotive News,* March 8, 2004, p. 3; "General Motors to Bring Oldsmobile Brand to an End," *Knight-Ridder/Tribune Business News,* December 12, 2000, www.chicagotribune.com; Rick Popely, "GM Claims Olds Owners Have Little to Worry About Except Resale Value," *Knight-Ridder/Tribune Business News,* January 21, 2001, www.chicagotribune.com; "A Year Left for Oldsmobile," *Ward's Dealer Business,* January 1, 2004, n.p.
15. Ann Harrington, "Who's Afraid of a New Product," *Fortune,* November 10, 2003, pp. 189+.
16. "Intel Unveils Next-Generation Pentium 4," *Information Week,* February 2, 2004, www.informationweek.com.
17. Ken Belson, "As Newcomers Swarm, Sony Girds for a Fight," *New York Times,* February 8, 2004, Sec. 3, p. 4.
18. James Gleick, "Get Out of My Namespace," *New York Times Magazine,* March 21, 2004, pp. 44+.
19. Bob Lamons, "Brand Power Moves BASF Past Commodity," *Marketing News,* March 15, 2004, p. 6.
20. Carol Matlack, "The Vuitton Machine," *BusinessWeek,* March 22, 2004, pp. 98+.
21. Don E. Schultz, "Understanding Total Brand Value," *Marketing Management,* March/April 2004, pp. 10–11.
22. Matlack, "The Vuitton Machine."
23. Johny K. Johansson and Ilkka A. Ronkainen, "The Brand Challenge," *Marketing Management,* March/April 2004, pp. 54+.
24. "Brand Extension, with Jacuzzi," *The Economist,* February 28, 2004, pp. 61–62.
25. Lauren Young, "A Suite for Fido," *BusinessWeek,* April 19, 2004, p. 129.

CHAPTER 7

1. Rob Furber, "The Independent," *MicroScope,* October 20, 2003, pp. 23+.
2. Roger O. Crockett, "Cell Phones," *Business Week,* April 26, 2004, pp. 48–49.
3. Jim Fuquay, "Travelocity to Unveil New Website Design, Logo," *Fort Worth Star-Telegram,* March 25, 2004, www.dfw.com.
4. Grainger David, "The Passion of the *Da Vinci* Reader," *Fortune,* March 8, 2004, p. 48; Jenna Schnue, "Adrienne Sparks and Suzanne Herz," *Advertising Age,* March 1, 2004, p. S4.
5. Mike Musgrove, "Gateway to Shutter Stores on April 9, Cut 2,500 Jobs," *Washington Post,* April 2, 2004, p. E2.
6. Leslie Chang, "China's Influx of Deluxe," *Wall Street Journal,* April 16, 2004, p. A9.
7. "Dell Sets Up Recycling Program for Computers," *New York Times,* July 10, 2003, p. C3.
8. "Global Business Briefs: Tupperware Corp.," *Wall Street Journal,* June 18, 2003, p. D4; "Brits Put an End to Tupperware Party," *Marketing News,* February 17, 2003, p. 8.
9. Russell Flanner, "'China Is a Big Prize,'" *Forbes,* May 10, 2004, pp. 163+.
10. David Strom, "Wired for Power," *VARbusiness,* March 15, 2004, pp. 54+.
11. Edward F. Moltzen, "Xerox Emphasizes Importance of Channel," *Computer Reseller News,* February 2, 2004, p. 14.
12. Kerry A. Dolan, "Outmuscling Wal-Mart," *Forbes,* May 10, 2004, pp. 80–81.
13. Martin Forstenzer, "In Search of Fine Art Amid the Paper Towels," *New York Times,* February 22, 2004, Sec. 3, p. 4.
14. David Welch, "Auto Megadealers: Running Out of Gas?" *BusinessWeek,* March 29, 2004, pp. 92–93; Alex Ricciuti, "eBay Motors Sees Growth in Top Markets," *Automotive News Europe,* April 5, 2004, p. 5.
15. Ricciuti, "eBay Motors Sees Growth in Top Markets;" William C. Symonds, "Thinking Outside the Big Box," *BusinessWeek,* August 4, 2003, pp. 62–63; Mary Ethridge, "Buyer of Cleveland, Ohio-Based OfficeMax Will Eliminate Jobs, Stores," *Akron Beacon Journal,* March 3, 2004, www.ohio.com/bj.
16. Carl Swanson, "Want Something Basic? Do Not See This Guy," *New York Times,* April 4, 2004, Sec. 9, pp. 1, 10.
17. "Royal Philips Electronics and Home Depot," *Private Label Buyer,* June 2002, p. 11.
18. Mike Troy, "PetsMart Unleashes Expansion Plans," *DSN Retailing Today,* October 27, 2003, pp. 7+.
19. Sunil Chopra and Peter Meindl, *Supply Chain Management 2e* (Upper Saddle River, N.J.: Prentice Hall, 2004), p. 73.
20. Wendy Zellner, "Wal-Mart Eases Its Grip," *BusinessWeek,* February 16, 2004, p. 40; Mike Troy, "Logistics Still Cornerstone of Competitive Advantage," *DSN Retailing Today,* June 9, 2003, pp. 209+; Michael Garry and Sarah Mulholland, "Master of Its Supply Chain," *Supermarket News,* December 2, 2002, pp. 55+; Jerry Useem, "One Nation Under Wal-Mart," *Fortune,* March 3, 2003, pp. 63–76.
21. Evan Ramstad, "China Has Cellphone Hangover," *Wall Street Journal,* September 2, 2003, p. B10.
22. Roy Furchgott, "Wi-Fi Technology Moves from Storeroom to Store," *New York Times,* August 25, 2003, p. C1.
23. Claudia H. Deutsch, "Planes, Trucks, and 7.5 Million Packages," *New York Times,* December 21, 2003, Sec. 3, pp. 1, 9.
24. Chuck Moozakis, "No-Slack Supply Chain: General Mills Maximizes Truck Loads to Cut Logistics Spending," *InternetWeek,* January 29, 2001, pp. 1+.

CHAPTER 8

1. Julie Schlosser, "Markdown Lowdown," *Fortune,* January 12, 2004, p. 40; "Zilliant," *Fortune,* November 24, 2003, p. 210.

2. "P&G Introduces Swiffer WetJet PowerMop," *MMR*, February 9, 2004, p. 19; Nancy Einhart, "Clean Sweep of the Market," *Business 2.0*, March 2003, p. 56.

3. Thomas T. Nagle and Reed K. Holden, *The Strategy and Tactics of Pricing 3e* (Upper Saddle River, N.J.: Prentice Hall, 2002), pp. 111–114.

4. Todd Zaun, "Big Money in Small Fashions," *New York Times*, April 23, 2004, pp. W1, W7.

5. Jeremy Kahn, "Beg, Borrow, and Steel," *Fortune*, March 8, 2004, p. 44.

6. Robert W. Poole, Jr., "What the Traffic Will Bear," *Forbes*, May 10, 2004, p. 44; "London Traffic Starts to See Benefits of Toll Levied on Motorists," *Wall Street Journal*, May 6, 2003, p. 1; "Ken Livingstone's Gamble," *The Economist*, February 15, 2003, pp. 51–53.

7. Thomas T. Nagle and Reed K. Holden, *The Strategy and Tactics of Pricing 3e* (Upper Saddle River, N.J.: Prentice Hall, 2002), pp. 1–10.

8. Robert Berner and Brian Grow, "Out-Discounting the Discounter," *BusinessWeek*, May 10, 2004, pp. 78–79.

9. Rob Walker, "The Payoff from a $29 DVD Player," *New York Times Magazine*, March 7, 2004, p. 28.

10. Joseph B. White and Norihiko Shirouzu, "At Ford Motor, High Volume Takes Backseat to Profits," *Wall Street Journal*, May 7, 2004, pp. A1+.

11. David Bank and Gary McWilliams, "Picking a Big Fight with Dell," *Wall Street Journal*, May 12, 2004, pp. A1+.

12. Wayne D. Hoyer and Deborah J. MacInnis, *Consumer Behavior 3e* (Boston: Houghton Mifflin, 2004), p. 262.

13. James Covert, "Monro Muffler Puts Focus on Trust," *Wall Street Journal*, June 11, 2003, p. B5G.

14. Philip Siekman, "The Struggle to Get Lean," *Fortune*, January 12, 2004, pp. 128(B)–128(H).

15. Daniel Lyons, "Skin in the Game," *Forbes*, February 16, 2004, pp. 78, 80.

16. Ian Mount, "If They Have to Pay, Will They Come?" *Business 2.0*, February 2003, p. 45; "WSJ.com launches Personal Journal," *Information Today*, January 2004, p. 40.

17. Matt Nannery, "Digital Depot," *Chain Store Age*, January 2004, pp. 18A+.

18. Mark Tatge, "Mayday," *Forbes*, March 15, 2004, p. 73.

19. Geoffrey Colvin, "Pricing Power Ain't What It Used to Be," *Fortune*, September 15, 2003, p. 52.

20. "Knockoff Pill Pushers," *Fortune*, May 3, 2004, pp. 168–170.

21. Berner and Grow, "Out-Discounting the Discounter."

22. Timothy J. Mullaney, "Jewelry Heist," *BusinessWeek*, May 10, 2004, pp. 82–83.

23. See Thomas T. Nagle and Reed K. Holden, *The Strategy and Tactics of Pricing 3e* (Upper Saddle River, N.J.: Prentice Hall, 2002), pp. 378–382.

24. Tim Matanovich, "Fees! Fees! Fees!" *Marketing Management*, January–February 2004, pp. 14–15.

25. Adam Edström, "By the Numbers: Fueling Speculation," *Fortune*, May 17, 2004, p. 32.

26. "California Drinking," *The Economist*, June 7, 2003, p. 56.

27. Sheryl Jean, "As Check Sales Slow, Deluxe Corp. Begins Selling Personal Accessories," *Saint Paul Pioneer Press*, January 15, 2004, www.twincities.com/mld/pioneerpress; Sheryl Jean, "Shoreview, Minn.-Based Check Printer Reports Third-Quarter Profit," *Saint Paul Pioneer Press*, October 17, 2003, www.twincities.com/mld/pioneerpress; Deluxe Chairman's Letter and Form 10-K for 2003.

28. Carol Matlack, "The Vuitton Machine," *BusinessWeek*, March 22, 2004, pp. 98+.

29. "The Asian Invasion Picks Up Speed," *BusinessWeek*, October 6, 2003, pp. 62–64.

30. Timothy J. Mullaney, "Hotel Crunch," *BusinessWeek*, May 10, 2004, pp. 86+.

31. Arundhati Parmar, "Redecoration: Bombay Style," *Marketing News*, March 15, 2004, pp. 9–10.

32. "Gillette Hits Mach 4,"*BusinessWeek,* November 127, 2003, p. 52; Charles Forelle, "Schick Puts a Nick in Gillette's Razor Cycle," *Wall Street Journal,* October 3, 2003, p. B7; Claudia H. Deutsch, "For Mighty Gillette, There Are the Faces of War," *New York Times,* October 12, 2003, Sec. 3, pp. 1, 11.

33. Paul Sweeting, "Netflix Out to Conquer New Worlds," *Video Business,* January 26, 2004, pp. 1+; "Netflix's Loss Widens on Rise in Subscriber-Acquisition Costs," *Wall Street Journal,* April 15, 2004, www.wsj.com.

34. "The Price Is Wrong," *The Economist,* May 25, 2002, pp. 59–60.

35. "The Commoditization of Brands and Its Implications for Businesses," *Copernicus* and *Market Facts,* December 2000, pp. 1–6.

CHAPTER 9

1. Suzanne Vranica, "For Big Marketers Like AmEx, TV Ads Lose Starring Role," *Wall Street Journal,* May 17, 2004, pp. B1+; Andrew Shotland, "The Integrated Advertisers," *Adweek,* May 10, 2004, p. 34; David Breitkopf, "'Wheel of Fortune' Colored Blue (Cash)," *American Banker,* December 10, 2003, p. 16; Lavonne Kuykendall, "Amex Gives Blue a Surname: Cash," *American Banker,* October 10, 2003, p. 6.

2. "Heineken Hispanic Marketing," Heineken 2004 Hispanic Marketing booklet, n.d.

3. Catherine Arnold, "Vox Venditori," *Marketing News,* March 15, 2004, pp. 1, 11.

4. Mike Schneider, "Fla. Citrus Dept. Stops 'Yuppie Girl' Marketing," *Marketing News,* May 15, 2004, p. 10.

5. "Media Multi-Taskers," *Marketing Management,* May–June 2004, p. 6; Don E. Schultz, "Include SIMM in Modern Media Ad Plans," *Marketing News,* May 15, 2004, p. 6.

6. Lexie Williamson, "Healthcare: Consumer Health," *PR Week (UK),* September 19, 2003, p. 14.

7. Stuart Elliott, "A Survey of Consumer Attitudes Reveals the Depth of the Challenge That the Agencies Face," *New York Times,* April 14, 2004, p. C8.

8. Richard Sandomir, "Spider-Man Web of Ads Unravels," *New York Times,* May 7, 2004, www.nytimes.com.

9. Donna De Marco, "BSO To Tune Up Its Pitch," *Washington Times,* May 17, 2004, p. C17.

10. Margaret Webb Pressler, "Turning the Job into a Party," *Washington Post,* July 6, 2003, p. F6.

11. Matthew Swibel, "Where Money Doesn't Talk," *Forbes,* May 24, 2004, p. 176.

12. Arundhati Parmar, "Attitude Adjustment," *Marketing News,* May 1, 2004, pp. 10–12.

13. "If It's Not Certified, It's Just Used," Ford ad in *Reader's Digest,* May 2004, p. 60G.

14. Erin White, "Look Up for New Products in Aisle 5," *Wall Street Journal,* March 23, 2004, p. B11.

15. Michael Krauss, "Monster.com Exec Shares Vision for Brand," *Marketing News,* May 1, 2004, p. 6.

16. "Field Marketing: Right People, Place, Time," *Marketing,* January 8, 2004, p. 23.

17. Belinda Gannaway, "Hidden Danger of Sales Promotions," *Marketing,* February 20, 2003, pp. 31+; Philip Kotler, *A Framework for Marketing Management 2e* (Upper Saddle River, N.J.: Prentice Hall, 2003), pp. 318–319.

18. "Back to Basics: Devising a Media Plan," *PR Week (US),* January 12, 2004, p. 22.

19. Scott Malone, "Gap Report Cites Action Against Violating Factories," *WWD,* May 12, 2004, p. 23.

20. Claudia H. Deutsch, "Shunning the Traditional Route for Trade Shows, Siemens Is Showcasing Its Technology by Railway," *New York Times,* March 26, 2004, p. C6.

21. Colleen Brrett, "Fasten Your Seat Belts," *Adweek,* January 26, 2004, p. 17; "Corporate Case Study: Southwest Airlines Keeps PR Course with Flying Colors," *PR Week (US),* January 26, 2004, p. 10.

22. "Heifer International Has Been Named the Winner of the 2004 Award," *Arkansas Business,* March 22, 2004, p. 10.

23. Paul Soltoff, "Taking the Spam Out of Your E-mail Marketing," *DSN Retailing Today,* November 10, 2003, pp. 10+.

24. Chris Penttila, "The Art of the Sale," *Entrepreneur,* August 2003, pp. 58+.

CHAPTER 10

1. Amy Garber, "John McDonnell: It's Showtime," *Nation's Restaurant News,* January 26, 2004, pp. 120+.

2. "Downturn in Fast-Forward," *BusinessWeek,* February 19, 2001, pp. 32+.

3. Michael Remez, "UTC Raises Revenue Forecast 3%," *Hartford Courant,* May 5, 2004, p. E2.

4. Philip Bligh, Darius Vaskelis, and John Kelleher, "Taking the Frenzy Out of Forecasting," *Optimize,* March 2003, www.optimizemag.com.

5. See David B. Whitlark, Michael D. Geurts, and Michael J. Swenson, "New Product Forecasting with a Purchase Intention Survey," *Journal of Business Forecasting* 12, Fall 1993, pp. 18–21.

6. Gary L. Lilien and Arvind Rangaswamy, *Marketing Engineering 2e* (Upper Saddle River, N.J.: Prentice Hall, 2003), p. 253.

7. Loren Gary, "Why Budgeting Kills Your Company," *HBS Working Knowledge,* August 11, 2003, www.hbsworkingknowledge.hbs.edu.

8. Andy Hemmer, "Entrepreneurs Clean Up," *Cincinnati Business Courier,* May 28, 2001, www.cincinnati.bcentral.com/cincinnati/stories/2001/05/28/smallb1.html.

9. Adam Lashinsky, "By the Numbers: Sales Data," *Fortune,* January 12, 2004, p. 34.

10. "Sara Lee Earmarks Global Growth Brands for Big Marketing Spend," *Marketing Week,* February 26, 2004, p. 8.

11. Russ Banham, "The Revolution in Planning," *CFO,* August 1999, pp. 47+.

12. Joe Stephens, "Overhaul of Nature Conservancy Urged," *Washington Post,* March 31, 2004, p. A1; John Sawhill and David Williamson, "Measuring What Matters in Nonprofits," *McKinsey Quarterly, 2001,* no. 2, www.mckinseyquarterly.com; Sean Madigan, "War Stories," *Washington Business Journal,* January 11, 2002, www.washington.bcentral.com/washington/stories/ 2002/01/14/story2.html.

13. Dave Antanitus, "The Business of Metrics," *Program Manager,* March–April 2003, pp. 10+.

14. Tim Ambler, "Why Is Marketing Not Measuring Up?" *Marketing,* September 24, 1998, pp. 24+.

15. Christopher Ittner and David Larcker, "Non-Financial Performance Measures: What Works and What Doesn't," *Wharton Knowledge,* October 16, 2000, www.knowledge.wharton.upenn,edu/ articles.cfm?catid=1&articleid=279.

16. Daniel Kruger, "You Want Data with That?" *Forbes,* March 29, 2004, pp. 58+.

17. Christopher Palmeri, "Toyota's Youth Models Are Having Growing Pains," *BusinessWeek,* May 31, 2004, p. 32; Yuzo Yamaguchi, "Upbeat Toyota Revises Forecast for Global Sales," *Automotive News,* July 28, 2003, p. 18; Michele Yamada, "Toyota Raises Global Forecast for Sales, Output," *Wall Street Journal,* July 23, 2003, p. B2.

18. Ittner and Larcker, "Non-Financial Performance Measures."

19. Gordon A. Wyner, "The Right Side of Metrics," *Marketing Management,* January–February 2004, pp. 8–9.

20. Jonathan Karp, "From Bricks to Clicks," *Wall Street Journal,* September 22, 2003, p. R7.

21. Reed Abelson, "For Glaxo, the Answers Are in the Pipeline," *New York Times,* May 4, 2003, Sec. 3, p. 4.

22. Banham, "The Revolution in Planning."

23. Toni Kistner, "One Smart Contingency Plan," *Network World Fusion,* October 6, 2003, www.nwfusion.com.

Credits

Chapter 1

Exhibit 1.3   Six Approaches to Growth
Adapted from Alan R. Andreasen and Philip Kotler, *Strategic Marketing for Non-Profit Organizations,* 6e (Upper Saddle River, N.J.: Prentice Hall, 2003), p. 81.

Exhibit 1.5   The Marketing Mix
Adapted from Figure 1.5, "The Four P Components of the Marketing Mix," in Philip Kotler, *Marketing Management,* 11th ed. (Upper Saddle River, NJ: Prentice Hall, 2003), Chapter 1.

Chapter 2

Exhibit 2.1   Environmental Scanning and Marketing Strategy
Marian Burk Wood, *Marketing Planning: Principles into Practice* (Harlow, Essex, England: Pearson Education, 2004), p. 40.

Exhibit 2.4   Competitive Forces Affecting Industry Profitability and Attractiveness
Michael E. Porter, *Competitive Advantage.* © 1985 The Free Press, imprint of Simon & Schuster. Reprinted with permission.

Exhibit 2.5   Judging Organizational Strengths and Weaknesses
Mary K. Coulter, *Strategic Management in Action* (Upper Saddle River, N.J.: Prentice Hall, 1998), p. 141.

Chapter 3

Sustainable Forestry Initiative
Used with the permission of the Sustainable Forestry Initiative.

Chapter 4

Lysol Sanitizing Wipes
Used with permission of Reckitt Benckiser, Inc.

Exhibit 4.4   Assessing Segment Attractiveness
Adapted from Graham Hooley, John Saunders, and Nigel Piercy, *Marketing Strategy and Competitive Positioning 3e* (Harlow, Essex, England: FT Prentice Hall, 2004), p. 345.

Chapter 5

Office Depot
Office Depot.com. Reprinted by permission.

Exhibit 5.1   Options for Marketing Plan Direction
Marian Burk Wood, *Marketing Planning: Principles into Practice* (Harlow, Essex, England: Pearson Education, 2004), p. 124.

Exhibit 5.4   Strategy Pyramid
Adapted from Tim Berry and Doug Wilson, *On Target: The Book on Marketing Plans.* (Eugene, OR: Palo Alto Software, 2001), 107.

Chapter 6

Exhibit 6.2   Designing a Service
Adapted from Christopher Lovelock and Jochen Wirtz, *Services Marketing 5e* (Upper Saddle River, N.J.: Prentice Hall, 2004), Fig. 1–5, p. 15.

Exhibit 6.6   Pyramid of Brand Equity
Adapted from Kevin Lane Keller, *Strategic Brand Management, 2/e* (Upper Saddle River, N.J.: Prentice Hall, 2003), p. 76, Fig. 2.5.

UPS
UPS Ad. Reprinted by permission of UPS.

Chapter 7

Chico's
Used with permission of Chico's.

Exhibit 7.2   Channel Levels
Philip Kotler and Gary Armstrong, *Principles of Marketing, 10/e* (Upper Saddle River, N.J.: Prentice Hall, 2004), p. 408.

Chapter 8

Exhibit 8.3   Cost-Based Versus Value-Based Pricing
Nagle, Thomas; Holden, Reed, *Strategy and Tactics of Pricing: A Guide to Profitable Decision Making, 3/e,* 2002. Reprinted by permission of Pearson Education, Inc. Upper Saddle River, NJ.

Exhibit 8.6   Break-Even Analysis
Tim Berry and Doug Wilson, *On Target: The Book on Marketing Plans* (Eugene, OR: Palo Alto Software, 2000), 163.

Exhibit 8.7   Alternative Reactions to Competitive Price Cuts
Framework of Marketing Management by Kotler, Philip, © 2001. Reprinted by permission of Pearson Education Inc., Upper Saddle River, NJ.

Chapter 9

Exhibit 9.1   Push and Pull Strategies
Armstrong, Gary; Kotler, Philip, *Marketing: An Introduction, 7/e,* 2005. Reprinted by permission of Pearson Education, Inc., Upper Saddle River, NJ.

Exhibit 9.2   Models for Audience Response to IMC
Adapted from Michael R. Solomon, *Consumer Behavior 5e* (Upper Saddle River, N.J.: Prentice Hall, 2002), p. 200–202.

Exhibit 9.4   The Media Mix
Clow, Kenneth; Baack, Donald, *Integrated Advertising, Promotion, Marketing Communication and IMC Plan Pro Package, 2/e,* 2004. Reprinted by permission of Pearson Education, Inc., Upper Saddle River, NJ.

Dove Shampoo
Used with permission of Unilever United States, Inc.

Index